TEACHING FOR THINKING

Theory, Strategies, and Activities for the Classroom

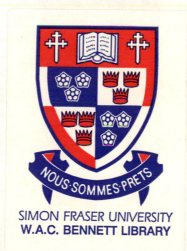

SECOND EDITION

TEACHING FOR THINKING

Theory, Strategies, and Activities for the Classroom

LOUIS E. RATHS

SELMA WASSERMANN

ARTHUR JONAS

ARNOLD ROTHSTEIN

Teachers College, Columbia University
New York and London

Published by Teachers College Press, 1234 Amsterdam Avenue,
New York, N.Y. 10027

Library of Congress Cataloging in Publication Data

Teaching for thinking.

  Bibliography: p.
  Includes index.
  1. Thought and thinking—Study and teaching.
2. Cognition in children. 3. Teacher-student
relationships. 4. Interaction analysis in education.
I. Raths, Louis Edward.
LB1590.3.T43 1986   370.15′2   86-5828

ISBN 0-8077-2814-4

Manufactured in the United States of America

91 90   3 4 5 6

This second edition is dedicated
to the memory of our teacher
Louis E. Raths

Contents

Introduction
to the Second Edition

When Teachers College Press asked for a new introduction to this second edition of *Teaching for Thinking*, Arnold Rothstein, Arthur Jonas, and I talked at some length about the nature of such a responsibility. Anyone who knew Louis Raths will immediately understand. He is a very tough act to follow. Yet in a new introduction we would have an opportunity to reexamine the theory of thinking originated by Raths through the lens of the 1980s. Do such ideas still have merit for the Information Age? Have we come up with any new data that undermine the validity of the theory? We would also have a chance to look at the applications of teaching for thinking to classroom practices over the past twenty years. What have we learned about classroom applications? How can we better help teachers to implement teaching for thinking in their classrooms? Finally, in such a new introduction we could once more pay tribute to our beloved teacher and friend—an educator of deep and profound wisdom; a theory builder who lived well in advance of his time. What began as an intimidating task became an attractive opportunity.

It is something of a paradox that *thinking* should have surfaced now as *the* educational cause célèbre, with all the fanfare and attention that was accorded "back to basics" just a few short years ago. Why now? Why thinking—and not more back-to-basics or son-of-back-to-basics? Why have professional educators, in their infinite wisdom, chosen only now to take notice of the shortfall between our rhetoric about the need to promote thinking and its lack of emphasis in classroom practice? The championing of thinking as though it were a new discovery is ironic, for it is almost twenty years since the original publication of this text, and seventy-five years since Dewey published his seminal work in the field.[1] It is even more ironic in view of the almost universal acknowledgment of thinking as an avowed educational goal.

Seminal ideas that point to the need for radical and far-reaching change in established professional practice have historically been met with resistance from professional institutions, no matter what the field. Think, for example, of Semmelweiss, whose research in antiseptic obstetrics brought down upon him the wrath and antagonism of the entrenched medical establishment, driving him eventually to madness. Although Semmelweiss made his discoveries about septicemia in 1850, it was not until fifty years later that antisepsis was fully accepted into medical practice. It's hard to know at what stage resistance gives way to enthusiasm—nor how long such a process may take. Perhaps professionals need many years of reflection before they are ready to embrace ideas that are perceived as radically different from traditional practice.

Whatever is moving *thinking* these days, let us not examine the gift horse too closely, lest it evaporate, like others before it, into the educational ether. Let us hope that teaching for thinking is an idea, like antisepsis, whose time has finally come.

TEACHING FOR THINKING: A VIEW FROM THE EIGHTIES

The children sit quietly, with impeccable good manners, around the table. They are beautifully groomed in their designer jeans and Nieman Marcus haircuts. But their scrubbed faces do not divert attention from the apprehension seen in their eyes. I pull a card from a large box of thinking activities and offer it for their examination.

"How do you suppose pigeons can be trained to carry messages and find their way home again?"

They are clearly stumped, and there is a long, pregnant silence. I wait. Finally Sharon timidly queries, "Could you tell us what you mean?"

I repeat the question, not willing to play into her transparent ruse of manipulating me into giving some clues to "the answer." Again I wait. After what seems to be an eternity, Des mumbles, "We didn't study birds yet."

Kevin is somewhat more bold. "A pigeon trainer?" He forms his answer as a question—perhaps to check out the accuracy of his thought.

These elegant, well-groomed children are having a great deal of trouble thinking for themselves about a question that is outside the domain of their grade 4 curriculum. Within the confines of their day-to-day classroom activities, they are considered the "good" students. And, observably, they are quite good at performing those hundreds of school exercises requiring single, correct answers that permeate just about every area of the curriculum. However, when it comes to functioning on a task that calls for a little imagination, for suggesting hypotheses, for connecting means with ends, for taking some cognitive risks, for extending their thinking into new territory, they flounder and fail.

How does this occur? How can it happen that bright young minds become so narrowed in functioning that the creation of ideas and intelligent problem solving become tasks quite beyond their capabilities? Why is it that in spite of our repeated affirmation of the educational goal of developing pupils' thinking skills, it is frequently the least emphasized activity in classroom practice?

Most teachers want the best for all their pupils. In citing their teaching goals, most teachers state that they hope their pupils will grow in their abilities to act thoughtfully and maturely, as well as to take on and deal effectively with the complex problems of life in the twenty-first century. Many teachers, in fact, consider the promotion of each pupil's capacity to think as a top-priority educational goal, more important today than ever before in the history of education.

The differences between our rhetoric—what we *say* we want—and the actual pupil outcomes are startling. We are *for* intelligent behavior, yet the data show we are graduating large numbers of students who are expert at memorizing and recalling factual information, but who lack the ability to use that information to make informed judgments.[2] In their extreme, dogmatic behavior, their quest for certainty, their insistence on simple answers to profound and complex questions, their inability to function intelligently in confronting new problems, and their general lack of wisdom, we see the results of an education in which experience in thinking has been lacking. In the twenty years since we originally wrote *Teaching for Thinking*, it is mainly the rhetoric about thinking that has flourished. The application of teaching for thinking to classroom practices still lags far behind.[3]

As we studied these phenomena, we learned about some of the obstacles that create barriers between what we say we want and what we do. Even though Raths' theory is "user friendly," the impediments to bridging the gap between theory and classroom practice are not easily overcome. There are many reasons for this.[4]

For example, classroom materials in widespread use still emphasize the acquisition of low-level cognitive skills. In terms of materials that are the staple of the instructional diet, we still keep buying and using texts and workbooks that give pupils extensive and exhaustive practice in the development of lower-order skills.[5] There is a virtual dearth of instructional materials that require pupils to practice and gain skill in the higher-order cognitive tasks.

Instructional strategies still place heavy emphasis on the dissemination of information. In most classrooms teachers do most of the talking. The art of using questioning strategies that call for students to think about rather than to resurrect information is largely absent from teachers' instructional repertoires.[6]

Teacher training has not helped the student teacher to come to terms with and develop competence in teaching for thinking. Most education courses are still bogged down in professors' talk about what teachers *should* do, with the assumption being made that listening to and reading about educational ideas will automatically result both in understanding and in competent classroom performance. Courses that give systematic training in how to implement teaching for thinking are few and far between.

The excessive reliance on standardized tests, with their emphasis on low-level cognitive skills, torques curriculum to that end. We "teach to the test." This is especially true where teachers' competence is being assessed by pupil performance on such measures. "Teaching for thinking is fine, in theory, and we all want it. But let's face it. It's impractical for the real world of the schools, where pupils' learning is measured, not by their competence as thinkers, but by their ability to recall what has been heard and read."

These are some of the more overt conditions that explain why teaching for thinking programs have failed to make significant headway in classroom practice. These conditions have proved most resistant to change, since they are woven tightly into the whole cloth of our educational practices. To make the changes, to allow teaching for thinking a toehold, requires nothing short of major reconstruction.

Yet, as we rapidly approach the turn of this century, we may no longer have the options that we did in the sixties, the options of passionately guarding the educational status quo yet expecting that schools will survive. The computer presence has thrust us, screaming and kicking, into the Information Age, making it possible for students to access information via computer software resources that multiply prolifically even as I write. Now that much of the information-dispensing and skill-drilling functions of the teacher can more than adequately be carried out by effective computer programs, who will choose to remain in a classroom listening to a teacher, when he or she could instead be at the PC console, learning from Turtle Geometry, Magic Spells, Algebra Arcade, or Fraction Factory?[7]

It need not mean the end of schools, as some experts have predicted.[8] Optimistically viewed, perhaps now that teachers can be freed from the laborious and time-consuming tasks of information dispensing, they can place emphasis on the more sophisticated and challenging tasks of developing students' thinking capabilities. Will it be the computer that forces us to reconceptualize the process of education and moves teaching for thinking from our rhetoric into the life of the classroom?

CLASSROOM APPLICATIONS

Putting teaching for thinking into classroom practice can be helped by understanding the few basic principles upon which such a program rests. These principles are far from exotic. It is likely that they have been seen before in other learning contexts. To understand them and their implications, however, is the key to successful classroom implementation.

The first principle is cheekily called "practice makes perfect." Not to be summarily dismissed, it is important to state explicitly that practice in a task over time works toward increased competence. Moreover, as the second principle explains, knowledge of the kinds of tasks one needs to practice to achieve the desired results is also required. The last principle involves knowledge of how teachers' interactions with students contribute to or diminish skill development. Each of these principles is discussed further in the following paragraphs, from the perspective of classroom applications.

Practice Makes Perfect

Throughout this volume, the theoretical position that experience in thinking contributes to more thoughtful behavior is extensively discussed. It is also shown that lack of experience with thinking contributes to behaviors that we associate with less thoughtful actions, such as extreme impulsiveness, overdependency, inflexibility of ideas, unyielding dogmatism, and inability to comprehend relationships. Conventional wisdom and personal experience tell us that "practice makes perfect." We do get better at those tasks that we spend lots of time practicing, whether it is playing the violin, working at the computer, figure skating, making omelets, or thinking. After cracking ten thousand eggs, you really get quite good at egg cracking. However, we may not make the mistake of believing that expertise in egg cracking alone will result in making perfect omelets. To make omelets, one must practice omelets. And although it is helpful to crack eggs skillfully in omelet making, a perfect omelet may result even from imperfectly cracked eggs.

We have learned that the mental processes called *thinking* occur in different forms and at varying levels of sophistication and rigor. Thinking is exercised when we try to "name that tune"; when we dig into memory for the year in which the Louisiana Territory was purchased; when we calculate that 32 divided by 5 equals 6.4. We know that thinking is required when we plan what to cook for dinner; when we try to remember where we put last year's income tax receipts; when we imagine what it would be like to holiday in Spain. Thinking is also necessary when we face the problem of finding the mistake in the checkbook; when we have to raise money for a new car; when we are deciding whether to buy a new house or stay in the apartment.

When we design experiments to help us in our search for a cure for cancer or to determine whether there is life on Mars, we are also thinking. It is immediately apparent that there are different ways of thinking and that some ways (designing experiments, for example) are more complex and demanding than others (like dividing 32 by 5, for example). Some theorists have chosen to call these different ways of thinking *higher-order* and *lower-order* mental processes.[9] (See the discussion on various ways of thinking presented in Part 3.)

If we agree that the ability to think is a learned set of skills, then we can see that repeated experiences "on task" will result in increased expertise in skill development. Therefore, the more we practice adding sums, recalling dates, doing double-digit multiplication, the better we are likely to get at those (lower-order) skills. However, just as expertise in egg cracking does not result in perfect omelets, neither does skill in adding sums or recalling dates result in the capability to design experiments. In order to develop expertise in designing experiments, we need to practice designing experiments. Furthermore, much as we may wish to believe otherwise, expertise in designing experiments is not dependent upon the ability to perform lower-order tasks successfully. The transfer of lower-order skills (egg cracking, recalling names and dates) to higher-order functions (creating new recipes, designing experiments) does not automatically occur.

Here, then, is the first principle upon which a teaching for thinking program is based: *Children need to spend many, many hours practicing higher-order thinking skills if they are to become successful thinkers.* To spend most of their school time at textbook and workbook exercises emphasizing recall of single, correct answers will result in expertise at just those lower-level skills.

Thinking Activities

In Part 1 of this text, a number of operations relating to thinking are described. It is also suggested that as students engage in one or more of these operations they are engaging in higher-order mental activities. It is also argued that such mental activities, performed on these tasks over time, contribute to the development of more thoughtful behaviors and a diminishing of those behaviors associated with thinking deficits. A number of studies were carried out to examine this theoretical position empirically, and the results lend strong support for the theory. These studies are cited in Appendix B.

Pencil-and-paper assignments consume a large portion of classroom time, and if students are to profit from them in terms of thinking-skills development, it follows that such exercises must stress the higher-order processes. In order to do this, teachers must learn to differentiate between those tasks that call for emphasis on the lower-order skills, and those that engage the higher mental processes. We may not, of course, pretend that lower-order exercises promote higher-order functioning; for example, we should not expect that the ability to multiply accurately will result in a pupil's ability to create innovative solutions to an entirely new kind of mathematical problem.

There are activities—and there are thinking activities. Activities, seen in abundance in most classrooms, whatever the subject being studied, generally emphasize the recall of information. In most cases, a single, correct answer is sought. Here are some examples of familiar items from elementary classroom activities:

1. Read the story and answer the question: What is Janine doing?
   a. Cooking
   b. Making tea
   c. Boiling an egg
2. Make a pendulum. Start the string moving. How many swings does it make in ten seconds? _____ Make the string longer. How many swings does it now make in ten seconds? _____
3. What are the three races?
   a. _____
   b. _____
   c. _____
4. In what year were metals first discovered? _____
5. Solve these problems:
   a. $65 \div 21 =$ _____
   b. $72 \div 24 =$ _____
   c. $335 \div 35 =$ _____
6. Which is the correct spelling?
   a. Labirynthe
   b. Labirinth
   c. Labyrinthe
   d. None of the above

It is important to state that activities emphasizing recall of information and the finding of "correct" answers are not being condemned as inappropriate to educational goals. Teachers will, of course, wish to ensure that pupils know their addition facts and multiplication tables, as well as the correct spellings of words. However, when such activities are used in over-whelming proportion to exercises in which pupils must process, rather than retrieve information, we cannot expect that pupils will grow as thinkers. To do that requires practice with thinking activities.

Thinking activities are derived from the kinds of thinking operations described in this text. These operations are inquiry-oriented: That is, the emphasis is upon the pupils' engaging in the generation of ideas rather than in retrieving information. In thinking activities, many different answers are acceptable and appropriate, and the answers may vary in substance and in form. Thinking activities do not require pupils to come up with a predetermined answer or set of answers. They require pupils to generate their own ideas and to support them with data from their inquiries.

For example, pupils might be asked to hypothesize why it was acceptable practice to burn "witches" in Massachusetts in the seventeenth century; to observe and report on the behavior of a spider building a web; to study a photograph of the ruins of Machu Picchu in the mountains of Peru and develop some hypotheses about the kind of people who lived there and about life in this community; to classify a list of spelling words that have certain letters, sounds, and other attributes in common; to identify the kinds of mathematical skills needed in the building of a duck pond; to imagine what life was like before the wheel was invented.

It becomes clear then, that some activities work toward helping pupils arrive at "right" answers. Such activities provide practice in those lower-order mental functions of acquisition and recall of information. On the other hand, thinking activities work toward the generation of ideas. The emphasis is on the processing of data. They provide pupils with practice in those higher-order mental functions of comparing, classifying, and interpreting data; problem solving; critical reflection; creating; designing investigations; comprehending ideas; identifying assumptions; hypothesizing; and observing.

Here, then, is the second principle of a classroom program emphasizing teaching for thinking: *Know the difference between activities and* thinking *activities. Use each type selectively—as is appropriate to the teaching goals.*

Teacher–Student Interactions

Teachers interact with their students hundreds of times each day, and their interactions take various forms. Sometimes the teacher is called upon to give information:

> *Student*:   What page is the math homework on, Miss Pilpul?
> *Teacher*:   You'll find it begins on page 72.

> *Student*:   How do you fold this paper?
> Teacher: First, you fold the top down, like this. And then you fold
> the sides over, like this.
>
> *Student*:   Why doesn't the gold side bend in?
> *Teacher*:   It's stronger, and it's more resistant to heat.

There are many times during the day when teachers are directive:

> "Your margins should be one inch wide, on the left side of the
> paper."
> "Do all the examples on page 117."
> "You can see how this piece of wood is floating and how that metal
> rod sinks."
> "We'll wait until Bobby is finished."

There are also times during the day when teachers are called upon to
make judgments:

> "I like your poem very much, Julie."
> "That's not quite right, Boris."
> "William's answer is wrong. Does anybody have the right answer?"
> "That's not the way to spell 'ghosts'."

Sometimes, teachers' interactions are directed toward managing pupils'
behavior:

> "Clean up that mess, Charlie."
> "If you do that one more time, Wilmot, I'll have to send you to the
> office."
> "Give me that ruler and sit down, Alice."
> "Is that any way to behave?"
> "We're not interested in that, Norma."

Teachers may also interact in ways that require pupils to think a little
more about their ideas:

> "Where did you get that idea from, Sheckie?"
> "What alternatives can you suggest?"
> "How can you explain it?"
> "Perhaps you can identify some of the assumptions you are making?"
> "You may have thought of some hypotheses to explain how that
> happened."

There are many ways in which teachers interact with pupils in order to
manage and direct learning, and perhaps that is why the act of teaching has

been called "an interactive process." It is only recently, however, that we have studied the nature of teacher-student interactions and their effects on pupil behavior and learning.[10] We now have some evidence to suggest that children's interactions with teachers and other significant adults have powerful and long-lasting effects on their lives. We know, for example, that children who are on the receiving end of many, many directive interactions over time are likely to become very dependent upon that direction and to suffer from impaired ability to function on their own. When pupils are faced with a long-term diet of consistently judgmental interactions, they are likely to need and depend upon external sources for determining what is right or wrong, good or bad, and lose confidence in their ability to make judgments for themselves. These children, too, suffer from impairment of functioning. They are more vulnerable to the influence of others and less able to rely on their own experiences to guide them in determining value and worth.

When children experience long-term interactions that are harshly critical, the effect is to diminish their self-esteem. They are likely to feel less worthy, less capable, and more fearful. They will have been undermined and their personal security threatened. The effect of harshly critical interactions, over time, is to diminish a child as a person and as a learner.

It is not being suggested that teachers ought never to be directive or that they ought never to make judgments about pupils' work. Neither is the teacher who expresses anger at a student's inappropriate behavior being condemned. We *all* get angry. And there are times when teacher direction and teacher judgments are both warranted and highly appropriate.

What is being suggested, however, is that when directive, judgmental, or excessively critical responses play the dominant role in the interactive process of teaching, the effects upon pupils, over time, will be a diminishing of their functioning. To be increasingly aware of the kinds of interactions being used and to use interactions appropriate to the learning goals being sought is another important dimension of a classroom program emphasizing teaching for thinking.

One of the primary goals of such a program is to increase pupils' confidence in themselves and in their ideas and to strengthen their ability to do their *own* thinking. As a consequence of their experience with thinking-related materials, pupils become strengthened in their sense of personal power and more capable of handling challenge. In such a program, the kinds of teacher-student interactions used in the classroom play a critical role.

Learning to listen to ourselves as we talk to our students is one important requisite of a teaching for thinking program, and it is a difficult skill to acquire. Without it, however, it is virtually impossible to make an accurate assessment of what we are saying and to modify those interactions so that they become more reflective and less directive. It is a retraining no less rigorous than learning to play a Bach prelude, and it is no wonder that many teachers, faced with the enormous pressures involved in their normal classroom duties, shrink from such an undertaking. However, without such serious practice in interactive skill development, teaching for thinking gains in classroom practice will be hard to come by.

The third principle, then, of an effective teaching for thinking program is, *Be aware of your teacher-student interactions. Learn to listen to yourself talking to pupils. Build more teaching for thinking responses into your interactive repertoire.*

WHAT CAN SCHOOLS BECOME?

Norbert Finster teaches grade 6 at the Archive School. He has been teaching for ten years, and his classroom contains many of the accoutrements of a modern school: a film library with cassette tapes, a language lab, an opaque projector. The shelves in his room are filled with multiple copies of books—not just one series, but several series of language arts, social studies, and science texts. If you count the hardware and software, you would say that Norbert Finster has it all.

A visitor to his classroom would notice immediately that no pupils' work is on display. A closer look reveals no sign of art nor of student projects of any kind. If pupils are involved in any hands-on projects or investigations, there is no evidence of such involvement to be seen in the room. In a three-hour morning session, almost the entire time is spent in activities that are dominated by the teacher. A language activity lasting over an hour consists of pupils being called upon to give the correct answers to a forty-item homework assignment emphasizing grammatical construction. Pupils do not speak unless they are called upon. Much of their time is spent waiting. This is a language activity in which the teacher gets most of the practice with language. Throughout the morning all activities flow from the teacher and are directed to the whole class. Only when the recess bell sounds does the class explode in frantic and frenetic behaviors out the door and onto the schoolyard.

In Finster's teaching there is little consideration for individual differences in learning style or in pacing, and little concern shown for individual interest or special talent. If curriculum is the stuff of life in the classroom, life here is withered, dry, gutless. Goodlad's study of schools is seen in microcosm in this room.[11]

Meanwhile, on the other side of town, the Learning Store is in full operation. It is a fully computerized individualized classroom that provides unlimited free machine time to students of all ages for remedial or enrichment work in subjects such as reading skills, spelling, basic arithmetic skills,

Logo geometry, writing skills, algebra, and the like. The Learning Store is open seven days a week, from 8:00 AM to 10:00 PM, and plans are being made for several neighborhood branches. The advertisement they send out to potential students is appealing:

> YOU SET THE SPEED AT WHICH YOU WILL LEARN!
> YOU REALLY MASTER YOUR SUBJECT!
> YOU PICK THE TIME YOU WANT TO COME IN.
> YOU LEARN ON A FAST TRACK—NO DIVERSIONS, NO DELAYS.
> YOUR SUCCESS IS ASSURED!

What could this mean for the Norbert Finsters of the teaching profession? Perhaps not very much. After all, his kind of teaching has endured for one hundred years. Isn't it likely that things will go on just as they are; that Finster and his style of teaching will continue to survive, as it has in the past, in spite of all the changes in the world around us?

Seymour Papert, professor of mathematics at MIT, suggests otherwise. Papert predicts that such classrooms will not survive the next decade. He claims that as the communication-of-information function of the teacher is increasingly being displaced by the silicon chip, schools as we know them will cease to exist.[12] "The computer presence will enable us to so modify the learning environment outside the classroom that much if not all the knowledge schools presently try to teach with such pain and expense and such limited success will be learned, as the child learns to talk, painlessly, successfully and without organized instruction. This obviously implies that schools as we know them today will have no place in the future."[13]

Is it possible that Papert is overstating the case? The IBM Write-to-Read program, which was tested in 105 schools in several states and involved over ten thousand five- and six-year-old children, has provided some supporting data. Children using this computerized language-learning program made higher scores in reading skills than 89 percent of their peers. What's more, over 95 percent of the children in the first grade have learned to write as well as read.[14] The implications of these data cannot be dismissed, for if this program realizes its full expectation, it is likely to eliminate the curse of reading failure altogether from the primary classroom. Think of it. No pupil will fail in reading. Think too, that all of this may done *without the intervention of a human teacher.*

The most significant and far-reaching change we have seen in the last twenty years has been the advance of computer technology. Today, there are probably more stores in the downtown area that sell computer hardware and software than there are fast-food outlets. Computer technology already exists to teach our students their "basic skills." Many of today's children are already computer literate. They play computer games instead of pinball in the amusement arcades. They choose computer camps for holiday fun, and they ask for Apples for Christmas. Surely changes of such magnitude have great and profound implications for the future of the schools.

It may be true that the very survival of schools is being threatened by these options and alternatives. It may be possible that it is the computer presence that has given rise to our current concern with teaching for thinking. For if mastery of content remains the single, most important educational concern, our schools will surely become obsolete in the next decades. It is in the area of teaching for thinking that human teachers may still potentially outclass even the most sophisticated and stylish computer program.

To finally move teaching for thinking into the classroom won't be an easy job. This much we have learned. It means shifts in our thinking, shifts in our awareness, shifts in our priorities. It means new ways of conceptualizing life in classrooms, and teachers who are trained to embark on these new courses of action. It means a shift not only in the kinds of curricular materials available for instruction but also a shift in the thinking of curriculum consultants, writers, and educational publishers. It will mean a major shift in the way teachers are trained, with an emphasis on teaching for thinking in college and university courses, and a need for college professors who know how to carry out this training. It will mean a change in what principals look for when they visit teachers' classrooms and a change in what activities parents expect children to do in school. It will mean a change in our thinking about tests and a change in the way we evaluate teachers' effectiveness. It will mean in-service programs that really deliver the goods, that train and support teachers in carrying out teaching for thinking programs. It will mean a problem-solving attitude on the part of professionals, to ensure that recommendations for change are compatible with these goals, and a rejection of politically motivated solutions that are inappropriate to our objectives. It will mean that a nation and its public schools will finally be moving from rhetoric into action—putting our "money where our mouth is"—showing what it is we really value for our children.

In spite of the obstacles, there are increasing numbers of teachers who have moved teaching for thinking into their classrooms, and the payoffs have been substantial and multifaceted. Children encouraged to think for themselves actually learn to do so and, in the process, develop into more thoughtful, more responsible persons. When their ideas are valued, they offer them more willingly and more imaginatively, and the results are often surprising and delightful. Teachers who witness the growth in pupils are even more strengthened in their conviction that teaching for thinking does work to produce the results claimed. There is an exhilaration about life in classrooms where teachers and pupils are partners in searching for meanings, in a true laboratory for learning, and such a working environment contributes sub-stantially toward teachers' added pleasure and satisfaction in teaching.

Putting teaching for thinking to work in classrooms may seem like a tall order, but it is within our reach. We have the work of Louis Raths to provide us with a framework, a theoretical structure that informs us and guides us into action. We have the means, the talent, and the resources. It may be time for us to decide how we are going to use them—and toward what end.

This is for you, Dudy, from the three of us, with love.

SELMA WASSERMANN
1986

Introduction
to the First Edition

In this book *thinking* is associated with *the whole man*. It is not restricted to the cognitive domain alone. It embraces imagination, it includes thinking to some purpose, it invites the expression of values, attitudes, feelings, beliefs, and aspirations. Throughout the book there is a recurring emphasis on questioning of implicit and explicit assumptions, on generalizations, on the easy attributions to other people of motives, feelings, and purposes. There is a stress on the meaning of the many ways in which life experiences may be clarified for their possible significance.

Through experiences with our family physician we are familiar with the distinction between *symptoms* and the probable underlying *causes* of those symptoms. We are helped by our medical adviser to realize that it is not enough to treat symptoms. It *is* important to investigate the causes of symptoms. For example, where a child exhibits unusual and persistent aggressive behavioral symptoms potentially or actually harmful to other children, we have come to believe that there are underlying causes that relate to the frustrations of very important emotional needs. We now believe that when these needs are met, the aggressive behavior is likely to diminish in frequency, or intensity, or both. Studies in the field of psychology have enabled us to gain insight into human behavior and to make generalizations that help us to understand the possible causes of behavior. This type of *theoretical* orientation is extended in this book to those human functions we ordinarily associate with thinking: Certain behaviors of people reflect an incompleteness or inconsistency of thought. These behaviors reflect experience with thinking that has not been adequately rigorous in terms of what is set forth in these pages.

Deprivation of certain kinds of experiences has consequences of a behavioral kind. Impulsiveness, for example, is generally associated with the function of thinking: One did not stop to think. A second illustration is reflected in the characterization that a student doesn't concentrate: At some moment in time he is not paying attention to what he is doing and hence meets failure in his work. It is commonly assumed that this is a neglect of rigor in the thinking processes. Where there is an emphasis upon thinking in the curriculum, students tend to modify their behaviors. Where there is frequent opportunity to engage in a great variety of processes that involve thinking, the frequency of impulsive behavior tends to decline.

It is important to note that we are not suggesting that teachers can or should teach children *how to think*. There is no "one way" of thinking. We tend to assume that in the normal population of the human family the capacity to think is present and that what is needed most are *opportunities to think*, and opportunities to discuss the thinking that is done. This book, therefore, has many, many suggestions for teachers at various levels of instruction for ways to provide opportunities that involve thinking.

In this book we are concerned with *theory* and *its applications* in an area that focuses upon thinking. In this context *theory* is taken to mean a statement of relationships between two or more variables where effort is made to define the variables. In this book the variables under consideration are *thinking* and *behavior*. It is maintained that a relationship exists between thinking and *some* kinds of behavior. Incompleteness or inconsistency of thought or limited experience with thinking is often reflected in certain kinds of human behavior that can be observed in the classroom. A theory is also thought of as an attempt *to explain* the connections between variables or throw light upon a problem. The thinking theory presented in this book is defined in terms of its ability to explain the behavior in question.

Another criterion often associated with a theory is that hypotheses may be drawn from it and put to the test. The theory set forth in this volume is amenable to such testing. Children with certain thinking-related characteristics may be identified. These children may be given many opportunities over a period of one semester to think, and then an assessment of their behaviors can be carried out a second time. To the extent that positive changes occur the theory is supported; to the extent that very little happens, doubt is thrown upon the theory. In other words, every teacher can be in a position to test what is here proposed as a workable theory.

We ask of a theory that it meet certain common-sense notions. Is it reasonable to suppose that if we are given many opportunities to think we might become different in our behavior? The theory has been discussed with thousands of teachers and has stood this test very well. There is substantial agreement that an emphasis upon thinking activities will encourage thinking and result in a decrease in what may be termed "immature" behavior. A theory that is worth its salt tends to grow out of observed facts. This theory has developed from classroom observations, from long years of work with teachers, and from experimental evidence.

At appropriate places in the text we suggest the tremendously sig⸜ role that physical health plays in influencing behavior. We also poin⸜ how significant emotional security seems to be in its influence on behavio⸜ We suggest that where there is a serious problem in learning that seems to relate to thinking, it is wise first to make some investigation of physical fitness and of emotional security. Mention is also made of the time and patience needed for application of this particular theory. Overnight results are out of the question. It is suggested that a minimum of one entire semester is needed to give the theory an adequate trial.

With these qualifications one might infer that the theory does attempt to explain too much. There is little doubt that it represents an oversimplified explanation of some complex behavior problems. Isn't it true, however, that in the early stages of its publication practically every theory in all fields is an oversimplification? One of the great values in formulating a theory is to bring it before the public of one's peers for experimental verification and for theoretical examination. Trials of the theory in many different situations, conducted by different experimenters, tend to subject the theory to very critical appraisal. Under these circumstances the theory may be modified or rejected. This is why, perhaps, theories are the subject of frequent debate: They challenge critical scrutiny; they open up channels for experimentation and for the exchange of data; they add zest and life to the related profession. In presenting a theory that relates clearly to the practice of education, what we have presented here will invite widespread criticism.

A further point bears mentioning. Widespread among educational leaders is the assumption that teachers *must* take responsibility for changing the behavior of children. In this book stress is given to the idea that teachers *must* take the responsibility for providing experiences that open up opportunities for students to change, if that is their desire. In other words, the teacher tries to create situations in which students have experiences that may or may not facilitate change. The teacher's job, and professional responsibility, is to provide richness of experience. The test of good teaching does not consist alone of changed behavior on the part of students. Good teaching is recognized, in part, by the quality of the experiences that are going on in the school. If students do *not* change, this does not mean that worthwhile experiences have not been provided. If students do not change, it means only that students have not changed. Other kinds of evidence are needed to answer the question: Have excellent experiences been provided?

If teachers provide a school life that is very rich in its opportunities for thinking, it is very probable that most children will reconstruct their own behavior. We are familiar with the fact that teachers often say to children: You should, you ought, you must, as ways of getting changes in behavior. Students learn what teachers want and give it to them. In this book we have

...where children have opportunities for thinking, where ...s are so much a part of the curriculum that they are present ...d week after week, they begin to change their own behavior. ...told to change it. They are not penalized for not changing it. ...rwhelming majority of cases they do change it.

...e same vein teachers are not heartbroken if the students do not ...e. Teachers get satisfaction out of knowing that they are presenting ...opportunities for children to experience decision making, comparing, summarizing, and the other operations mentioned in this book. While they hope for change, they do not demand it. While they look for change, they do not manipulate children in order to get change. The teachers are looking for change that is self-directed on the part of students. The responsibility for change lies with the students. The responsibility for richness of experiences lies with the teachers. Where change is taking place under these circumstances, progress on the part of students is evidence of their achievement, and it is also evidence that the curriculum is providing experiences that enable them to make decisions about their behavior.

It is *experience* that contributes most significantly to the process of maturing. Teachers cannot guarantee that any particular activity will become an experience for students in the classroom. Teachers can and should guide in the continuing process of developing a curriculum that seems to be rich in the qualities associated with the concept of experience. Opportunities to think belong in this category.

Perhaps something more should be said about the many subtle and not so subtle ways of manipulating students to get changes in behavior that are wanted. Those of us who have observed teachers at work have been surprised by the tendency of teachers to make judgments about what students say and do. Instead of accepting an explanation, an example, a dissent, a rebuttal, or a question as part of an encounter with the child's life, there is the tendency to use praise or blame for almost everything a student might say or do. Under these circumstances it becomes very clear to students what they "should do." In this book there are hundreds of examples that illustrate opportunities for students to think. If, in using these examples, teachers are going to make judgments, favorable or unfavorable, about every response made by students, a disservice will be done to the larger concept of providing opportunity for freedom to think. Instead of approving or disapproving, it is hoped that the teacher will relate what is being said to the purpose that is governing the encounter. There is no need for distributing applause or disapproval for what children say and do. In unusual circumstances it is appropriate. Where adults are exchanging ideas, or raising questions, or dissenting, we do not think it necessary for a continuing presentation of praise and blame for what is being said. Where we live with students in situations that have meaning for them and for us, we diminish the significance of those encounters by the overuse of praise and blame. It is high time that we respected these students more and respected ourselves more. If we focus upon the thinking that is being done and raise questions about it at times and accept it at times, we shall be doing what is required by the situation.

In this book *thinking* is conceived as processes associated with inquiry and decision making. Where the process of *comparing* is purposeful, we see it as one way of acquiring facts about likeness and difference; we see it as a step toward weighing similarities and differences in preparation for choosing. Where *summarizing* is taking place, we see the process as involving analyzing, abstracting, ordering, organizing, and synthesizing. And so too with the other operations discussed in the pages that follow. The emphasis is upon *opportunities to think*, so that inquiry may go forward, and so that decisions and conclusions may be more soundly based.

With John Dewey we believe that one of the most important aims of inquiry is to arrive at warranted assertability. Most of us want to make assertions that will stand critical scrutiny; we want a minimum of holes in our arguments. In a great many life situations we do not expect "to prove" something as absolutely true or false. Most often we do not have the time or the facilities, and quite often we may not have the needed training or experience in the area under discussion. A child in grade 4 may find a way to estimate the area of a circle. An acceptable *proof* might involve the use of calculus. For *his* purposes, the method used by the child may be satisfactory, and the conclusion *warranted* in terms of that purpose. The thinking operations described in this volume represent activities that involve many kinds of thinking. Little or no attention, however, is given to rigorous proofs or to designs of research appropriate to the exact testing of clearly formulated hypotheses. We are emphasizing *opportunities to think*, and opportunities *to share our thinking* as inquiry is carried forward in terms of purposes important in these situations.

The thinking operations emphasized in these pages, all of them, can be used to develop habits of thoughtful inquiry. Where they are consistently employed to enrich the experience of young people, we are entitled to hope that a contribution will be made to the maturity of our world.

The theory underlying this book and the many thinking operations set forth have been explored for several years. During that time many questions have been asked about the theory and the materials. We have lived with these questions and have tried to answer them to our own satisfaction, and we share a number of them with our readers.

Are we concerned purely with the intellectual processes? We believe that emotional security is very important and a necessary condition in the learning processes associated with school life. It is a necessary but not a sufficient condition to explain human behavior in total. Not *all* behavior can be explained by the weaning processes carried on in early childhood! We have emphasized the importance of physical health and emotional health, and we have stressed the importance of thinking. We have suggested that thinking enters into many facets of life; that man is not compartmentalized; that thinking must be thought of in its relationship to values, and that values must be looked at in terms of choices and consequences. As we see it, young people have not been given many opportunities to think in our schools. We suggest that children and grown-ups have great capacities for thinking, and that if thinking is stressed in our schools, there will be an increased tendency to use thinking operations in the solution of many life problems.

Why have we not given much more space to the many people who have written about thinking? The reason is a simple one: We have restricted ourselves to a theory that relates thinking to a number of behavioral symptoms and to a number of thinking operations. We have tried to bring together the materials relevant to this theory, and we have reported a number of the researches that bear upon the theory. The book is intended to clarify this theory and to illustrate it.

After long and intensive work with the materials and operations relating to the theory, some teachers have asked, "What is new about this. . . . Doesn't everybody know this?" A new theory often is greeted in this way. When it is clearly formulated, many people wonder why it was not formulated years earlier! The newness is associated with a different organization of materials, with clear-cut hypotheses that can be tested by classroom teachers, and with many illustrations of thinking operations that are applicable to almost any type of organization of the curriculum. One might turn the question around: If the theory and its applications are so obvious, why shouldn't we find many evidences of its use in normal classroom functioning? Perhaps educators have given a lot of lip service to thinking in the past without concomitant emphasis on thinking in the classroom.

Ideally, shouldn't a book that emphasizes thinking also emphasize the problems that should be thought about? We have many examples in the book that have bearing upon important problems, but we do not believe that we should be prescriptive about curriculum content. The book emphasizes method, student behavior, and operations. The stress is upon teaching for thinking and how to go about it. A very large number of problems become significant as these operations are used and the processes applied. Where the faculty has a voice in policy making that is concerned with curriculum, where teachers are free to think, and where thinking operations can be applied to curriculum development, progress can be made.

As more work is done with this theory and its applications, we certainly anticipate that changes will be recommended. Some of the categories may not stand up; others may and probably will be added. Many other thinking operations may be suggested as appropriate for trials of the theory. The thinking operations overlap considerably. Some of the behavioral manifestations overlap. We do not consider this too serious in the actual applications of the ideas to classroom practice. We do not offer the materials as a syllabus to be adopted. We offer a series of suggestions to teachers as a basis for their further thinking.

In *Webster's Twentieth Century Dictionary, Unabridged*, second edition, thinking is defined in a number of ways. The first meaning is "to bring the intellectual faculties into play; to use the mind for arriving at conclusions, making decisions, drawing inferences, etc.; to perform any mental operation, to reason." The second explanation for the word *think* is "to judge, to conclude; to decide; to hold as a settled opinion; to believe; as to *think* nobly of a person." The third meaning says: "to purpose; to intend; as I *thought* to help him." A fourth interpretation: "to muse; to meditate; to reflect; to weigh something mentally." When we are asked to define a term, ordinarily we try to give boundaries to the term, to fix limits to it. We aim to be precise. We hope to make clear what is included and what is excluded. Where we describe, we intend accuracy and perhaps vividness. As we look again at the definitions quoted, we are perhaps puzzled by the vagueness, by the lack of precision, the lack of clarity, the comprehensiveness of what has been suggested as the meaning of *thinking*. The authors of this book are unable to define thinking in a brief paragraph that would suggest the breadth and the depth of the concept as it is used in the pages that follow. We agree that man is a thinking being and that thinking is inextricably mixed with feeling and valuing and purposing. We see it as being influenced considerably by chemical and physical reactions within our bodies.

Instead of trying to "fix" a definition of this large concept in a small space we have devoted many, many pages to a clarification of some of the many things that we associate with thinking. By and large our efforts are twofold.

First we suggest that many examples of our behavior are indicative both of thought and lack of thought. With respect to the latter we emphasize eight rather common behavioral syndromes as associated with an habitual disregard for thinking processes.

1. Impulsiveness
2. Overdependence upon the teacher
3. Inability to concentrate
4. Rigidity and inflexibility
5. Dogmatic, assertive behavior
6. Extreme lack of confidence
7. Missing the meaning
8. Resistance to thinking

Many instances are given throughout the book of positive evidences of thought: caution in generalizing, recognition of assumptions, grounding inferences by reference to data that are publicly available. There are dozens of these instances in the pages that follow. The point is that we make inferences about thinking from the behavior of people. We make inferences about "the mind" by the traces available of a mind at work. In much the same way we make inferences about the thinking of an individual. In part, therefore, thinking is defined as having a relationship to examined behavior.

Our second effort at a definition of thinking is embraced by the listing of many thinking operations. We say explicitly that the listing is not complete. We say in clear fashion that when these operations are carried on, a favorable situation has been created for the *eliciting* of thinking by those who participate. We say that *comparing, interpreting, observing,* and *summarizing* are some thinking operations in the sense that their intelligent use elicits thinking. We give fifteen such categories of action for use in teaching with an emphasis on thinking.

Our definition is behavioral in part, procedural in part, conceptual in part. While it cannot be pinpointed, it can be clarified in terms of emphasizing the objective in school practice. Teachers can probably incorporate these suggested operations in their teaching practices and, as they are applied, will probably agree that they are eliciting and emphasizing thinking. In the utilization of these processes teachers are apt to experience and to conceptualize what they mean by thinking and what students mean by the term. We could not ask for more.

Part 1 of this volume deals with an exposition of a theory of thinking. Part 2 deals with applications of the theory on the elementary school level. Part 3 deals with the applications of the theory in the secondary school. Part 4 is concerned with the role of the teacher in the application of the theory. Part 5 contains a recapitulation of the theory, research evidence, and some final comments. There are appendices that contain instruments and selected readings.

High school teachers may wish to bypass Part 2, which deals with the elementary school, and go directly to Part 3, where they will find an extended discussion of applications to secondary school programs. Conversely, elementary school teachers may concentrate on Part 2 and skip over Part 3. All teachers may profit from Part 4, which deals with issues and concerns relevant to all instructional levels. We hope this treatment is sufficiently comprehensive to enable all school personnel to work more effectively in developing programs that emphasize thinking.

The book was written primarily for classroom teachers and for those who are preparing to teach. It should also prove informative and useful to members of boards of education and to administrators and supervisors who prize emphasis upon thinking and who are seeking practical ways of bringing that emphasis into being.

LOUIS E. RATHS
1967

TEACHING FOR THINKING
Theory, Strategies, and Activities for the Classroom

Man is but a reed, the feeblest thing in nature, but he is a thinking reed. The entire universe need not arm itself to destroy him. A vapour, a drop of water suffices to kill him. But were the universe to crush him, man would still be more noble than that which slays him, because he knows that he dies and the advantage which the universe has over him; of this the universe knows nothing.

All our dignity lies in thought. By thought we must elevate ourselves, not by space and time which we cannot fill. Let us endeavor then to think well; therein lies the principle of morality.

BLAISE PASCAL
1623–1662

PART 1

A Theoretical Framework

It has been said that for hundreds of thousands of years the primary aim of man was to survive, and most of early man's thinking probably served this end. And then a time came when man could plan not just to live, but to live better. And this called for the recognition of new alternatives for the dreaming of dreams and the alteration of the environment in pursuit of the dreams. Man became social, and in that process he also created social problems. These problems in turn called for solution, and man's thinking was again challenged. There was, and there continues to be, no end to the problems that confront humankind, and the need to emphasize thinking in the education of young people was never so urgent as it is today.

There is widespread verbal recognition of the importance of thinking. We want our students to be able to think for themselves, to be self-directing, considerate, and thoughtful. We don't want them to be rash or hasty in their judgments. In situations that are new to them, we hope they will be able to apply knowledge that they have gained in the past. We hope they will be able to see through the propaganda that is directed toward them. We hope that they will come up with new ideas, new inventions, new dreams. We hope they will have an attitude of thoughtfulness in many situations that are problematic in character.

Why do we want all of this? Partly because we think that survival depends upon it. Perhaps because we realize that men cannot be both stupid and free. The free society that we have been trying to build demands a free intelligence. A population that cannot or will not think about its problems will not long remain free and independent. Respect for the personalities of others, a readiness to share, and faith in the use of intelligence are the cornerstones of a democratic society.

All of the social institutions of a society play an important role in the shaping of that society. As they create purposes, devote their energies to certain projects, reward and penalize certain kinds of behavior, they are engaged in creating a certain kind of society. Means and ends are thus integrated. As you sow, so shall you reap. Every hour of every school day we are not only living through that hour; we are helping to create a world. Will it be a thoughtful world? A free world? A sharing world? A world that has respect for the personality of each individual?

Schools contribute to the development of a society as they work with pupils. The United States has led the world in the direction of free, public education for all students. We spend a great deal of money and time on education, and we do so in the belief that it will make a better world to live in. If thinking is emphasized, will this probably enhance the contribution that schools make?

As children grow older they mature physically. It is our hope that they also mature emotionally, socially, and intellectually. We have learned much about the requirements for good physical development, and we are doing our best to find out what contributes most to the all-around maturity of young people. We used to assume that it was learning itself that matured people: If we could make children learn, we were contributing to their maturity! We are beginning to see the great importance of experience in the maturing processes. We are beginning to believe that it is experience that matures people, and we are examining the role of the curriculum in providing those experiences most likely to contribute to maturity.

There are a great many words and phrases in use to describe immature behavior. It is not surprising to learn that many of them are associated with thinking activity or, more properly, its neglect. We may say of a person that he or she is like a child, forever leaning upon an adult for help in thinking; or again, we might say that a person is very impulsive and doesn't take time to think and that in this respect he or she seems not to have grown up. Or we say that the person has never learned to concentrate, and we imply that in this respect he or she hasn't matured. Many such phrases are used, and more will be said about them later. All of them suggest the absence of those experiences that discipline behavior. There is also the subtle implication that if the experiences had been lived through, had been endured, the behavior of the individual would have been different.

We do not mean to suggest that the solution is a simple *either–or* choice: either learning or experience as the only basis for maturity. We are talking about *how* one learns. Some teachers have the idea that a student must *learn the facts first*, and *then* be asked to think about them. These same teachers often assume that learning the facts is largely a process of memorizing, of repetition and drill, until the facts are firmly fixed. They overlook the importance of the many processes by which facts may be acquired. When we are in a situation where a choice between two objects is necessary, we compare them and evaluate them in terms of the purposes they serve. *As we compare* we are acquiring facts, and if our purpose is to make judgments of better, or worse, or equal, we are discovering facts that are of great importance for making the final decision.

Thinking is a *way* of learning. Thinking is one way of inquiring for facts, and if the thinking is to some purpose, the facts so found will be relevant to that same purpose. We then have purposeful learning, and a person is maturing when his or her activities are disciplined by purpose.

If we grant the importance of thinking for the growth and maintenance of a free society, and if we acknowledge the contributions that thinking experiences make to maturity, we may well ask why the schools do not spend much of their time in efforts to extend greatly the opportunities for thinking.

There is no easy answer to this question. For different communities, for different schools, for different teachers, the answers may vary considerably. Superintendents and principals may be chosen because they have a reputation for stressing memorization, drill, homework, the three Rs. If the elite positions of a system go to those who do not stress thinking, an example is being set for the teachers and the students. If promotions and praise go to those who most neglect thinking, this fact too will be learned by all those who work in the schools. If the rewards go to those teachers who keep the children quiet, who raise no questions about the curriculum or about experimentation, teachers will soon learn that inquiry, reflection, the consideration of alternatives are frowned upon.

Why should this be so? There is something unsettling about thinking. It raises questions about the status quo. It suggests that the text, or the teacher, or the superintendent, may not have considered adequately all of the alternatives. It suggests that the learners will have an opportunity to add alternatives of their own before they make a choice. If alternatives are to be considered and weighed and chosen, this takes time. The so-called course of study may not be completed, and if pages in a text or topical headings have the highest importance, then thinking experiences may be sacrificed to subject matter coverage. Here again, the choice is not necessarily *either–or*, but it is often assumed to be, and many school systems elect to emphasize the so-called factual content. This is sometimes rationalized by saying that the children or the students are not yet mature enough to think about these matters! Can we deplore the immaturity of children and contribute to it, at one and the same time? When will they be mature enough?

Another reason given for the lack of emphasis on thinking in our schools is associated with the work and attention that are involved. Where thinking is stressed, the teacher must of necessity supplement the existing texts by exercises that call for thinking. The available textbooks are notably deficient in their attention to thinking. Developing curriculum materials is a difficult task, and it is easier to follow the book. Moreover, if thinking is to be stressed, one must pay close attention to what the children say and write; a teacher must also pay close attention to what he or she is saying and writing. How does one read a paper with attention to the thinking that is expressed? What does one listen *for*, as he or she listens to children?

Underemphasis upon thinking may also be related to ideas of power and authority. If students are allowed to think—indeed, are encouraged to think—perhaps they will think some things that they shouldn't! If students raise alternatives, if they criticize, they may be questioning power that properly belongs to those in authority. This suggests that we may prefer to encourage docility and meekness, obedience to the power figures. It suggests that day by day, we are not zealous in our efforts to create a free society. It may also imply that we are afraid to face up to the consequences of thinking.

Still another reason given for our neglect of thinking processes in our schools may be associated with a lack of skill and appreciation on the part of teachers. We have talked with hundreds of teachers about this matter, and the overwhelming majority have indicated that their college education prepared them most inadequately for appraising and encouraging the processes of thought. This was as true of the liberal arts graduates as it was of the graduates of teachers' colleges. If teachers are not well prepared by their own education to put an emphasis upon thinking, one can understand the neglect of thinking operations in the lives of school children.

In several ways the educational testing movement has influenced the trend toward underemphasis on thinking. It has been easier to improvise tests of information that have statistical evidence of reliability. A kind of snowball effect has taken place: As more of these tests were used, more and more were asked for. Educational accomplishment tended to be measured in objective type, short-answer test questions. Leaders in the field concentrated largely upon simple questions of fact derived from analyses of widely used texts. Teachers, children, and parents soon discovered that it paid to learn what was regarded as the most important kind of information. Curriculum and instruction quite naturally began to be oriented to the testing.

The post–World War II society displayed a very conservative trend, and this influenced the teaching of thinking in two very powerful ways. In the first place, there was a desire for simple solutions to very complex problems. If there was something wrong with society, it probably had its origins in the schools; and if the schools were at fault, it was probably because of the way that schools taught reading! Hence, it followed that more and more attention must be paid to the mechanics of reading, to the testing of reading, and to the methods by which reading was taught! As a matter of fact, so far as test scores were concerned, the available research showed that children were reading as well or better than comparable samples of ten, twenty, and thirty years ago. This is not to say that the teaching of reading should not be improved. It is to say that if there is anything wrong with the schools, the causes are probably multiple and complex, and solutions will not be found in a new approach to the teaching or testing of reading. With the greatly increased emphasis upon reading, there was not much time or interest for a new emphasis on thinking.

The postwar era, with its emphasis upon simple solutions to complex problems, carried with it a disdain for intellectual processes. The term *egghead* came into being, and it was almost always used derisively. A thoughtful person was often called a *longhair*. There was much evidence of belief in guilt by association; a great deal of name-calling and labeling took place. Society wanted action, action, action. It wanted desperately to go backward, to a time of peace, quiet, and order; it looked about for scapegoats and found them. In these circumstances it was hard for many school officials to come out openly for a greatly increased emphasis upon thinking.

For all of these reasons, and probably for many more, thinking continued to be neglected in our school curriculum. Now the decks seem to be clear again. We are ready for a new look at the place of thinking in our schools. In the long interval there has been considerable research into ways of encouraging thinking. There has been a serious examination of the relationships between certain kinds of behavior and thinking. In the pages that follow, an attempt is made to clarify what is meant by an emphasis upon thinking and what is meant by the changes in the behavior of children that can occur when thinking is emphasized.

What can we do to put an emphasis upon thinking? What kinds of assignments can we make that will call for thinking, or that will probably evoke thinking? What kinds of questions can we ask that stress thinking?

THINKING OPERATIONS

Perhaps most people will agree that thinking is an important aim of education and that schools should do all that they can to provide opportunities for thinking. How can this be done? What are some of the ways that excellent teachers do it? What kinds of assignments and class activities tend to put an emphasis on thinking? Many of the suggestions that follow are not at all new to teachers everywhere. What may be instructive is the organized focus. The headings below can be used by teachers as a checklist to monitor their own teaching. At the end of a morning, and again at the end of the school day, a teacher might look at the list and ask himself or herself to what extent he or she has practiced any of the listed suggestions. It is not implied that the listing is complete, nor is it implied that every single morning and afternoon should include some of these activities. The list is suggestive rather than inclusive. It does, however, contain many ideas that are widely used for giving emphasis to thinking.

Comparing

When we ask students to compare things, we are putting them in a situation where thinking can take place. Students have the chance to observe differences and similarities in fact or in contemplation. They examine two or more objects or ideas or processes with the idea of seeing what relationships one has to another. They seek points of agreement and of disagreement. They observe what is present in one and missing in another. What they see and report will often depend upon the purposes underlying the assignment. As purposes vary, it is highly probable that the reports of comparisons will vary.

The assignment *to compare* can vary tremendously in difficulty and scope—from a comparison of two integers to a comparison of modern music with modern art; from a comparison of two coins to a comparison of two philosophies. One may ask high school students to compare the early Hemingway novels with the later ones, or to compare Hemingway with Joyce. One may ask mathematics students to compare two proofs; in science one may ask students to compare two scientific experiments; in foreign languages, to compare two translations or two styles of literature. Each subject is rich in possibilities for comparing. And the possibilities are as great at the level of kindergarten and first grade as they are at the level of senior high school and college.

If the whole class has been given the same assignment, it is sometimes interesting *to compare* the comparisons! Students can learn from each other. As they see others noting likenesses or differences that they overlooked, their sensitivity may increase.

This process of comparing involves abstracting and holding the abstraction in the mind while attention is paid to the objects being compared. Where it is done superficially and only *for the sake of doing it*, it can be almost as dull as ordinary routine lessons. But where there is real purpose in the analysis, where there is a real motive for this searching for like and unlike, the quest proves to be interesting and stimulating both to teachers and to students. It should perhaps be noted that the comparisons of even trivial objects probably yield more in motivation and content learnings than the assignments that put great emphasis on recall alone. As an item in a checklist, the reader may ask himself or herself: Have I asked my students to make significant comparisons in recent days?

Summarizing

If you were asked now to summarize what has been presented thus far in the chapter, you would quite likely agree that to summarize requires thought. The idea of a summary is to state in brief or condensed form the substance of what has been presented. It is a restating of the gist of the matter, of the big idea or ideas. There is a requirement of conciseness without the omission of important points.

To do this one begins by reflecting upon the experience. One thinks back, and this can be done in a great number of ways. It is possible to recollect in terms of a time sequence: what came first, second, third, and so forth. One might start with an enumeration of the big ideas and then briefly report on each one of them. One might summarize a discussion by indicating which individuals stood for certain points of view. There is no one way of summarizing, and different students may do the same task in different ways.

When students are asked to tell about a trip they have taken, when they are asked to report on a TV program, when they are asked to review a story or a book, when they are asked to tell briefly their experiences at a concert, they have opportunities to communicate in summary form.

Some students seem to have great difficulty in carrying out this kind of assignment, and they need help. This is sometimes given by showing them how to outline what they are going to say or write. Emphasis is given to the point that one puts down the big ideas, the important concepts, and then talks about each of them. A last paragraph might then consist of recounting the main ideas.

Frequently there is opportunity to combine the operations of summarizing and comparing. The latter is often done in terms of a series of specifics, and students can be asked to sum up what has been said about likenesses and differences. This training in sensitivity to what goes together, what is relevant and what is irrelevant, what is of greater and of lesser significance is a contribution to development of discrimination. It is a slow process, but teachers can make daily efforts to add to each child's growth in this area.

Thus far two kinds of thinking assignments have been briefly discussed. Assuming that they are important points in a checklist of thinking activities, do you use them regularly?

Observing

Behind the assignment to observe, there is the idea of watching, of noting, of perceiving. Usually we are paying strict attention; we are watching closely and for a purpose; we are involved in something, and we have good reason for noting carefully. On some occasions we concentrate on details, at other times on substance or on procedures, and sometimes on both. Sometimes we are concerned with great accuracy of observation and sometimes only with approximations.

When students are asked to compare objects of almost any kind, observation is involved. Observations can also be focused upon an event. One may observe an experiment, an art exhibit, a sculptor at work, one's mother baking a cake. One may observe another student who is solving a problem. One may go to the window, look out, and tell what one sees. One may observe animals at play, an aquarium, or an herbarium. One may observe exhibitions and demonstrations. One may go to another classroom and make an observation. One may observe techniques of swimming, batting, painting, throwing, weaving. There are literally countless opportunities to *observe* what is going on in the world around us.

Are we teaching young people to make use of their eyes and ears? Are they employing all of their senses as they grow through our schools? Is it important that they should have opportunities to check on the accuracy and comprehensiveness of what they see, hear, feel, smell, and taste? Perhaps we are overemphasizing the bookishness of learning? To observe is a way of discovering information, a part of the process of reacting meaningfully to the world. As we share our observations with others, we notice our blind spots and the blind spots of others. We learn to see and to note what we had not perceived before. We develop discrimination, and it is very important that we should have opportunities to grow in this area. It leads toward maturity.

We must be sure that observations are worthwhile. We should rarely assign them as busywork. There should be important reasons for making the assignment: There may be crucial points to observe, and at particular times. On most occasions there should be opportunities to share the observations made. One should be careful about not prodding too much by saying, "And what else did you see; what else, what else?" If there is a long pause, one might ask if there is anything more; one might sum up what has been said and ask if the student wants to add to it. If the purpose of the observation is clear, children are less apt to clutter up their reports with a lot of irrelevant detail.

The idea of keeping notes of one's observations, of making an outline from the notes and then summarizing, is a common method that incorporates comparing, summarizing, and observing. They tend to go together rather naturally. There is a discipline to observing, as there is to comparing and summarizing; the process should be disciplined by purpose. Our observations should be directed by purposes. This does not mean, of course, that other observations should always be excluded. It does mean that the reasons for their inclusion should be weighed.

Should you include assignments dealing with observations if you are stressing thinking? Should *observing* be an item on a checklist for monitoring your own teaching? Think back on the classroom activities of the past several days. Did you give your students opportunities to compare, to summarize, and to observe?

Classifying

When we classify or sort things, we put them into groups according to some principle that we have in mind. If we are asked to classify a collection of objects, or ideas, we begin to examine them, and when we see certain things in common, we start by putting those objects or ideas together. We keep at it until we have a number of groupings. If the remainder seems unclassifiable according to the system we are using, we are apt to say that a different system might have to be used if they are to be included, or that they may be thought of in a grouping called "miscellaneous."

Children are exposed very early in their lives to systems of classification. The kitchen cabinets and the china closets are organized in certain ways: The plates go here, and the cups go here, and the saucers here, and the glasses here. In putting away the silver, the forks have a special place; so do the knives and the spoons and the ladles. The rooms of a home have different labels and functions: a dining room, bedrooms, kitchen. Oftentimes things "belong" in a room. Clothing has its groupings: clothes to play in, to sleep in, to work in, for school wear and for party wear, for summer and for winter. The idea of "what's mine and what's thine" is a simple *either–or* classification and sometimes difficult to teach!

In preschool, in kindergarten, and in first grade, children have opportunities to work with blocks, paper, and beads of differing sizes, shapes, and colors, and as one observes them at work and play, one sees them improvise schemes of classification. In subsequent years of schooling, children have fewer opportunities to make their own systems of classification. Usually they are set forth by the text, and one has to "learn" them!

In the earlier years teachers sometimes give the groupings or headings or categories to children and supply the children with a collection of objects or words to be distributed within the given classification system. Sometimes the collections alone are given, and the children are asked to work out ways of grouping the items. Here again, as children share their ideas for groupings, they learn from each other. They perceive new and different ways of handling the data that have been given.

In junior and senior high school, requirements of a classification system can be developed and more rigor applied to the task of devising a system. Seeing what belongs and what doesn't, the work involved in "thinking up" possible headings, the business of trying things out and discarding them when they do not work out—these are purposeful exercises.

To classify is to bring order into existence; it is to contribute to the meaning of experience. It involves analysis and synthesis. It encourages children to make order out of their own world, to think on their own, to come to their own conclusions. It is an experience that can contribute to the maturing of young people.

In other chapters of this volume there are many examples of possibilities for classifying at all the levels of public education. Thoughtful teachers will use these as guides and will soon see in their own curriculum many other opportunities for providing this kind of experience. There is general agreement that an exercise of this kind should be included in a program that stresses thinking. Do your students have experiences in observing, summarizing, comparing, and classifying?

Interpreting

When we interpret an experience, we explain the meaning it has for us; interpreting is a process of putting meaning into and taking meaning out of our experiences. If we are asked how we got a particular meaning out of our experience, we give supporting details in defense of our interpretation. Students may have presented to them graphs, tables, charts, pictures, cartoons, caricatures, maps, reports, and poems. When they are asked, "What meaning do you get out of this experience?" they are being asked to interpret. Meanings are also the outcomes of interpreting trips and excursions, of making comparisons and summaries, of relating rewards and punishment to behavior. Wherever there is reaction to experience it is possible to check one's inference against the facts to see if the data support the interpretation.

Many inferences need qualification. We accompany the meaning with such words as *probably, perhaps, it seems,* and other such words. At other times an inference is much more sure, and our language conveys this degree of conviction. On occasion there is little clearcut meaning that can be ascribed to or drawn from an experience. Under these circumstances we indicate that the data are too limited.

There is a tendency for young people (and for adults, too) to generalize on the basis of insufficient evidence. Also, there are tendencies to attribute causation, validity, and representativeness to data where these qualities are in doubt. On occasion children will use unwarranted analogies and metaphors. They sometimes extrapolate far into the future, and often they attribute meanings to words with a conviction that is not supported by the given data.

Sometimes when we interpret, we first describe and then explain the meaning we have received. Often we separate our interpretations into those that are reasonably sure, those that we think are probably true, and those that seem to us "hunches"—meanings that are possible but that go much beyond the available facts.

Some teachers use data-based articles from which the author's conclusions have been removed. The teacher then asks the students to write out the meanings they see in the data. Later, the teacher presents the students with the author's inferences. The students now have a chance to compare their interpretations with those of the author. They begin to see the limits of what meanings can be drawn from a given set of facts. This is excellent training for intelligent living. It disciplines us and makes us more respectful of facts and of the need for facts.

In this connection it may be worth noting that in a number of school experiences children may be taught *not* to respect facts or the need for them. In some science laboratories students will carry through a prescribed experiment, and if their results do not agree with the answer in the lab manual, they are apt to change what they themselves have discovered. Students have learned that they are "expected" to get answers very similar to those in the manual. In other words, they are apt to have little respect for what they themselves have seen, weighed, or measured. The very fact of difference, of disagreement with the lab manual or text, sets the stage for further thinking, but all too often it is not so interpreted.

Most textbooks are out of date. They need to be supplemented by currently valid materials. Evidence pertaining to the local community, to its incomes and expenditures, to its products and what is imported and exported, to its population trends, to its budgets for human welfare, to its growth or decline—all these and many more are possibilities for exercises in interpretation. As students interact with data of these kinds, they are acquiring facts that can be of great importance to their own lives and to the life of the community.

The accumulation of meaning in life adds to the richness of living. To ask students to interpret trivia, to have them do it more as an exercise than as a chance to organize their own thinking, is to miss the significance of this thinking operation. Under a competent, informed, patient teacher, learning how to interpret life's experiences is an important milestone along the road to maturity. We may well ask ourselves how often we give our students opportunities to interpret significant data.

Criticizing

When we criticize, we make judgments; we analyze and make evaluations. We do this in terms of some standards that are implicit in our statements, or we state the standards explicitly. Criticizing is not a matter of finding fault or of censuring. It involves critical examination of the qualities of whatever is being studied; hence, it is a designation of elements of worth as well as an indication of defects or shortcomings. Ordinarily we have a basis for any criticisms that we make. This basis represents the standards by which we judge. Where we have little or no basis for judging, our criticism is weakened.

Students like to criticize. They like to be asked for their judgments, for their appraisals of objects, of processes, of people's work. They are often able to criticize stories and comics and TV programs; they have a background for criticism of movies, of radio programs, of assembly programs. They may criticize write-ups of sports events, letters to the editor, or editorials. They often have judgments to offer about political, social, and scientific events.

When students are formulating criticisms, it is well to ask for evidence in support of the comments made, to search for the standards that the critic is using, and to contrast them with alternative standards that could be applied. It is well to accept criticism from students and to encourage them to reflect upon and to examine the critical comments that they have made. Children should be heard as well as seen, and we can profit much by listening closely when criticisms are being made. In our relationships with young people, we should convey the impression of respect for them, and this includes an acknowledgment of their right to criticize, their right to share in formulating the values that will direct their lives.

Some attempt should be made to encourage students to make a comprehensive examination of the subject under scrutiny. We should not lead students into indiscriminate faultfinding as if this were a process of criticism. It is not *balance* in the pros and cons that is sought, but a search for the qualities that are present, and this searching must include the good and the worthy and the average, as well as the poor and unworthy.

Should this be included in your checklist of thinking operations? If you were to criticize a book, or a play, or an educational experiment, as you see it, is thinking involved? Is it an activity that should be present frequently in the life of students? Where it is done often, and done well, students learn that they should have a basis for what they are saying. As they share with each other, they also learn about the existence of a variety of standards, and the evaluations of these standards by their classmates. Here again, there is a probable contribution to the development of discrimination and sound judgment that, in turn, lead toward greater maturity.

Looking for Assumptions

In the elementary school the word *assumption* is not often used, but the underlying idea is operative. By definition, an assumption is something that is taken for granted. We may, for example, take for granted that something is probably true or that something else is probably false. We think of a fact as true, as obvious, as not to be questioned in a particular context. An assumption, on the other hand, may be true, or probably true, or false, or probably false; we don't know for sure, and hence our need to "assume it" in the absence of factual support. We may be *unable* to investigate the relative truth or falsity of the assumed statement; it may take too long to investigate it, and we may need to assume it in order to go ahead with our plans.

The simplest example to come to mind relates to the boy who went to a store and bought two pencils for ten cents. The question is asked: How much did each pencil cost? If we limit ourselves to whole numbers, the answer may be represented by pairs of numbers that add up to ten. If we are to accept five cents as the appropriate answer, we have assumed that the pencils cost equal amounts. It doesn't say so in the statement of the problem. Unless we make some sort of assumption, we cannot emerge with one answer.

In this instance, as in many others, the assumption is concealed or implicit in the solution. We may say that a motorist went one hundred miles in two hours and then ask how far he went each hour. Unless some assumption is made, it is quite impossible to answer the question.

In *every* situation where a conclusion is drawn, one or more assumptions are being made. On occasion it is great fun to look for them. When we buy things, the decision to buy is based on facts and needs and assumptions of one kind or another. We may be assuming the integrity and sincerity of the vendor or the advertiser or the manufacturer. We may be assuming the competency and experience of those who are advising us; we may be assuming that their use of certain words and phrases is the same as ours; we may be assuming causal relations of one kind or another. Always, always, always—there are assumptions involved in the decision-making process. We can help students to gain skill and competence in recognizing assumptions.

When we make critical judgments, usually there are standards that have been assumed. When we compare two things, we have assumed that they should be compared in terms of the qualities we have chosen. When we say that something is better because it costs more, we are assuming a relationship between quality and cost. When we measure the educational accomplishments of students by standardized short-answer tests, we are making a number of assumptions.

In mathematics we may look at a proof and analyze the assumptions that are being made. We can look at translations and see the assumptions that a translator probably made. We may look at a scientific experiment, and its conclusions, and look for the assumptions. Usually, assumptions represent gaps in what would constitute proof. They are the things that we take for granted when we accept the conclusion.

The American public is thought of as gullible, as easily persuaded by rather shoddy propaganda, as lacking in critical acumen. Perhaps if the schools spent more time in a critical search for assumptions, the students would develop more discrimination, more discernment, and more resistance to propositions that are poorly based.

What about this assignment of looking for assumptions? Does it have a place in a checklist of thinking operations? Should it be a part of a steady educational diet that emphasizes thinking? It should be added that a number of teachers eschew the word completely. Sometimes a phrase like the following is used: If you believe this answer is true, *what else* do you have to believe? Occasionally an arithmetic problem with its solution is presented to the class. They are asked to examine it and to answer the above question. Students see it as a game, at first, and then see its tremendous import in the decision-making process. Sometimes, too, they spend much time on listing what seem to be rather silly assumptions.

These, however, have to be listed, looked at, and evaluated. Through a process of respectful scrutiny students come to see which assumptions are critical; it is this kind of discrimination that is important. Here again there is the possibility of a significant contribution to maturity.

Imagining

To imagine is to form some kind of idea about that which is not actually present; it is to perceive in the mind what has not been wholly experienced. It is a form of creativeness. We are released from the world of fact and reality and are free to roam where, perhaps, no one has ever been or ever will be. But we roam in fancy. We make mental pictures. In other words, we imagine.

Is this a form of thinking? Do we sometimes describe thinking as imaginative? And do we mean much the same thing when we use the phrase "to think creatively"? Imagining takes a readiness to leave what is prosaic; it involves inventiveness and originality, a freedom to entertain what is new and different.

When we ask for the release of the imagination, we then cannot ask for supporting data. The imagination goes beyond data, beyond our experience. It takes flight from reality. We may ask students in an art class to draw a headache! We may ask for an imaginative account of life in outer space. We may ask what one would do if he or she had twenty-four hours to live. We may ask for imaginative accounts of the daily life of a cavewoman. We may ask students to project themselves one thousand years into the future and write about the life of that time. We might ask them to imagine history if some event had *not* taken place. We might ask pupils to invent a language and to try to use it.

To imagine, to invent, to pretend, to create, are ways of liberating us from the demands of the day. We should not want a steady diet of imagining, but surely it has a place in our total scheme of things. It is difficult to defend as a "thinking" operation, but many of us sense intuitively that it is associated with and allied to thinking in a larger sense. Whatever is imagined should be accepted as "imagined." The sharing of what we imagine may introduce flexibility into our ways of thinking. What's more, it's fun.

Collecting and Organizing Data

We seldom give students an opportunity to do independent work. By "independent" we mean work that starts out with a student's own curiosity, a student's own questions, his or her own seeking. We have a tendency to supply students with information and to ask them to assimilate it. There are times, of course, when our assignments require them to examine several books and to collate the findings. This is one example of collecting and organizing data. Sometimes a problem may require interviewing, and this in turn may require planning a series of questions. It also requires some planning to determine how the replies to the questions are to be treated. Sometimes students may formulate some simple questionnaires to distribute to a population from which information is sought. When the questionnaires are returned there is the problem of how to organize the materials and how to present them. Sometimes students collect information that is relevant to a long span of time, and the data tend to be organized chronologically. Wherever data are collected, however, there are a number of ways of organizing them, and students should have an opportunity to be confronted with problems of this kind. In doing tasks that involve *comparing*, students have an opportunity to see different objects, or processes, or people. When they abstract from each and begin to summarize, they are getting into the problem of organizing the data. Sometimes the audience for whom one is preparing the materials will suggest methods of organization. If we are preparing a report for publication, we might think of several ways of organizing the data. If we are to make an oral report to the class, we might use exhibits. If we have a great deal of time, we might organize our data in great detail. Collecting and organizing data presents challenging thinking situations, and our students need many more opportunities for both. Do you provide opportunities for your students to collect and to organize data?

Hypothesizing

A hypothesis is a statement that is proposed as a possible solution to a problem. It suggests a way of going at something. Very often it also represents an effort to explain why something will work, and it operates as a guide in going ahead to find the solution to a problem. It is tentative and provisional.

It represents a guess. Sometimes we restrict the term, as in the phrase "a working hypothesis." When we are faced with a puzzling situation, an obstacle, a block of some kind, it is almost natural for us to conceive some way out of the dilemma. These hunches or ideas constitute hypotheses. As we become resourceful in suggesting possible solutions to our problem, we become more self-reliant and more independent in our work. Instead of depending upon others for direction, we ourselves suggest possible directions through the formulation of a guiding hypothesis. A resourceful teacher oftentimes presents a problem to a class and asks them to suggest various ways of attempting to solve it. The teacher writes these hypotheses on the blackboard, and students are then asked to consider each of them or some combination of them. Students try to anticipate what would be involved if each were tried and what the consequences might be. This constitutes a preliminary intellectual testing of the idea. If one or several hypotheses seem sound by this testing, further steps are taken. We may have hypotheses about solutions; we may also have hypotheses about sources of data, about the length of time necessary to work on the matter at hand, about the availability of personnel or money, about the relative values that are at stake with different problems. There is little doubt that this imaginative projection of possible solutions to an enigmatic situation is thought provoking. Those who use this kind of assignment find it challenging and interesting to the students. They find also that it emphasizes thinking.

Applying Facts and Principles in New Situations

This is one of the most common ways by which we now emphasize thinking. Somewhat helpful in this area are textbooks and a few of the workbooks that are available. A situation is presented in which a solution to some problem is required. Some data are given. The student is to "work it out." Math and science problems come to mind almost immediately as classical examples of this kind of assignment.

In general, a student is supposed to have learned certain principles, rules, generalizations, or laws. He or she is also supposed to be familiar with relevant facts. The situation that is presented is supposed to be new and to be a challenge. Does the student know which principles are applicable here? Does he or she know how to apply them? Can the student supply the relevant facts, if any are missing? Can he or she disregard irrelevant data if the teacher has purposely included some?

Sometimes a situation is described, and a student is asked to predict what will happen in the given circumstances. After making a prediction, the student is asked to give his or her reasons. Presumably, these reasons are the principles and the relevant facts. Sometimes the student is given a description of some past event, and is told the result. The student is asked to explain the result in terms of any principles or facts with which he or she is familiar.

Situations relevant to language and literature, to social studies and the arts, may be improvised in much the same manner. Generalizations or principles from these fields are then supposed to be applied to the solution of the problems.

In general this type of thinking tests our ability to apply facts and principles in situations that are new to us. We have learned them in one context, and we are now being tested to see if we can make use of what we have learned in another context. This involves seeing relationships; noticing what "belongs together" in this new context; discriminating what is relevant from what is irrelevant.

It requires *thought* to see the relevance of principles in a new situation, and to be successful subsequently in applying a principle is a valid measure of a sound understanding of the principle. Do your students have opportunities to apply principles in new situations?

Decision Making

This is much like the previous operation, with one major exception. In the previous section much emphasis was placed upon laws, principles, generalizations, or rules. In decision making, these are not omitted, but increased emphasis is given to the role of values. What *should* be done and why? In this case, the *why* is supposed to be revealing of the values that the student cherishes. Some teachers, when presenting opportunities for decision making, say to their students: "No matter how this problem may be solved, what *values* do you wish to protect in the solution?" This assumes that values are as, if not more, important than facts in problems that are related to social matters and to personal matters.

Thus far in the history of humankind, we have not paid very much attention to the role of values in the solution of all kinds of problems. Since the time of the Greeks and before, we have been aware of the possibility (at least) of creating a society in the image of values that we cherish. We have gone beyond the stage of living better and are in a position to create a world after our heart's desire. What do we really want? What are the values we hold dear? What do we prize? Few of us really know what we prize most. Few of us really know the kind of a world we want. And schools pay little or no attention to clarifying the values held by students.[1]

It is here assumed that if we were to present more decision-making situations to students, if we were to ask more frequently for those values that the student wants protected in the problematic situation, and if these could be shared and examined in a free give-and-take classroom discussion, we might be helping to create a world in which values have a chance to operate.

Are values important in the thinking operations? We think that they are. Our desires, our hopes, our purposes most often generate the power to think. We think in order to achieve ends we hold precious. But all too often, we are unaware of the goals we prize, or we conceal the motives of our actions. It is here assumed that strong lights should be shone on the values that impinge upon problematic situations. These are matters of choice, and choosing is often best served by comparing, observing, imagining, and all the other operations heretofore mentioned. Certainly decision making deserves a place among the thinking operations and should be on our checklist for monitoring our own teaching practices.

Designing Projects or Investigations

This assignment may be thought of as more appropriate for junior and senior high school students, but it is also given in the upper grades of the elementary school. A project is a large-scale assignment. It usually involves many different activities, takes longer to complete, and is complex enough to call for some kind of preliminary outline before work is started on it. Sometimes a committee assignment is made for the completion of a project, and this involves the planning of a division of labor and the integration of the timing of the several tasks.

A project involves a desire for execution of the task, and students, for the first time, get a good idea of the importance of design. If certain questions are to be answered, certain kinds of data have to be gathered. If these data are not gathered, the question cannot be answered. Hence, the project starts out by an attempt to formulate a problem. One way of beginning is to list a series of questions that seem to be worthy of investigation. After some time an attempt is made to sort or to classify these questions. A cluster or group of questions sometimes transforms itself into one large problem.

If this happens, the individual or the committee is asked to study the problem further. If it is to be solved, what are *all* of the questions that have to be answered? These questions are then analyzed in terms of locating the sources of information that are available. The library in the school is almost always one such source. Newspaper files often constitute another. Appeals are sometimes made to other students to find out if there are materials available in home libraries.

Sometimes a question cannot be answered by appeal to written sources. Authorities have to be found, and letters have to be written to them. If the authorities are local, plans can be made to interview them. Where this is a necessary part of the project, students are taught something about interviewing: how to formulate their questions clearly, how to open the interview by introducing themselves and indicating the purpose of the visit and the investigation, how to close the interview and to thank the authority for his or her time and trouble.

Before students go out for the interview, the teacher goes over the questions and asks the students how they will use the responses when writing up their results. Do they just want yes and no answers? If so, perhaps they could formulate a short questionnaire and mail it to the authorities. Are they going to quote the authority? If so, what about taking notes during the interview? Will they read back the exact statement to the authority before the close of the interview, or will they write later and ask permission for a quote that they are enclosing?

Some investigations involve the polling of students and teachers. Usually people are not asked to sign their names, and this brings up a question of a facing sheet. Should each respondent indicate his or her sex, grade level, and other information that might be useful in interpreting the results?

Where students are required to make a preliminary outline of the work of the project, where they are asked to indicate the order in which the separate tasks are to be attacked, where some due dates are established for completing different parts of the investigation, the work is apt to proceed smoothly.

As the data gathering nears completion, questions are raised about planning the final report. How will it be done? Is it to be an oral report? If oral or written, how will it be organized? If it is a committee report, who will lead off, who will follow, and who will sum up? Are comments to be solicited from the class? Should it be presented to an assembly? If the report is a written one, can it be filed in the library for use by other students in the school?

Some teachers find this kind of curriculum activity exciting, profitable, and very stimulating as far as thinking is concerned. If students are working on a project that is their own, that involves *their* purposes, they are apt to work hard and long at the task. Almost always a significant project involves all of the other operations of thinking that have been discussed—comparing, summarizing, observing, interpreting, looking for assumptions, applying principles, and decision making, imagining, and criticizing. There is no doubt that designing projects and investigations offers a rich potential for engaging in many thinking operations.

Coding

When students hand in written *work*, it is a common practice today *to correct it* and *to grade it*. Under these circumstances, what are the students learning? Mistakes are found by the teacher and are pointed out to the student, who is asked to correct them, to supply the preferred response. In some situations this is an acceptable procedure. However, it should not be the only way of marking the written papers of students. Assume that we wanted to increase the responsibility that students take for their own thinking. Instead of *grading* the paper, or red-penciling it, could we code it?

If so, how shall we code it? Most of us are familiar with codes that are shorthand methods for indicating various and sundry stylistic shortcomings. How could it be done for thinking?

ALL OR NOTHING

We may be interested in the extreme statements used by students in their writing. As we read a student's paper, we will be alert to such words as *all, every, each, always, never, nobody, everybody*; we will also look for superlatives: *the best, the worst, the biggest, the nicest, the tallest*, and so forth. We might place an X near the word or in the margin of the line where it occurs. We could ask the student to take a clean sheet of paper and copy down each sentence with which an X is associated. The student is to answer two questions: (1) Does he or she wish to change any of the sentences, and if so, which ones and how; and (2) In what way are the sentences alike?

Some students may not wish to change any of their "extreme" statements and will say so. *We should accept this decision without objection.* We have given to these students a *second* opportunity to read what they have written, and they have judged it to be appropriate. Each is saying to his teacher: "I will take full responsibility for what I wrote. I want to leave it as it is. I do not wish to change anything."

These students may be embarrassed by the coding and express this feeling by being defiant. Some may not be sensitive to the extremes that have been coded. Some may not care. A class sharing of reactions tends to be positive. The common response is to wonder why such an important matter has not been called to their attention before. Teachers who have used this approach report that subsequent papers reflect a more serious consideration of "extreme" statements.

EITHER–ORS

We look for the little word *or* and perhaps circle it. We look for such expressions as "There are two ways of doing . . . or three ways or four." Sometimes students will use the expression: "*The other way* of doing it," and this is a concealed *either-or* type of statement. The statement is not marked wrong. It is called to the attention of the student. Does he or she want to change it? Will the student take the responsibility for the statement as it stands? We are trying to teach students to be responsible for what they say. If they are to learn to take responsibility, they must be given the responsibility to decide for themselves. In the previous section concerned with extreme statements, the students might have used the word *only*, and the teacher may have placed an X beside it. If the student believes it to be appropriate, he or she does not change it, and *the teacher accepts this decision*, even if at the moment the teacher believes that the student should change it.

It is important for the teacher to code *all* of the extreme statements and *all* of the *either-ors*; not just the ones about which he or she has some doubts.

QUALIFYING WORDS AND PHRASES

In their writings students use such words and phrases as *it seems*, *it appears*, *it's my opinion*, *perhaps*, *maybe*, *might*, *probably*, and many similar expressions. These might be coded with the letter Q, signifying qualifying words. Again, the student is asked to recopy the sentences with which the Q is associated and to indicate how the sentences are alike and any changes he or she wishes to make. Some students will ask, "Why are these words coded at all, when you seem to be opposed to all (?) kinds of extreme statements?" One has to say often that the code does *not* indicate that the teacher opposes the word or phrase. The code suggests that the student should take a second look at what he or she has written.

Another way of reacting to qualifying words is to have someone make a tabulation of all the qualifying words used by the class and to classify them into groups that have approximately the same meaning so far as degree of conviction is concerned. Under these conditions of self-examination, some students will find that they use certain qualifying words or phrases over and over again to the point of monotony. Some will find that they have a three-point continuum, noting that things are either *true, false*, or qualified with the expressions *it seems* or *it appears*.

The teacher may draw a long, horizontal line on the blackboard. At the extreme left end of the line, the teacher writes the words "absolutely true and absolutely false." At the extreme right end of the line he or she writes "complete uncertainty." The teacher asks the class for phrases or words that are very close to these extreme positions and then works the process toward the middle of the line. Students begin to see the meaning of such expressions as *almost without exception, with very few exceptions, almost always, in the large majority of instances, in general, in more cases than not*, and so forth. The idea is to say what we believe and to believe what we say. If we are more sure, our words should indicate that degree of sureness. If we are less sure, we should qualify our statement the more. We should use words with care, so that we communicate our thinking as best we can. We should be developing habits of accuracy of expression, not habits of slovenliness in communication. As teachers we can pay close attention to the ways students use qualifying expressions. We can help them to take a second look at their work, and we can give them the responsibility for deciding upon possible changes.

VALUE STATEMENTS

Very often students will indicate what they like or dislike, what they want or don't want, what they prefer and what they do not prefer. Value expressions are usually associated with nouns. A teacher might place a V near the word that stands for the value. If something is disliked, it might be a V minus (V−) and if it is liked it might be a V plus (V+). Students are to list these words and classify them; then they are to write a summary paragraph about the value expressions they have used. Sometimes they are asked if they have been consistent all the way through. Often they are asked if they have omitted some important values that they would now include.

On many occasions students will not be aware that they are revealing value indicators. They may have been writing a report of an observation in which they were supposed to restrict themselves to sense impressions. Value judgments expressed by students demand attention. What do our students cherish? When the value indicators are placed on the blackboard, students get some idea of what others cherish. More alternatives come out into the open, and sometimes there is debate about their *value*. It is also a way of getting to know more about oneself. If the teacher helps students to see what they stand for, they may, on reflection, reject their own positions, but even if they reaffirm their statements, they know a little more about themselves.

Where there is a paucity of value statements in the writings of students, a different type of assignment may help. The decision-making kind of assignment is apt to yield many affirmations and denials. As one reads papers with special alertness for value expressions, one begins to know the students better. This is one way of finding out "what makes them tick." If the problems and issues are of great importance to them, they will reveal much about themselves. This is especially true in circumstances where their values are not criticized, or marked wrong—where they are accepted for what they are: value expressions.

ATTRIBUTIONS

In their writings students often give attributions to others. They attribute motives, causes, preferences, feelings, attitudes, beliefs, hopes, aspirations, authority, responsibility, skill, sincerity, hypocrisy, and scores of other human strengths and weaknesses. They are seldom aware that they are "attributing." It seems to them that they are stating "facts." After examination they see how difficult it is to be reliably informed about motives or feelings and how greatly such expressions need to be qualified. These attributions may also be thought of as assumptions and examined for their reasonableness. Teachers code these expressions with an A+ or an A− and ask the students to list and classify their attributions and to comment upon their expressions.

Where this is started in the elementary grades and carried forward, students will have many opportunities to examine their habits. As with the other codings, in an atmosphere of acceptance and self-examination students may become much more discerning, discriminating, and responsible in their use of language. This leads to more self-direction toward maturity.

OTHER CODINGS

Some teachers want students to be sensitive about their use of generalizations. Wherever students generalize, the teacher codes the sentence with a G. Some teachers have used special codes for analogies and metaphors. Codes are sometimes used for vague and ambiguous constructions. Some look for the little word *if*, which usually is followed by *then*. Such a statement is often a great oversimplification of the case. Upon reexamination the student may see that the *then* does not logically follow if the *if* is fulfilled. It may take many different *ifs* to meet the situation. Some teachers look for statements indicative of suspended judgment. Some look for carefulness in defining terms. Some look for direct correlation statements, such as "To the extent that a student studies, to that extent he or she will get high grades."

In the elementary grades some teachers code nouns, or adjectives, or verbs and have students examine their use of these terms. In higher grades infinitives and gerunds may be coded to be reflected upon. The opportunities are almost unlimited, and what a teacher decides to use will be guided by his or her own cherished aims and the needs of students.

Coding Other Papers

When students have become somewhat familiar with a few coding symbols, they may be asked to code some paper that has been selected by the teacher. This may be part of an editorial, a page from a text or a novel, a selection from a student newspaper or magazine. Students are directed to look for the extreme statements in the article, for the value statements, for the *either-ors* and *if-thens*, for the attributions and generalizations, for name-calling and propaganda statements. After they have coded the paper, they are asked to write a critical summary paragraph. This type of assignment teaches observation, summarizing, interpreting, criticizing, and, of course, responsibility. The students are held responsible for the coding they have done and the criticisms they have made.

One cannot make use of this coding operation on *every* paper that a student turns in. Like most assignments, overuse of this one can produce boredom and monotony. There is little doubt, however, that its selective and discriminating use makes a contribution to a program that aims to stress thinking. To respond to the coding made by a teacher and to code the writings of others puts an emphasis upon some of the cruder and more common errors of thinking. It deserves a place in a checklist for teachers to use in monitoring their own curriculum materials and their own teaching.

BEHAVIOR AND THINKING

What are some symptoms of human behavior that reflect inadequate experiences with thinking? How significant are these "symptoms"? Do they tend to cut off opportunities to learn and to grow? Are students at all aware of these traits in themselves? Can the present habits or dispositions to act be modified? We have some evidence to indicate that certain behaviors of young people change after the introduction of a program that emphasizes thinking. We shall begin by discussing some of these behaviors.

Impulsiveness

There are some students who seem to react on the spur of the moment to many kinds of stimuli. Teachers often say of them that they go off "half-cocked"; they jump the gun. They begin to respond before the question is asked. In the minds of many teachers, this behavior is closely related to thinking. They say that impulsive students should stop to think, that they should take time to consider the problem and its alternatives. In this volume it is hypothesized that if students had many opportunities for thinking, the tendency toward impulsiveness would diminish. There is research evidence to support the hypothesis that this behavior can be modified (see Part 5).

Overdependence upon the Teacher

In practically every classroom there are students who seem to be forever stuck. As soon as the teacher gets the group started, such students will immediately raise their hands. They are indicating that they need help. The teacher responds by telling them how to proceed with steps 1 and 2. A short time later these students are in trouble again! Steps 1 and 2 have been completed, but more help is needed on how to go ahead. When this happens again and again, the teacher is quite apt to warn these students that in their lives there will be many occasions when a teacher will not be present and that they had better soon learn to think for themselves. Here again, the teacher relates this overdependence to a lack of experience and training in thinking. Research evidence suggests that when thinking is given an emphasis in classroom work, this kind of behavior is modified. The students make changes in their habits.

Inability to Concentrate

There are students who seem to start off all right in their efforts, but soon something happens. Their minds seem to wander; sometimes they seem to be woolgathering; they do not "pay attention" to their work. Connections between means and ends are missed. A rather thoughtless slip may ruin what was otherwise a good piece of work. Teachers often say of these students that they can't concentrate. It is common for teachers to tell these students over and over again that they should keep their minds on their work, that they should *think* about what they are doing. Notice that teachers connect the behavior directly with thinking. What is needed is a curriculum that puts an emphasis on thinking. *Telling* a pupil to think doesn't seem to work. We need classroom activities that require thinking operations, and we need to emphasize them year after year.

Missing the Meaning

Teachers say that some students get very little meaning out of their work. If these pupils are asked to give the gist of a story, they are quite apt to tell the whole story in great detail or to sum it all up by a sentence or two that does not convey much sense. If a joke has been told and many students are smiling or laughing, these pupils are apt to ask, "What are they laughing at?" These pupils don't seem to see meanings in their experiences; they have little sense of big ideas. Teachers say that they are superficial, not thoughtful; that thinking is over their heads; that it's too deep for them. Yet, when pupils so characterized have had frequent opportunities to think under the guidance of an informed teacher, they begin to change. A start has been made on the reconstruction of a habit that has interfered with maturation. Notice again the direct way in which teachers relate this behavior to thinking.

Dogmatic, Assertive Behavior

In almost every class there are students who seem to have all, or almost all, of the answers. They are frequent users of *either–ors*. Sometimes they are thought of as class "loudmouths." When they encounter differences of opinion, they try to outshout the opposition. They seldom qualify responses. Many of their statements are of the *all-or-nothing* kind. They are not sensitive to nuances of expression, to shades of meaning. Where things are probably true, they are apt to assert their unconditional truth. They may be equally assertive about propositions where evidence is lacking. They are sure in situations where thoughtful people entertain a doubt. These students know in some way that what they do is not quite right; they know that they need help, that something needs to be changed. The teacher knows this, too. The need is for curriculum materials and methods that stress thinking. Such students need a concentrated diet of thinking activities. The research evidence indicates that a semester of work in which almost every day puts forth a requirement for varied kinds of thinking results in noticeable changes in behavior.

Rigidity, Inflexibility of Behavior

Some students seem to be like little old men and women long before their time. New ways of doing things seem to frighten them. If the teacher attempts to show these students another way to subtract, they are apt to respond by asking if they can't do it the way they were shown last year. They like to act in terms of a formula, and they persist in a rigid manner. Some of these pupils, when asked to redo problems that were incorrect, even repeat their previous mistakes. There is a resistance to new ideas, new materials, new ways of doing things, new situations. There is a preference for the old ways, the known ways, the familiar ways. To think suggests a fresh look at a new situation; to think involves an examination of alternatives and often means the trying of a new hypothesis. These students are in great need of help in meeting situations that involve thought. Teachers relate this behavior to thinking habits and are aware of the need for a continuing emphasis on thinking.

Extreme Lack of Confidence in One's Own Thinking

In this group are the students who almost never volunteer a response to a question that involves thought. If there has been a discussion in class, such students are apt to come to the teacher after it is all over and say that they wanted to say something but didn't know if it was correct or didn't know what the other students might say in criticism. There is a misunderstanding of the purposes of sharing our thinking. There is the idea that one's thoughts must be absolutely true or they should not be uttered. There is a timidity about revealing oneself; a lack of confidence in self. As these students experience many thinking situations, see others respond to them, are guided daily in many kinds of thinking operations, they will be apt to share their thinking with colleagues. Extreme lack of confidence in one's own thinking is here regarded as a symptom that is modifiable by a curriculum emphasizing thinking operations.

Unwillingness to Think

Most of us have had experiences with students who just don't seem to want to think. They want the teacher to outline for them what is to be done, and then they will do it. They detest independent work, projects, discussions, research. They are the lesson learners of our school society. They don't want to be in any doubt about standards of accomplishment. They believe that the teacher should do the thinking and that students should give the right answers, which are to be found in the texts. These students have habits that tend to make them resistant to change and difficult to work with if the curriculum emphasizes thinking. Steady exposure to many kinds of thinking operations, rewards judiciously applied, and informed, thoughtful guidance all help in getting the processes of change started.

SOME QUALIFYING COMMENTS

Only eight categories of behavior were listed in association with lack of thinking experience. These were the most frequently mentioned by classroom teachers when so-called thinking-related behaviors were discussed. Are there more? Almost surely there are many more, and thoughtful teachers will recognize relationships between those other behaviors and thinking. Are these offered as ironclad categories with no overlapping? Not at all. We do not have categories of behavior of that kind. These categories represent a rather crude way of going about a diagnosis. A student does not fit exactly into one of the categories; he or she approximates it. He or she is not *just like that* all the time and in all situations. Teachers, however, have found these categories helpful in pointing a direction for teaching.

Is it certain that the "cause" of the foregoing behaviors is always and in every instance related to thinking? The contrary is probably true. Wherever a student is having difficulty in learning, the first step should be a careful physical examination by competent, thoughtful, informed medical doctors. We should rule out from our "nonthinking" group those students who are ill. In the second place, some students have deep emotional needs that are not being met, and these students too should be ruled out as having thinking-related behaviors. Where students are unusually and abnormally aggressive, hostile, or belligerent, where they are excessively shy and withdrawn, where they are submissive and meek, and where there is evidence of frequent regression to behavior that represents an earlier stage of development, we infer the presence of unmet emotional needs.[2]

In the preliminary trials of the materials and methods that receive extended treatment in the next two parts of the book, a number of teachers commented on the necessity for developing a feeling of security in children before emphasizing assignments relating to thinking. This seems to be sound advice. Thinking is sometimes unsettling; doubt is often disturbing; the trying out of new ideas has suspense and anxiety as correlates on many occasions. Where students are emotionally insecure, emphasis should first be placed upon the meeting of emotional needs.

The eight categories of behavior described above are associated with inadequacies in thinking. Students whose behavior seems to coincide with the descriptions in one or more of the categories have probably practiced these particular habits for a long period of time. Helping a student change a habit is not the work of a moment, or an afternoon, or a week. It is a cooperative venture that may take many months. It requires a continuing exposure to thinking situations. In addition, it also requires the thoughtful, friendly, patient, careful work of a competent teacher who identifies with the student in need of help. On the other hand, a teacher with all of these qualifications may experience frustration unless he or she is familiar with materials and practices that relate to the thinking processes. It is the integration of the two that promises most in terms of change.

Why is it that one child in a family may show one or more of the behaviors described in these eight categories, while brothers and sisters will not? We have no good answer for this question. Though children in the same family are said to have the same environment, this is questionable on many grounds. The same question is unanswered with respect to illnesses and particularly to communicable illnesses. It may be that without our being aware of it, some children miss having frequent opportunities to carry on thinking processes.

What happens to students if no special emphasis is placed on thinking? We cannot answer the question with respect to a particular student, but there is evidence that indicates that a student who is described by the teacher as impulsive, for example, will probably be categorized the same way in the following year by his or her new teacher. In some schools where comments about students' habits and character are solicited from teachers annually, there is a surprising amount of repetition. In some quarters this is accepted as evidence that the student is not yet ready for change!

Piaget and others have been much interested in the changes that take place from year to year in the ways children think. Their conclusions are often generalized by age levels and by stages of development, and in several instances have been associated with the history of human development from the earliest time. It should be quite clear that the evidence pertains to children who have had little or no instruction in thinking and little guidance in the development of habits that stress thinking. Probably the results have more to do with neglect and chance than with the "natural" evolution of man.

Isn't it true that in human development good things tend to go together? Aren't those who remember the facts the best more likely to be the best thinkers? At the college level the correlations between scores on information tests and scores on thinking tests tend to be low. At the elementary school level even the scores on intelligence tests tend to correlate with thinking test scores at a level of .50 or below, and oftentimes at the level of .30. As a matter of fact, when teachers begin to emphasize thinking operations, they find that certain students who were not doing well with the routine exercises now begin to excel and some students who have excelled at memoriter tasks need much help in assignments that emphasize thinking. There is probably some correlation among the "good" traits and habits, but it is not so high as is generally posited. Certainly one cannot take for granted that a person who does well on an examination testing retention of facts will also do well on a test that requires thinking.

Is it the responsibility of teachers to change the behaviors of children? What about the parents? What about other social institutions that have contacts with children? In one sense, to aim at the changing of children suggests that we will manipulate them in ways to satisfy our own ends. Who is to decide if and how children are to be changed? Shall we consult with parents and get their consent to our aims? Should we ask them how they want the schools to change their children?

Schools and teachers don't do just as they please. Through a board of education, in cooperation with educational leaders, broad policies are determined. Almost always such statements of educational aims include items associated with self-direction and independent thought. As we see it, teachers have a real responsibility to develop a curriculum that provides many opportunities for thinking. This is a major task. The school need not take responsibility for change; the student will take that responsibility if the educational diet is rich in experiences associated with a variety of thinking operations. But it is hard to see how a student can take this responsibility if the school does not have trained, insightful, thoughtful, considerate teachers, who supply thinking opportunities.

There is much evidence from research into test results that children forget a great deal of what they learn in school. R. W. Tyler and James E. Wert conducted some studies into the lack of recall of college students. They found that the thinking skills that were learned—interpreting data and applying principles—were not forgotten, but the specific facts that were learned were not retained very well.[3] This may be another reason for putting an emphasis upon thinking: It is a skilled habit that is likely to be retained.

CONCLUSION

Fifteen ways of emphasizing thinking have been presented in this part of the book. Nowhere has it been suggested that this is an all-inclusive listing. Although many thinking operations are frequently used in our class-rooms, it is also probably true that few teachers consistently emphasize their use. On the other hand, in typical school practices one is apt to see as much emphasis upon these operations in the kindergarten as in a junior high school or college classroom.

It is not uncommon to find high school teachers who will say that their students are not ready to think about problems; hence, these same teachers tend to emphasize a teaching function that puts great emphasis upon impart-ing information. The concept of *higher mental processes* may suggest to some that the mental processes operative in high school youth are quite different from those carried on by children in the elementary school. When one finds, however, that nearly all of these operations may be observed in the very early grades of elementary school, it raises a question about what is meant by higher mental processes. It probably means processes that distinguish human beings from lower orders of animals. It does not mean uniquely different processes for different age levels in the development toward maturity. Children in elementary school, adolescents in secondary school, and older students in college all need continuing practice in these thinking operations.

If we emphasize these operations more in the early years of education, we shall develop students who employ more caution in making judgments and drawing conclusions. We shall have students who see more than one course of action. We shall have students who are looking for alternatives and delving for assumptions. We shall have students who prize doubt. They will be more open-minded and perhaps more ready for change in a great number of areas. They will probably have a more experimental outlook on life, and instead of being resistant to problems, they will probably welcome them. There is little doubt that the beginnings of a great university are to be found in the public schools of a nation. The better our base, the more we can look forward to the flowering of a compassionate and intelligent study of humankind and our problems. To put an emphasis upon thinking is to take a first long step toward an improvement of the human situation.

PART 2

Applications
in the Elementary School

Marilyn Ziti teaches third grade at the Steveston Elementary School. This school year, encouraged by new administrative policy, she will begin a classroom program emphasizing thinking. The thinking skills program will represent a major departure from her customary teaching style, and although she is an experienced teacher, she is somewhat anxious about doing a good job. She is also concerned about the potential impact of teaching for thinking on the behavior of her students. Are there ways of helping Ziti to move teaching for thinking into her classroom practices with a minimum of stress for her? Are there guidelines that can be used to smooth her transition as well as the transition of her students? Can there be teaching for thinking without tears?

BEGINNING A TEACHING
FOR THINKING PROGRAM

One of the more exasperating as well as challenging aspects of teaching is that there are rarely any clear-cut, definitive, and explicit instructional strategies and organizational schemes that are universally applicable. It is frequently a source of great chagrin to teachers who query, "How shall I do this?" to be told, "Well, it depends." Teachers must often feel they are walking on shifting sands. Are there *never* any clear-cut answers? Is every teaching moment afloat on a sea of undulating variables?

Teachers with years of experience dealing with these shifting variables will immediately understand. There are few hard and fast rules that can be applied to all situations. Teachers usually take into account numerous considerations before making a decision requiring action. That is likely why books advocating a "cookbook" or "formula" approach to innovation are doomed to failure. Scheme A implemented in P.S. 173 Brooklyn may be a wonderful

31

innovation; parachuted holus-bolus into the public school system of Yakima, Washington, it may be a hopeless failure.

We have learned that the most important consideration in a teacher's acceptance of an innovative approach is how closely it is connected to that teacher's belief system. Teachers must truly believe in the proposed ideas, as well as the instructional strategies being advocated. A new program must not create too much dissonance for the teacher, either in theory or in classroom application.

There are many ways to implement teaching for thinking programs, no one of which is the "right" way. Although certain principles must be maintained, which have been spelled out in detail in Part 1 of this text, these principles provide much latitude for variation in application. As there are several different yet effective ways to teach reading, so are there differences in the approaches one may take in teaching for thinking. If you are planning to begin a teaching for thinking program in your classroom, you are encouraged to consider the variations presented in the rest of this section regarding grouping organization, as well as the extent of application. Then select procedures that feel most in harmony with your personal beliefs and values about running a classroom. In making the choices, ask yourself:

> Do I feel I will be able to exercise the controls that I need if I choose this approach?
> Do I believe that this approach is compatible with the background of experience of my pupils?
> Will this approach fit in with the organizational scheme of my classroom?

As you reflect on the choices, you should take into consideration variables of pupils and their backgrounds of experience, instructional materials available, administrative support, your own level of tolerance for ambiguity (that is, how stressful it is for you to try out new ideas), and your need to exercise classroom control.

The variations that follow are presented as suggestions. You may wish to select an approach from among those presented here, create an amalgam of your own from what is offered, or invent an entirely original design.

Grouping for Instruction

One of the ways in which teachers may differ in their applications of teaching for thinking is through their classroom organization. Different teachers prefer different organizations, each scheme offering its own idiosyncratic benefits and limitations.

WORKING WITH THE WHOLE CLASS

If most of your classroom activities are carried out with the whole class, it may be more manageable, at the outset, to use a whole class approach in teaching for thinking. This approach has clear advantages, as well as distinct limitations. Whole class instruction requires the least classroom reorganization. It is a familiar, and for many teachers, an entirely comfortable way of teaching. The chief drawback, as many teachers discover, is that the one-to-one teacher-student interactions so critical in furthering an individual student's thinking cannot be "played out" effectively in a whole class setting. In adopting a whole class approach, the following procedures ought to facilitate implementation.

1. Begin by introducing the pupils to the thinking operation upon which the exercise or activity is based. (Strategies for introducing thinking operations are presented in the next section, "Introducing the Operations.")

2. When the children have a good understanding of what the operation entails, select an activity from among those presented in this chapter for that operation.

3. In making your selection, consider the following criteria:

Does the activity give the pupils a chance to practice this thinking operation in a clear and unambiguous way?

Will the activity be appropriate to the children's background of experience?

Will I be more comfortable using a thinking activity in this particular area of the curriculum?

Does the activity relate to what is being studied in my class?

How does the thinking activity contribute to furthering specific skills and concept development in the area being studied?

4. Decide if the activity is to be done with oral or written responses.

5. Present the activity to the class. If hands-on materials are to be used, make sure that all the children get a chance to observe and handle them. If photographs or illustrations are to be used, make sure that all the children can see the data clearly.

6. Give the pupils adequate time to study and reflect upon the requirements of the exercise.

7. For activities requiring written responses:

Ask the children to complete the task recalling what the operation requires them to do. Make sure you allow sufficient time for children to think.

When pupils have completed the task, ask them to share their ideas with you. Respond to each pupil's statement with the kinds of teaching for thinking responses that attend to and accurately reflect the idea that the pupil is conveying. (These responses are described in detail in Part 4, in the section "Reflective Responses.")

Ask pupils to give their reactions to the exercise. Use data from the students' evaluative comments to strengthen your teaching for thinking skills.

8. For activities requiring oral responses:

You may wish to record the children's ideas on the chalkboard or on chart paper.

Invite the pupils' responses to the task, and respond to each pupil's statement by attending to and accurately reflecting the idea that the pupil is conveying. Avoid responses that bring closure or that limit pupil thinking. (See Part 4, "Teacher-Student Interactions.")

Be sensitive to the interest of the students in the activity. Don't carry the activity on after pupil interest is noticeably exhausted.

Ask for pupils to give you feedback on the activity. Use data from students' evaluative comments to help you increase your teaching for thinking skills.

SEVERAL SMALL GROUPS WORKING SIMULTANEOUSLY

Small group work, in contrast to the whole class approach, allows for more interaction among the children and is a helpful format for stimulating inquiry. "Group think" in a small group setting can be a provocative way to brainstorm ideas, but it is not productive in the more formal, whole class setting. Also, children who have difficulty talking out in a large group setting may volunteer their ideas more readily in the small group situation.

Working with small groups may require some classroom reorganization, especially for those teachers who are accustomed to large group instruction. Problems may arise in working out the formation of the groups (e.g., what children work more effectively with each other), in determining how to get children to follow effective group work procedures, and in helping groups to keep on task. There are no hard and fast rules for assigning pupils to groups, and there are no clear advantages to grouping according to academic ability. You may wish to try several different grouping arrangements to see which results in more productive on-task work.

If you select a small group instructional format, follow procedures 1, 2, and 3 above, as you would for working with the whole class. Then,

4. Prepare copies of the thinking activity for distribution to each group.

5. Divide the class into cooperative learning groups of about four or five members.

6. Make sure that the groups understand what the thinking operation requires them to do.

7. Distribute copies of the activity to each group. Ask the children to talk together about their ideas and to work together to complete the activity. Ask that each group select a recorder to be responsible for recording the group's ideas.

8. When the groups have finished, ask each recorder to present the group's responses to the rest of the class, or the recorders may transfer the responses to the chalkboard. Invite class discussion on the differences and varieties in each group's response. Avoid making judgments about the value of each group's ideas, and do not encourage these from the pupils. Use teaching for thinking interactions to encourage pupils to think more deeply about the responses they have made. (See the section "Teaching for Thinking Responses" in Part 4.)

WORKING WITH A SINGLE GROUP

Some teachers have found the single group approach more manageable for the following reason: It allows the teacher to work more productively with a small number of pupils and heightens the effect of the one-to-one teaching for thinking interactions. Since the major payoff occurs as a result of the teacher's facilitative interactions with the ideas of a single student, it is clear that the most advantageous setting for this is the small group instructional format. A slight drawback to this approach is that the rest of the class must be productively occupied so that the teacher may work with a minimum of interruption with the "thinking group." Teachers who have had experience working with reading groups will already have ideas of how this may be done. Here are some steps to consider in carrying out the single group approach:

1. Decide in advance which children you will work with. It may be interesting to try a very heterogeneous mixture and note the responses of the different pupils. A good working group should have no more than about six pupils. The more students in the group, the fewer one-to-one interactions are possible.

2. Decide in advance what the rest of the class will be doing. Of course, they may be working individually, or in small groups, on a thinking activity. They may also be reading, writing, or working on another type of assignment.

3. Select a thinking activity from this chapter that is appropriate for the group. In making your selection, consider the criteria presented in the

previous section on whole group instruction, item 3. Make sure that the children have a good understanding of what the operation entails.

4. Present the activity to the group. Allow them sufficient time to examine the activity and to talk together about their responses to the task. Avoid intervening at this time, if possible. Do not begin your teaching for thinking interactions until you are satisfied that the group has exhausted their self-directed inquiry.

5. Invite the pupils to discuss their ideas with you. What have they found? As they respond to you, listen carefully to each idea and reflect to each child the meaning of the idea that he or she is presenting. Carry on these reflective interactions for at least five minutes, or for as long as you think productive. Avoid telling children their ideas are "good" or even "interesting." When the session is over, thank the children for sharing their ideas with you.

6. Set up a schedule for rotating the groups so that all the pupils eventually have an opportunity to work with you in a small group session.

WORKING WITH INDIVIDUAL LEARNERS

Some teachers may prefer to organize teaching for thinking in an individualized program. This would not be a radically different approach from an individualized reading program. Instead of choosing books, pupils would select thinking activities from a large collection. Activities for selection would, of course, reflect the curriculum of the grade as well as accommodate for the range of abilities of the pupils.[1] The following implementation procedures should make this approach clearer:

1. Select about fifty activities from this chapter that you think are appropriate for the students in your class. (As you gain experience with teaching for thinking, you will likely wish to create your own activities, tailor-made for your class.) Write clear instructions to the students for each activity on ten- by fourteen-inch cards. Use photographs and illustrations cut from magazines and old books to make the cards more attractive and the activities more explicit. For example, here is a science activity in which individual children are asked to design their own investigation.

DESIGNING AN INVESTIGATION

You will need some materials for this investigation: a rubber band, a piece of wood, a piece of paper, and a piece of string.

Design an investigation to show how you can make sounds with these materials. Show how you can change sounds and make them soft, loud, higher, and lower. Then, write about what you found.

2. This collection of cards will become your resource file of thinking activities. Categorize the activities under subject area headings. Put the cards into containers that make the activities accessible for the pupils.

3. Require the children to select at least one thinking activity card per day to complete individually. You can decide to either let the children choose any activity they wish or specify the subject area from which the choice is to be made.

4. Completed thinking activities are turned in to the teacher, who then reads the work and responds in ways that facilitate pupil reflection. Figure 2.1 shows an example of how this might be done and presents a format which may be useful.

Extent of Application

Teaching for thinking has been represented throughout this text as a way of emphasizing the higher-order mental functions within the subject matter of the grade. Implicit in this statement is the idea that thinking per se is

FIGURE 2.1. Example of Student and Teacher Responses to Thinking Activity

---

Pupil's Name   Ardent T. Thinker
Date   February 10
Thinking Activity No.   12, Comparing Eyes and Ears
Subject Area   Science
Thinking Operation   Comparing

Alike: Both are found on the head.
Both are senses.
Both are important.
Both are complicated systems.

Different: One is for seeing, and one is for hearing.
Eyes come in different colors.
Eyes take in light; ears take in sound.

TEACHER'S COMMENT

Dear Ardent:
You have written that eyes and ears are both *senses*. Please help me to understand what you mean by defining that term. Also, the differences you listed are primarily differences in functions. There might be other differences that you might wish to consider—for example, differences in structure. Please think about these, and see if you wish to add to your list.

---

not a separate school subject; it is rather a way of teaching a subject. Using a teaching for thinking approach in each area of the curriculum would be the primary objective in classroom implementation.

However, teaching for thinking may be a new approach for many teachers. Since one must walk before one dances, we may need to proceed more slowly before we can achieve larger leaps. That is why teachers should also consider to what extent they initially wish to incorporate teaching for thinking into their classroom programs. The question of extent of application should be considered in conjunction with choices about grouping for instruction; no choice in either area precludes selecting any of the alternatives given in the other area.

TEACHING FOR THINKING IN A LIMITED FRAMEWORK

To what extent will you feel comfortable in using a teaching for thinking approach? What curriculum area will allow you to experiment with these ideas while still feeling safe about achieving the required learning goals? What curriculum area seems to you to offer the richest opportunities to engage pupils' higher-order thinking? One way of incorporating teaching for thinking into your classroom is to begin with emphasis in a single curriculum area and to use this to sharpen your skills, to increase your awareness, and to build your feelings of success in implementation. Once you have generated increased confidence in using this approach, you will want to consider extending the application into other areas of the curriculum. If you choose teaching for thinking in a limited framework, you may consider a whole class or a small group organizational scheme as indicated above. You may also modify the individualized program approach to suit this limited application. Here are some guidelines that may be helpful:

1. Decide on the subject area that best allows, for you, a teaching for thinking emphasis.
2. Choose an activity representing that curriculum area from among those presented in this chapter. The following criteria may help you to make an appropriate choice:
      Is the activity related to what is being studied in that subject?
      Is the activity within the realm of the children's background of experience?
      How does the activity help to build specific skills?
      How does the activity help to deepen pupils' understandings about the topic being studied?
3. Make sure that pupils understand what the thinking operation entails. (You may wish to refer to the section "Introducing Thinking Operations," which follows.)

4. Present the task to the students. Allow them adequate time for their inquiries.

5. Pupils' responses may be made orally or in writing. Follow the procedures suggested above, in the section "Working with the Whole Class," items 7 and 8.

6. Work on building your skills in using teaching for thinking responses. As you call for pupils to share their ideas, and as you respond to each, concentrate on attending to and reflecting back the main ideas of each pupil's statement.

7. After you have developed confidence and skill in using reflective responses, begin to extend your response repertoire by including appropriate analysis and challenging responses. (See the section "Teaching for Thinking Responses" in Part 4.)

8. Use at least one thinking activity per day in the curriculum area of your choice.

EXTENDING TEACHING FOR THINKING APPLICATIONS

As you grow more comfortable with an emphasis on thinking, begin to work thinking activities into a second and then a third subject area. Work at a pace that is comfortable for you following your own schedule of classroom implementation. Monitor your own reactions to the way the program is going. If you feel strong, confident, and capable, and if you experience a sense of healthful professional growth in using these classroom strategies, the pace you have set is likely appropriate. If you feel stressed, unhappy, and frustrated, and if you experience a sense of confusion and turbulence, you are likely to have moved too rapidly and taken on much more than is appropriate to your own learning pace. Hurrying teaching for thinking into action may be counterproductive, if it is done at the cost of increasing the stress in teachers' lives. Proceeding at a pace and in a fashion that will allow for continued professional growth is the key to successful implementation.

Designing Your Own Approach

The approaches to implementing teaching for thinking programs that have been described above are not all-inclusive. In no way is it intended that they be considered the only ways to initiate teaching for thinking in your classroom. They are proposed as helpful paradigms that we hope will serve as guidelines to your own creations, which may incorporate features of what we have described or may depart entirely from them, resulting in new creations. Again, we emphasize that the approach you choose should be one that is educationally viable for you—and one that allows you the degree of freedom you need to grow and learn with your students about the delightful, intriguing, and challenging facets of teaching for thinking.

INTRODUCING THE THINKING OPERATIONS

It has been suggested in the previous section that it is important for children to be introduced to a thinking operation before they undertake more extensive work with thinking activities. For example, before pupils are expected to carry out activities where classifying data is called for, they should have some prior experiences that help them understand what classification involves; specifically, that classification calls for the setting up of groups and the placing of items with similar attributes into these groups. Background of experience of pupils and the difficulty of the operation itself are two factors that should be taken into consideration in determining the nature and extent of the introductory experiences. For example, children's experiences with comparing and the familiarity of the comparing process should make this operation relatively accessible to most elementary students. Suggesting hypotheses, summarizing, and looking for assumptions, on the other hand, may present more formidable challenges in introductory lessons.

Since most elementary school children learn abstract concepts best when these are presented in concrete situations, it is suggested that the introduction of each operation be done, first, through the presentation of a concrete example, which is then used as a basis for drawing meaning about the operation. Charts, posters, or other illustrative materials, as well as manipulative materials, are all good ways to begin concretely. After meaning has been extracted and pupils appear to comprehend what the operation calls for, it is helpful to follow up with practice exercises. These may then be examined and appropriate feedback given to heighten pupils' understanding. Pupils' questions about the thinking operation may also be addressed in these introductory sessions.

In the pages that follow, numerous examples of how each thinking operation may be introduced are presented. Once again, these are to be considered guidelines, rather than as "the method" of introducing thinking operations.

Introducing Comparing

Begin with photos (for example, a fish and a butterfly) or with concrete materials (for example, a pair of scissors and a pair of pliers), and set these up so that all may see them. If manipulative materials are being used, the children should be able to handle them.

Ask the children to think of all the ways in which these items are alike. Then ask them to think of all the ways in which they are different. Working together, generate a list of all the similarities and differences that the children can think of.

When the children's ideas have dried up, explain that they have been comparing. Tell them that comparing means finding the ways in which two items are alike and finding the differences, too.

Ask the children to think of other items that may be compared, and if time permits, try another practice exercise. Ask the children to consider how learning to compare may be a valuable skill, and invite their ideas about it.

Introducing Observing

Use a photo from a social studies or science text that is rich in detail. Or use something concrete like a kite, a thermometer, or perhaps a musical instrument.

Ask the children to make observations about it. Encourage them to study the illustration (or object) and to note as many details as they can. If they seem to be going beyond the data, or making great impetuous leaps, ask them to support their statements with data from their observations. That is, what can be actually seen that allows them to make that statement?

When the observations have been collected and noted, explain that they have been observing and that observing means making a careful study of what you see, what you hear, and/or what you can gather from several senses; that it means noticing details and reporting your findings; that it means keeping reports of your observations free from assumptions and personal opinions.

Ask the students to think of other objects or illustrations that may yield fruitful observations, and try another practice exercise. Can the children think of times in their own experiences when they were called upon to make some observations? What happened? Can the children tell you how learning to observe may be a valuable skill for them to possess? How does knowing how to observe help us in our lives? Why might it be important to be able to keep observations free from assumptions? What are the children's ideas about this?

Introducing Classifying

Begin with a collection of manipulative materials that have some relationship to each other. For example, a collection of buttons, a collection of Christmas cards, or a collection of pictures of foods would be appropriate to use with introductory exercises.

If you choose buttons, allow the students to examine them, and ask them to create some groups. Ask them to place each of the buttons in a group. Ask them to identify the name of each group according to its particular attribute. Buttons may be classified according to the number of holes; according to size, and according to color. The groups may then be given names relating to the common characteristic; for example, the "two-holed button group."

When the buttons have been classified, ask the children if they can think of other ways to group them. What other kinds of classification systems can be established? How does each classification system serve us in a particular way?

When the possibilities for grouping the buttons seem to be running out, explain to the students that they have been classifying. Tell them that classifying means finding ways of arranging things in groups. It means that all the things in a particular group are alike in some common way.

Ask the children to think of other objects that may be classified, and if time permits, try another practice session. Ask them to think about a time in their lives when they were called upon to do some classifying. How did they do it? What happened? How did their classification system work? Ask them to consider how learning to classify may be a valuable skill in our lives. How does classifying help us to bring order into our lives? What are their ideas?

Introducing Imagining

Begin with a task that may be fun for the children. For example, ask them to invent a new holiday. Then, ask them to tell, write, or draw about the kind of holiday it is and what is going to be celebrated.

Ask the children to share their ideas with the group. Note the very many and different kinds of ideas the children have. Tell them that imagining means creating and inventing new ideas, new schemes, new forms. Explain that when you imagine, you are free to fantasize and create wonderful new images from your mind.

Invite the children's ideas as to why imagining is an important skill in our lives. How does imagining help us? What can a good imagination do for us?

Introducing Hypothesizing

Present a hypothetical situation to the students or one that is drawn from classroom experience. For example, can the children think of some ideas to explain why it is that two of the students in the class have such a hard time working together? When the teacher puts them into the same group, they almost always get into a fight. What might be some reasons for this? Why does it happen? Ask the children to try to think of as many possible explanations as they can. Make a list of the children's ideas.

When the list contains sufficient and varied possible explanations, tell the children that they have been suggesting hypotheses; that hypotheses are possible explanations to help us to understand why something might be happening. Since we don't know for certain what the real explanation is, the hypotheses are stated as *possible* explanations. Hypotheses are also used when we are trying to find ways to understand a particular problem.

Can the children think of other situations in which hypothesizing may illuminate our understanding of what might be going on? What are their ideas? If time permits, try another practice session using a situation coming from a pupil's suggestion.

Ask the students to reflect upon how learning to hypothesize might be a valuable skill in our lives. How can it help us?

Introducing Criticizing and Evaluating

Begin with a simulation or an example taken from the children's experience. For example, ask the children to give their opinions on whether boys and girls should join the Boy Scouts/Girl Scouts. What would be some good experiences for children who belonged to these groups? Why would these experiences be good ones? Would there be any reasons for children *not* to belong to these groups? Ask the children to state their opinions and to support their ideas with examples.

When the practice exercise has run its course, explain that the children have been criticizing and evaluating; that criticizing and evaluating mean offering opinions about value. When we criticize (or evaluate), we tell whether we think something is "good" or "bad," and we may also tell if we think it is "more worthy" or "less worthy." Explain to the children that when we criticize (or evaluate), it is important to make the criteria for our judgments specific. That is, if we are saying something is "good," we also need to say why we formed that opinion. What standards had to be met in order for this to be considered "good"?

The introductory session should be concluded with some discussion of why it is important to learn this thinking skill. Can children give examples of times, in their own experiences, when they were called upon to evaluate? How did they do this? What happened? Ask the children to tell why learning to criticize and evaluate are important skills to have. How do these operations help us in our lives? What are the pupils' ideas?

Introducing Identifying Assumptions

Begin with a practice exercise like the following: Draw a picture on the chalkboard of an ice-cream cone, with the caption, "Giant ice-cream cone, 75 cents." Ask the children what they expect when they go into a store to buy an ice-cream cone after they have seen such an advertisement. Ask them what assumptions they make. Ask them to talk about other times when they have seen advertisements in which they have made assumptions that turned out not to be true.

Explain that identifying assumptions means looking at what is being taken for granted. It means being able to tell the difference between what is true (*fact*) and what is guessed to be true (*assumed*).

Ask the children to consider how learning to identify assumptions may be a valuable skill. How might this skill help in our lives? What are the children's ideas?

Introducing Designing Projects and Investigations

An introductory exercise for primary children in designing investigations might be the planning of how to build a sandbox. This beginning exercise would be carried out as a brainstorming session, with children's ideas invited, and culminate in a set of plans for action. Whether the actual building of the sandbox would follow would be entirely up to the teacher. As children present ideas in the design stage, it would be important *not* to reject any idea as being inappropriate. Instead, when ideas are presented, it might be more effective to ask, "Why do you think that would work?" Or, "How do you suppose that would help?"

Intermediate grade children might be asked to design an investigation to determine whether a traffic light is needed at a school crossing. Once again, this beginning exercise would be carried out as a planning session, where children lay out the design, rather than actually carry it out. Whether the plan moves into action would be up to the teacher, but it is not a critical aspect of the introductory lesson.

Younger children generally do better with hands-on types of investigations in this operation. Children in the upper elementary grades may engage in more sophisticated and more abstract types of investigations.

In drawing children's attention to the meaning of the operation, explain to them that they are using several different thinking skills together. When designing projects and investigations, pupils will sometimes gather data and draw conclusions from the data. Sometimes plans or designs have to be created, tried out, and evaluated.

Conclude the introductory session by asking the children how learning this skill may contribute to more productive lives. Why is this a valuable skill for us to have? What are the children's ideas?

Introducing Interpreting

Introduce the operation by asking the children to study the graph in Figure 2.2. Ask them to think of at least five statements that can be made on the basis on the data in the graph. List the students' statements on the chalkboard. Ask the children to examine each of them to see how the data in the graph support the statement. Questions such as "What information are you using to make that conclusion?" and "How do you know that for sure?" may be used in helping students to verify their statements.

When the activity is over, explain to the students that they are learning the skill of interpreting; that interpreting means drawing meanings and inferences from data. When we interpret data, we try to find the differences between what is true and what we *believe to be true*; what is false and what we *believe to be false*.

Ask the students to give instances from their experience in which they were called upon to interpret data. Ask them how this skill helps them in their lives. Why is it a valuable skill to have? What are their ideas?

Introducing Decision Making

Begin with a simulation, such as the following (or a situation based upon some recent classroom experience). Ask the children, "What is the right thing to do?" For example: Bobby saw Michele throwing the garbage from her lunch onto the playground. What should Bobby do? What's the right thing?

FIGURE 2.2. Number of Hours Children Spend Watching Television (per Week)

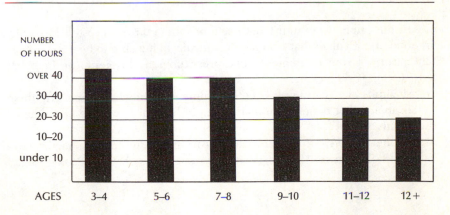

In eliciting their ideas, help students to determine for themselves what they believe is right and what they believe is wrong. The teacher's role in responding to children's ideas should be as value-free as possible. If you subtly lead children to make the "right" decision, the choice is being made by the teacher, and children's opportunities to examine the issues for themselves have been reduced.

Explain to the children that they are learning about making decisions. When they do this, they are going to be looking at the beliefs, attitudes, and feelings that lie behind the choices they make. They are going to be asked to decide for themselves what they consider to be important and also to examine the possible consequences of their choices for themselves and for others.

Ask the children to think about experiences they have had in which important decisions had to be made. How did they make these decisions? What values did they hold which were being protected in that decision? Why was the decision hard? Easy? What were some consequences of that decision? How did they feel in retrospect?

Ask the children how learning to make decisions more thoughtfully might be of some help to them in their lives. What are their ideas about this?

Introducing Summarizing

Begin with an exercise like the following. Present these statements to the pupils, with the summaries of the statements in close juxtaposition:

> This is the door you use when you want to leave.
>   (*Exit*)
> This is a dangerous part of the road. You might have an accident
>   here if you go too fast.
> (*Caution! Proceed slowly*)

Ask the pupils to examine both sets of statements and to tell how they are different. Explain that summarizing means being able to take the important meanings from a statement and express them in a briefer form. In effect, it is "telling it shorter."

Ask pupils to give examples of other summaries they have seen. Ask them to talk about what benefits summaries might have over writing or telling all the details.

Ask the students to consider how learning to summarize might be a valuable skill to have. How might it help in our lives? What are their ideas?

Introducing Problem Solving

Begin with a simulated problem, such as the following, and present this to the class for discussion:

> Marvin and four of his friends are planning a weekend bicycle trip to Pender Harbor, a seaport village about 20 miles from where they live. What kinds of problems are involved in such a trip? What are some good strategies for dealing with those problems?

Ask the children to suggest answers to these questions. List the problems and the proposed strategies on the chalkboard and ask for the implications of each. Ask the children to consider which of the potential solutions seem more reasonable; which seem less so? Ask the children to think about how the solutions chosen might be evaluated. That is, how can we know if they are good solutions?

Explain to the students that they have been engaging in a practice exercise in problem solving; that problem solving requires making a careful study of what the problem is about. It requires thinking about the steps that must be taken in the solution of the problem. It requires making good judgments about what might work and being able to evaluate afterwards whether the solution chosen was a good one. Ask the students to discuss problems that they have faced in their own experiences, and solutions that worked and didn't work. Ask for their ideas about how they might better have proceeded with solving those problems.

Ask the children how learning to solve problems more effectively can be helpful in their lives. Why should we learn to do this well? How can it help us? What are their ideas?

THINKING ACTIVITIES IN THE CONTENT AREAS

In the pages that follow you will find hundreds of examples of exercises that we call *thinking activities*. Thinking activities are different from other school exercises in several ways. First, they are open-ended, in that no single, "correct" answers are being sought. In thinking activities many answers are acceptable and appropriate. Second, each activity calls for the exercise of one or more higher-order mental functions such as those described in Part 1 of this text. In a thinking activity, pupils are asked to compare, to observe, to classify, to suggest hypotheses, and so forth, and they are asked to perform these functions in relationship to the subject matter and curriculum topics for that grade. Third, thinking activities place emphasis upon pupils' generation of ideas, rather than on their retrieval of information. In a thinking activity, pupils are asked "what *they* think," instead of asking them to remember the thinking of others.

Thinking activities are created by identifying a concept or skill that you wish to teach the students, and by casting it in a framework in which higher-order operations are called for. This may be done in virtually every subject area of the school curriculum. Good thinking activities should lead to pupils' increased insights about the subject; they may also be used to sharpen specific subject-matter skills.

Teachers who have used thinking activities have pointed out that some operations are less appropriate at certain instructional levels. For example, comparing, observing, classifying, imagining, suggesting hypotheses, designing projects and investigations, making decisions, and solving problems can easily lead to the creation of thinking activities that are suitable for both primary and intermediate grade pupils; but the operations of criticizing and evaluating, identifying assumptions, interpreting, and summarizing are likely to be conceptually too difficult for most children in the primary grades. In addition, since some operations are likely to be more familiar to most students (for example, comparing, observing, classifying, suggesting hypotheses, imagining, and decision making), it may be a good idea to begin a teaching for thinking program with activities that emphasize these mental processes and to introduce the others later, after pupils have had initial success with the first group.

In selecting thinking activities for your classroom from among the many examples in these pages, consider the following guidelines:

1. *Does the activity reflect the level of abilities of my students?* Is the activity too difficult for my students to grasp conceptually? Have I selected something which requires them to deal with material that is too abstract or too complex for their level of understanding? For example, if you were to ask a group of first graders to hypothesize about how sound is transferred onto magnetic tape, it is likely that they will not have sufficient science background to think productively about such a problem. Such a thinking activity may well go beyond the scope of most primary graders.

2. *Does the activity reflect the background of experience of my students?* Is it within the realm of their experiences? For example, if you ask students who rarely read newspapers to compare two newspapers, it is not likely that they will be able to bring much depth of thought to the task.

3. *How does the activity relate to the curriculum of my grade?* Will it lead to new insights and conceptual understandings about the topic being studied? Will it bring new meanings? Will it provide opportunities for students to develop specific skills? For example, students may, of course, compare apples and oranges to some benefit. If, however, "energy" is being

studied in science, it may be more productive for students to compare solar energy with wind power or to imagine alternatives to the internal combustion engine.

4. *What are my goals for the pupils in selecting this activity?* What do I expect them to learn? For example, if you are planning to use the activity so that students acquire specific information, instead of as a basis for thinking about the issues, your work with the activity may become more directive and be less productive for getting at students' ideas.

The thinking activities are presented primarily as examples to the teacher, not as a curriculum to be serially followed in a daily school regimen. It is our hope that by presenting so many examples, teachers will find some that are especially useful for what is being studied in their classrooms. It is also our hope that the examples will serve as illustrations of how thinking operations are emphasized in the content areas, so that not only may teachers selectively approach what is available in their own curriculum textbooks and teacher guides, but ultimately they may create their own activities to emphasize thinking in every subject of the school curriculum.

Language Arts Activities

The language arts activities in this section have been grouped by thinking operation. No division has been made to differentiate those more appropriate for primary or intermediate grade pupils. Thinking activities may have a broader application than other curriculum tasks, and teachers are likely to see, upon scanning the list, how an activity lends itself to the development of a particular skill regardless of grade level. For example, a teacher who wanted to give a teaching for thinking emphasis to word analysis might choose the activity in which pupils compare two "sound alike" words, such as *road* and *rode*. This task may be suitable for young children; it may be equally suitable for certain intermediate grade pupils. A teacher who wished to promote comprehension about character development might ask pupils to do the activity that requires them to observe the behavior of a character in a story and make a list of descriptors that would help in our understanding of that character. While this activity can be challenging for intermediate grade students, it may also be suitable for some primary pupils.

OBSERVING

The opportunity to exercise the higher-mental process of observing in the language arts will benefit pupils in several ways. It will help pupils to become more critically aware, to "sharpen their senses," to differentiate between what is fact and what is speculation. To become a thoughtful, intelligent observer in the language arts is one of the main objectives of the exercises that follow. Primary grade students can begin to be intelligent observers if they have sufficient practice with such tasks. Intermediate grade students may benefit enormously as they sharpen their skills in this area.

1. Present two words to the students, such as *and* and *said*. Ask them to make some observations about each word. Ask them to tell (or write) everything they can about these words.

2. Present a word that is spelled differently from its phonetic construction, such as *straight*. Ask the pupils to make some observations about the word. Ask them to write (or tell) five "truth statements" about the word. (A "truth statement" is one that is fully supported by the data in the observation.)

3. Present two spelling words that sound alike but have different spellings, such as *which* and *witch*. Ask the students to make some observations about the spellings of these words. Ask them to share their observations.

4. Present these four pairs of words: read and red; seen and scene; pane and pain; eye and I. Ask the students to make some observations about the pairs and to report on what they have noted.

5. Choose a story that the children like, and read it aloud to them. Ask them to tell what words or phrases make the story exciting. What words make the story sad? What words add beauty to the story? These words and phrases can be recorded on the chalkboard and reexamined.

6. Ask the students to study the behavior of a character in a story. Ask them to make a list of descriptors that may help in understanding this character a little better.

7. Ask the pupils to study a poem. What words were used in the poem that contribute to its effectiveness?

8. Ask the children to study the local newspaper. Have them work in cooperative learning groups of four to five students and make careful observations of the paper. Ask each group to record their findings.

9. Again have the pupils work in groups, and ask them to carry out the same task as 8 but use a glossy magazine instead of a newspaper.

10. Ask the students to study the following poem and make observations about how the words are used and how the poem is constructed:

> Don't tell anyone,
> but
>   I have a
> fat guardian angel
>   with an electric halo   and
> burnt out bulbs.[2]

When the children have completed their observations, you may wish to extend the activity into the imagining realm and ask them to write a poem about their own guardian angels.

11. Select a set of instructions from a workbook, a textbook, or other classroom aid. Ask the students to make observations about the clarity of the instructions. Ask them to report on their findings.

12. Ask the pupils to make observations of someone at work on a word processor. Ask them to report on their findings.

13. Ask the children to observe a particular event being broadcast on television. Ask them to pay particular attention to details of content, form, style of presentation, camera work, and language usage. Have them discuss their findings in small groups. Then ask each pupil to make a report of his or her observations.

14. Ask the students to study a television commercial. Ask them to pay attention to the visual as well as the verbal messages. Ask them to report on their observations.

15. Ask the pupils to listen carefully to a particular speaker. Ask them to pay attention to the message that the speaker is communicating. Ask them to note his or her nonverbal behavior during the speech. Have them report their findings.

COMPARING

Learning to sharpen the higher-order skills of comparing in the language arts allows pupils to become more critically aware of similarities and differences and, consequently, of the data upon which judgments are made. When we call for students to compare, we require them to attend to the specifics of comparative points; we call attention to the necessity of sharpening distinctions. Learning to be critically aware of similarities and differences increases the data base used to make judgments.

Comparing is a relatively comfortable beginning operation for both primary and intermediate grade students.

1. Select two words that the pupils may confuse, such as *road* and *rode*. Ask the children to compare them. In what ways are the words alike? How are they different? Ask the children to think of as many similarities and differences as they can.

2. Select two characters from a story that the students have read. Ask them to tell how these two characters are alike. How are they different? Encourage the pupils to think of as many similarities and differences as they can.

3. Present this list of words, in two columns, as shown:

A	B
hat	hate
pet	Pete
dim	dime
hop	hope

Ask the children how the words in column *A* and the words in column *B* are alike. How are they different? In what ways are the words in each of the rows across alike? How are they different?

4. Present these two stories to the group:

BRIAN'S STORY

The Yo-Yo Family. My family is red. They live in the sewer. They eat slugs and worms. They can't talk because they are deaf.

DEBBIE'S STORY

The Windy Night. The night was here. The night that we went to camp. It was windy and it was howling. The skakes were sticking in to the grass. All of a sudden we ran out of gas. We had a phone luckily. And then the gas truck came and filled us up. Then we drove off.

Then ask the children in what ways the stories are alike. How are they different? Ask them to think of as many similarities and differences as they can.

5. Ask the students to compare two books (or two stories or two poems) they have read. Ask them to tell how they are alike and how they are different.

6. Ask the pupils to compare two films they have seen.

7. Have the students compare two television programs.

8. Ask the children to compare the following openings to two stories:

She was tired. She had just spent twenty hours on the bus traveling home. In her head the after-images of her experiences in Winlaw made purple and dark-blue pictures, . . . like the rerun of an old nightmare. She would never forget what she had seen there.

Maria opened the door and called out to her mother. What a nuisance to find nobody at home after cheerleading practice. Now she would probably have to get her own dinner. She dropped her schoolbooks and reached for the phone.

9. The students may also compare the following:

> Two newspapers
> A cartoon and a comic strip
> A comic book and a children's news magazine
> A library book and a school reader
> The writing styles of two authors

CLASSIFYING

The operation of classifying allows us to bring some order into our lives. It allows us to develop and use systems that make life easier. In the language arts, the dictionary is one example of a system of classification that helps us through the maze of thousands of words. The card catalogue in the library is another classification system that facilitates our searching for and locating needed reference material. Life without classification systems would be a terrible muddle, and helping students to grow in this valuable skill can be an integral part of language experience.

Here are some examples of how students may be involved in developing classification systems in the language arts, which may be used to illuminate important conceptual understandings about language.

1. Present a group of sound-alike words such as the following:

back	sack	snack	tack
track	stack	black	crack
flack	lack	pack	

Ask the children to arrange these words into groups. Ask them to tell how each of the words belongs in that group.

2. Ask the students to make a list of all the stories in the reader or in library books that they have read to date. Ask them to classify the books or stories. Ask them to tell how each story or book belongs in that particular group.

3. Present a group of seemingly unrelated words, which may come from the vocabulary of the class reader, such as:

satellites	promise	hero	five
potatoes	secret	ghost	junk
moving	funny	giant	
battle	scary	kiss	

Ask the pupils to arrange these words into groups. Ask them to tell how each word belongs in that group.

4. Present the children with a list of the spelling words in the last three workbook units. Ask them to classify the words by arranging them in groups.

Ask them to identify the attributes of the words in each group and tell why each of the words belongs in that group.

5. Classifying some of the things in the following list should give pupils some additional practice:

> Stories in the reader
> Books read during the school year
> Vocabulary words
> Poems
> Jokes and riddles
> TV programs
> News programs
> TV commercials
> Magazines
> Video games

SUGGESTING HYPOTHESES

In the area of language arts, the higher-order skill of hypothesizing may be particularly valuable. Being able to suspend one's judgment, being able to suggest several possible ways to explain an event, and being able to move from positions of dogmatic assertion to reflection lead to keeping an open mind—a key element in becoming literate.

The exercises presented below are some examples of how students might be engaged in language arts activities that call for practice in suggesting hypotheses.

1. Present the students with the following problem: Michael has a hard time learning how to spell the word *e-l-e-p-h-a-n-t*. Why do you suppose this is such a hard word to spell? How can you explain it? Think of as many possible explanations as you can.

2. Ask the pupils to study the following words:

> elephant   fame
> telephone   left

Ask them how to explain why you may use the letters *ph* to spell out the sound of *f* in some words when at other times you just use the letter *f*. How can pupils know which to use? What hypotheses can the students suggest?

3. Ask the students how a computer might help them to improve their writing skills. Ask them to think about this and to write their ideas.

4. When a story that the pupils have been reading has been finished, ask them why they think the author ended the story in that way. How might this ending be explained? What hypotheses can the students suggest?

5. In studying a story, the children might also be asked why they think the author began the story in that way. What hypotheses can they suggest to explain it?

6. Ask the students why they think some pupils prefer reading comic books to library books. How do they explain it? What hypotheses can they suggest?

7. Ask the students to suggest some hypotheses to explain why some children enjoy horror movies.

8. Ask the pupils to suggest hypotheses to predict how the word processor may affect our reading and writing habits. What are some of their ideas?

9. Ask the students why they suppose Judy Blume is such a popular writer. What are their ideas?

10. Ask the pupils to suggest hypotheses to explain how a person might learn to write beautiful poetry. What are their ideas?

11. Ask the children to suggest hypotheses to explain why so many people enjoy a particular TV program. What are their ideas?

12. Ask the students to tell how they think a person can learn to improve his or her spelling. What hypotheses can they suggest.

IMAGINING AND CREATING

Imagining and creating are at the very heart of language arts. From imagination come stories, poems, plays, and all means of literary inventions. Imagining and creating allow us to push the boundaries of accepted practice into the new and innovative. The greatest gifts of literature come from the brilliant imaginations and the creative efforts of our most cherished writers. In promoting pupils' creative skills we may hope that new literary masterpieces may one day emerge from their talents in this realm.

Following are some examples of activities for the language arts that give pupils practice in imagining and creating.

1. Present the following words and ask the pupils to draw pictures of what each one might mean:

labyrinth   funicular   pseudonym

2. Ask the children to imagine what it might be like to be a particular character in a story. Ask them to describe their feelings as that character or to write about their experiences as that character.

3. Ask the students to think of other ways that a story might have ended. Ask them to tell their ideas or to write their alternate endings.

4. Ask the children to invent a new character for a story they have read.

How would this character fit into the story? Ask them to tell or to write their ideas.

5. Ask the pupils to think of the scariest nightmare they have ever had and to write about it.

6. Ask the children to imagine and write their ideas about what it would be like to be

    A character in a story
    A famous rock star
    A writer of mystery stories
    A maker of TV commercials
    A cartoonist

7. Ask the students to create

    A poem using only two words
    A slogan that would persuade people to buy a particular product
    A new way to say, "It was the ugliest thing I ever saw!"
    Twenty different ways to describe the feeling of sadness
    A mystery story that is a real thriller

DECISION MAKING

The ways in which students employ and use language is central to the process of language development. Becoming more critical about language usage, whether one's own or that of others, is an important dimension of a good language program. Helping pupils to examine language from the vantage point of values and beliefs, as well as from potential consequences of language usage, adds great power to a language arts program.

Included below are some activities that will encourage children to examine language arts from a decision-making perspective. Ask the children to consider these situations, to talk together about them in small groups, and to come to a decision about what they would do.

1. Half of a class wants to do *A Christmas Carol* as the Christmas play. The other half wants to do an original play made up by the class. Students in the first half say, "Everybody loves the *Christmas Carol*. Let's do it!" Those in the other half say, "Everybody is sick and tired of the *Christmas Carol*. Let's do something new." How can this issue be decided? Is there a way to agree on a decision so that nobody's feelings are hurt?

2. Which is better: seeing the movie of a book or reading the book? What do the students think? What reasons can they give for their opinions?

3. Mei Li is a new pupil in the class. English is a new language for her, and she makes a lot of mistakes when she talks. Some of the children are worried that if they keep correcting her English, she might feel stupid. Yet

they want to help her. What should the students in Mei Li's class do? What are some important considerations in this situation?

4. The teacher has asked Marvin to make a book report on a biography. Marvin hates reading biographies. What should he do? How can he decide?

5. Fred has an opportunity to learn how to use a computer to write his stories. It means spending one hour a day after school learning how to do it. Fred has a lot of other activities that he enjoys after school, such as playing ball with his friends. What should Fred do? What are some potential consequences of the decisions being proposed?

INTERPRETING DATA

The operation of interpreting data can be a valuable exercise in promoting comprehension about a story, an article, a report, or other written material. When children are asked to make interpretations of written language, they must exercise rigorous thinking in using data from the content to support conclusions. The following example shows how almost any paragraph from any text can be used to develop interpreting data exercises.

Present the paragraph below to the students. Ask them to read the text and respond to the statements that follow, using only the information in the paragraph. If a statement is true, that is, if the statement is clearly supported by data in the text, students should mark it with a *T*. If a statement is false, that is, if the statement is clearly refuted by data in the text, students should mark that with an *F*. If there is insufficient information in the text to determine if a statement is true or false, students should mark those statements with a question mark (*?*) to indicate that we can't tell if the statement is true or false.

The letter drops from my locker gratings with a soft flop onto the floor. Bonnie is off at the water fountain with loudmouth Frank. I'm secretly hoping Frank will drown there sometime before this afternoon's caper. I know right away that the letter is from Klutzy. I could tell her scrawl anywhere. I read, with a thudding, sick feeling in my throat: "Dear Mitch, . . ."[3]

1. Bonnie and Frank are less important characters in the story. (*?*)
2. Mitch didn't know who the letter was from. (*F*)
3. The letter fell to the floor when Mitch opened his locker. (*T*)
4. Mitch found the letter at school. (*?*)
5. The letter made Mitch's heart pound in his throat. (*T*)

EXAMINING ASSUMPTIONS

Language arts activities seem to be a natural place for the examination of assumptions. When our spoken or written language is laden with assumptions posing as facts, our statements are not only sloppy, but they misrepresent and cast doubt on the quality of our thinking. Examining assumptions in language arts activities offers us a chance to help students to become more rigorous in their thinking and, as a consequence, in what they say and what they write. It also provides students with training in becoming more thoughtfully critical of the written and spoken language of others.

Following are some practice exercises in examining assumptions.

1. Ask the students to identify the assumptions that they make when they hear the words:
> It's wrong.
> He's starving.
> You're my best friend.
> She's the smartest girl in the class.
> I'll never do it.

2. Ask the pupils what assumptions they are likely to make when they see a book with a flashy jacket displayed in the window of a book store.

3. Ask the students what assumptions they might make when a best friend says, "That's a great book. You should read it!"

4. When a teacher says, "This book is one of the most significant books of its time, and everybody should read it," what assumptions are pupils likely to make?

5. When students read an article in a newspaper about a person or an event, what assumptions are they likely to make about that person or event?

6. When pupils hear that a certain movie is breaking box office records, what assumptions are they likely to make about it? When pupils line up in a crowd of hundreds to see that movie, what assumptions have they made?

CRITICIZING AND EVALUATING

The language arts seems a rich curriculum area for the carrying out of the higher-order mental processes of criticizing and evaluating. Students read poems, stories, books; they see movies, television programs, plays; they listen to the stories of their classmates—and inevitably they make judgments about the quality. The operation of criticizing and evaluating offers students opportunities to practice the sharpening of their critical capabilities, to raise their qualitative standards, and to appreciate higher quality from language experiences. It helps them to move from the trivial, "It was good," to a more thoughtful examination of the criteria that allows such a value judgment to be made.

Here are some examples of activities in which students may practice criticizing and evaluating in the language arts.

1. Ask the pupils to work together in small groups to study a poem, story, book, or television program. Ask them to tell what they liked about it. Ask what made it a good reading or viewing experience for them. Ask them to be specific in identifying the positive characteristics of the experience.

2. Present an example of a student's poem, story, or essay to a group of students for study. Ask the students to work together and to think about what might be said to the writer in order to help him or her improve.

3. Ask the pupils to work together in small groups to suggest some plans for offering criticism to a classmate who had written a poem or story. They should try to figure out how to offer helpful criticism that would not hurt his or her feelings.

4. Ask the students to work together in small groups to discuss how they are able to decide if a movie or TV show is good or bad. What do they look for in deciding qualities of good or bad? What criteria are being used?

5. Present the following example to the pupils: Fred and Bill both went to see the movie, *Soft Rock Cafe*. Fred said, "It's just a piece of junk." Bill said, "Wow! It was great!" Ask the students who is right. How can we know for sure? How is it possible for two people to have such different ideas about the same movie?

SUMMARIZING

There are several important reasons for learning to use the higher-order skill of summarizing in language arts. Often we are called upon to give the main ideas of a story, a movie, or a dramatic production. We are asked to reflect upon a speech, a news event, or a report, and we are called upon to extract the important ideas from the larger body of thought. To be able to distill what is important from a larger context and to be able to do this with some accuracy and validity gives us credibility as thinkers and as communicators.

Below are some activities to provide pupils with practice in summarizing in the language arts.

1. Ask the students to summarize a book, a story, a play, a film, a TV program, an editorial, a news article.

2. Ask the pupils to examine some cartoons. Ask them to work in small groups to come up with some good captions for them.

3. Have the students work together in pairs or in small groups. Present them with a newspaper article from which the headline has been removed. Ask them to work together and come up with a good headline for the article. Then, give them the original headline, and ask them to compare their headlines with the original.

DESIGNING PROJECTS AND INVESTIGATIONS

Projects and investigations are most effectively done in small groups where pupils are able to work cooperatively in the planning, creating, and evaluating stages of project development. The language arts offers fruitful opportunities for many different kinds of such higher-order experiences.

Following are some suggestions of how students may gain experience in designing projects relating to the language arts.

1. The students may work together to make up an original play, television commercial, or puppet show.
2. They may work together to put out a class newspaper or magazine.
3. They may undertake a project in which they learn to give directions clearly, such as travel directions.
4. They may do group work in learning to report events accurately.
5. They may undertake an investigation about the "truth" in advertising.
6. They may make plans for increasing their vocabulary. They may carry out their plan and identify ways to see if it is effective.

COMBINING SEVERAL OPERATIONS IN ONE COMPREHENSION TASK

Practice with thinking operations need not only occur within separate categories. Reading comprehension activities may incorporate questions that call for several operations to be carried out in a single exercise. The following example, an adaptation of a familiar exercise, illustrates how a paragraph may be followed by several types of higher-order questions, instead of the lower-order, information retrieval type that are usually found in such exercises.

> Johanna thought that she had a good idea when she saw the lost kitten. She thought she would take it home and keep it until she heard about who might have lost a kitten. Her mother had another idea. When she saw the kitten she said, "We'll call the SPCA and they can keep the kitten until it is called for by the owners." Johanna hated her mother's idea. She was already working on a plan to get her mother to change her mind.

> 1. What would be a good title for this story? (A question calling for summarizing)

2. Why do you suppose Johanna's mother wanted to call the SPCA to take the kitten? (A question calling for suggesting hypotheses)
3. What might Johanna try to do to get her mother to change her mind? (A question calling for solving problems)
4. What would you do if you found a lost kitten? (A question calling for making decisions)
5. What would be a good ending for this story? Write your ideas. (A question calling for imagining and creating)

Social Studies Activities

Some teachers have said that the social studies is *the* logical place to emphasize pupils' higher-order thinking skills. If the major objective in teaching social studies is to prepare children to play active, intelligent, and thoughtful roles as an informed electorate in a democratic society, then surely a good case can be made for the value of such emphasis.

Weaving opportunities for thinking into a social studies curriculum can be done with a minimum of upheaval. There is no need to allocate additional time or to add more content to an already overcrowded day. If your lesson is to deal with the Bill of Rights, see if there are ways of requiring pupils to observe or compare or summarize the data in the Bill. If you are planning a lesson on the Middle East, see what comparisons can be made that may deepen pupils' understanding about similarities and differences: for example, comparing countries (Iran and Egypt), comparing cities (Beirut and Jerusalem), comparing cuisines (Syrian and Yemenite), comparing geography (Israel and Saudi Arabia), comparing governments (Iran and Lebanon). If your class is studying jobs and work, what comparisons can be made about jobs? What observations? What hypotheses can be generated to explain productivity? Lack of productivity? Poor quality products? What imagining can occur about the kinds of jobs people will do in the future?

More than one hundred examples of thinking activities related to social studies are presented below. Each of them provides practice in a particular thinking operation. Each reflects, in some way, a topic or issue that is normally studied in the elementary school. From this list you may be able to select several that would reflect both the specific studies of your class and the abilities of your pupils. They may also serve as illustrations for the development of your own materials.

COMPARING

Have the children

1. Compare two holidays
2. Compare two famous people

3. Compare a factory and a farm
4. Compare the job of a police officer and that of a teacher
5. Compare Chinese food and Mexican food
6. Compare living in the suburbs and living in the city
7. Compare a supermarket and a restaurant
8. Compare a park and a playground
9. Compare working in a group and working alone
10. Compare two cities, two countries, two states, two rivers
11. Compare life in the Artic with life in Hawaii

OBSERVING

1. Take the children for a walk around the school building. Ask them to make observations of what is seen.
2. Take the children for a walk in the neighborhood of the school. Ask them to make observations of what is seen, heard, smelled, and/or felt.
3. Select a group of students to visit the principal's office. Ask them to observe and report on the kind of work being done there.
4. Ask pupils to make observations about some photographs in the social studies text. What "truth statements" can be made about what is seen in these photographs?
5. Take the children for a visit to the supermarket. What observations can be made about the variety of food found there? What observations can be made about quality? Prices? Ask them to report on their observations.
6. Select a team of students to make observations of a person at work at a particular job. What kind of equipment is needed? What kinds of skills are being used? What kinds of activity can be seen? Ask them to report on their observations.
7. Take the pupils on a walk in the neighborhood of the school. Have them make some observations about the kinds of residences seen. What kinds of building materials are used? What kinds of construction? Have them report on their observations.
8. Ask the students to make observations of geographical phenomena in the area of the school. What is the nature of the land? What natural phenomena can be found? What natural materials have been used in construction? Are there rivers to be observed? Mountains? Plateaus? Swamps? Oceans? Prairies? Have them report on their observations.
9. Ask pupils to make observations of the kinds of recreational activities each child participates in after school. Ask them to report their findings. What "truth statements" can be made about recreational activities in the neighborhood?

CLASSIFYING

1. Working together with the class, generate a list of occupations of parents of pupils in the class. How can these occupations be classified? How many different types of categorizations can be created?

2. Have the students make a list of stores in the neighborhood (or at the neighborhood mall). How can these stores be classified? What can be learned about the stores from this classification? In what other ways can the stores be classified?

3. Work with the pupils to make a list of foods eaten by the children for breakfast. How can these foods be classified? What can be learned about children's eating habits from this classification?

4. Have the students make a list of instruments used for communication. How can these be classified? What kinds of classification systems can the children create?

5. Ask the pupils to make a list of all the games children play. How can these games be classified? What can be learned about children's games from this classification?

6. Have the students make a list of all the kinds of clothing we wear. How can these items be classified? How many different kinds of classification systems can be developed?

7. Have the pupils make a list of all the famous people they can think of. How can these names be classified? What can be learned about these people from this classification?

8. Work together and generate a list of vehicles used for transportation. How can these vehicles be classified? What can be learned about transportation from this classification?

9. Ask a group of children to make a list of all the items found in the classroom trash. How can these items be classified? What is learned about life in our classroom from doing this classification?

10. Children may also classify: lists of bodies of water, islands, states, countries, heads of state, famous historical personages, cities, sports, toys.

IMAGINING AND CREATING

Ask the pupils to

1. Imagine a computer that would help them to learn in school. How would it work? What would it do? Ask them to write or draw their ideas.

2. Imagine living on an island where there was no electricity. What would their lives be like? Ask them to write or draw their ideas.

3. Imagine growing up in a village on the top of a mountain. What would their lives be like there? Ask them to write or draw their ideas.

4. Imagine they could live wherever they wanted to. Where would they choose? What would their lives be like? Ask them to write or draw their ideas.

5. Imagine what it is like to be a grown-up. Ask them to write or draw their ideas.

6. Suppose they had three wishes. What would they choose? How would their lives be changed?

7. Imagine what would happen if we used up all the oil in the world and we could no longer make any gasoline. What do they suppose life would be like for all of us? Ask them to write their ideas.

8. Imagine what would happen if people never had to worry about having enough money. What would life be like? Ask the pupils to write or draw their ideas.

9. Imagine what it would take to clean up our environment. What would we have to do? How could we get it done? Ask the students to write their ideas.

SUGGESTING HYPOTHESES

Ask students the following questions. Have them suggest hypotheses as possible explanations.

1. Why are some boys and girls shy?
2. How are mountains formed?
3. Where do rivers begin?
4. Why do some people prefer to live in the city? In the country?
5. Why do some people litter the road (park, playground)?
6. How do you get to be a famous person?
7. How is it that people come in different sizes? Shapes? Colors?
8. Why are some people very poor and others very rich?
9. Why do some nations start wars as a way to deal with problems?
10. Why do you suppose Columbus set sail for the Americas?
11. Why do you suppose the population of some states has increased while that of other states has decreased?

EXAMINING ASSUMPTIONS

Have the children work in groups of four or five. Use the following questions to generate group discussion. Ask each group to write out its list of assumptions. Then ask the groups to share their ideas with the class.

1. When we see a person who is wearing shabby clothes, what assumptions might we make about him or her?
2. When we see a person who is old, what assumptions might we make about him or her?
3. When we see a photograph of a famous rock star, what assumptions might we make about his or her life?
4. When we hear that the population of China is over one billion, what assumptions are we likely to make about life in China?
5. When we hear that Mrs. Jones earns $100,000 a year, what assumptions might we make about her?
6. When we hear that Georgie got a C − in science, what assumptions might we make about him?
7. When we hear that our class is getting a new pupil—a girl who has just come here from Vietnam—what assumptions might we make about her?
8. When we hear that Winnie is moving to Hawaii, what assumptions might we make about her life there?
9. When Norman says that his family does not believe in celebrating Thanksgiving, what assumptions might we make about them?
10. When a person in native costume is shown in a photograph in the social studies text, what assumptions might we make about life in that country?
11. When people display the American flag in front of their house, what assumptions are we likely to make about them?

DECISION MAKING

The following types of situations all involve making decisions based upon personally held values. Any of these may be presented to the class for discussion and for thinking about the value positions upon which decisions are based. In some instances, the question of potential consequences of a decision may also be raised.

1. If your grandmother gave you five dollars for your birthday, what would you do with the money?
2. What rules do we need in this classroom? What are some ways to decide about the rules?
3. After school, Peter can play with his video game, or he can go to Robert's house. He wants to do both. How might he choose? What are your ideas?
4. When Phyllis sees Fiona pushing other kids on the playground, what should she do?
5. When Michael sees Sarah throwing her trash from her lunch onto the playground, what should Michael do? What is Michael's responsibility?

6. When Simon's mother asks him to help her with the dishes and he wants to watch his favorite TV program, what should he do?

7. When nobody wants to sit next to Audrey and neither does Marissa, but she feels bad about it, what should she do?

8. When Alice took Marjorie's pencil, and Sam saw her do it, what should he do?

9. When Philip says to Don, "Can I come to your house?" and Don's mother has said, "No kids here this afternoon!"—but she is not going to be home—what should Don do?

INTERPRETING DATA

Almost any written social studies material can be used as a basis for developing exercises to provide practice in drawing meanings from data. The following example may serve as an illustration.

Instruct the pupils to read the paragraph and respond to the statements that follow, using only the information in the paragraph. If a statement is true, that is, if the statement is clearly supported by data in the text, students should mark it with a *T*. If a statement is false, that is, if the statement is clearly refuted by data in the text, students should mark that with an *F*. If there is insufficient information in the text to determine if a statement is true or false, students should mark those statements with a question mark (*?*) to indicate that we can't tell if the statement is true or false.

FOOD FOR HUNGRY PEOPLE

Did you know that most people in the world do not get enough to eat? Did you know that hunger is one of the world's biggest problems?

Scientists are trying to solve this problem. They believe that man can grow more food on land by bringing water to dry places with irrigation. They also believe that the sea can supply many animals and plants that are good to eat. Someday perhaps there will be enough food for all, when we use the land and the sea to feed many more people.

1. Many people in the world are starving. (*T*)
2. Salt water is not a good source for increasing food supply. (*F*)
3. If we solve the problems of food production, people will be happier. (*?*)
4. Even if we can get more food from the sea, people will still prefer to eat steak and potatoes. (*?*)

5. Scientists are trying to solve the problems of feeding the world population. (*T*)

SUMMARIZING

Before summarizing activities can be carried out, it is assumed that pupils will have had some prior experience in gathering and organizing information about the social studies topics chosen. Some examples of summarizing activities follow.

Ask the students to summarize

1. The events leading up to the Second World War
2. The historical development of your town, city, or state
3. The exploration and settlement of the American West
4. The growth and change of the American South
5. The growth and change of the United Nations
6. The life and times of Martin Luther King
7. The growth and development of Japan since World War II
8. The relationship between Native Americans and white settlers from colonial times to the present day

CRITICIZING AND EVALUATING

Pupils' more effective participation in these tasks is largely dependent upon the extent of their information base. It may be helpful, therefore, to encourage pupils to collect and organize data about social studies topics prior to their engaging in criticism or evaluative activities. Here is a list of possible activities that exercise this higher-order skill.

Ask the pupils to criticize/evaluate

1. The immigration policy of the United States
2. The work of Mother Theresa
3. The nature and extent of U.S. military intervention abroad
4. The nuclear arms race
5. The relationship between two major world powers

DESIGNING PROJECTS AND INVESTIGATIONS

Projects and investigations in the social studies are more effectively done when students work cooperatively in small groups. In this way, their thinking is engaged through discussions, through the sharing of ideas, and through examining evaluative comments. The resultant work is the outcome of cooperative group effort. Possible ideas for social studies projects or investigations include

1. The traffic patterns on major avenues near the school
2. The differences in prices in various shops
3. The recreational facilities of the neighborhood
4. The urban growth or decline of a nearby large city
5. The patterns of population growth and decline in the immediate area
6. The growth or decline of school population in the district
7. Housing development in the areas near the school
8. Job opportunities for young adults in the area
9. Facilities for "senior" citizens in the area

Science Activities

Mary Budd Rowe has written that "science is a journey into the unknown with all the uncertainties that new ventures entail."[4] To "do" science, therefore, is to inquire into that unknown—to raise hypotheses, to test ideas, to observe data, to interpret phenomena judiciously, to make order out of the mess of disorder. In short, it is to have experiences in thinking.

In a strange series of events, science at the elementary school level has been transformed from experiences in thinking to practice in repeating so-called "experiments" to discover what is already known. For example, children are asked, "Can sound travel through a liquid?" They are then told to "Knock two blocks together in a pail of water. You will see that the sound in the water is clearer, louder." If children's findings do not match the sought-for outcomes, they are expected to repeat the "experiment" until they do. Science as a journey into the unknown has been replaced with pseudo-inquiry where we require children merely to follow the directions of others. Not only is thinking *not* required; it is actually condemned. Children learn *not* to trust their own findings; they learn instead to accept with blind faith the findings of others.

A teaching for thinking approach may help to restore elementary science to its intended function; that is, to open children's minds to the wonders of scientific discoveries, to prize the search for meanings, to learn the process of inquiry. All this may be done, of course, without losing the emphasis on content.

The thinking activities in this section are designed to elevate students' awareness of scientific concepts within an inquiry-based instructional framework. Used selectively, they should provide for learning to think about science, as well as learning to think. When these exercises can be carried out with actual hands-on materials, the potential for real scientific investigation is vastly increased.

As in the previous sections, activities are grouped according to operation, and no distinction has been made between primary and intermediate grade tasks. Once again, it is left up to individual teachers to select those tasks most appropriate for their own pupils.

OBSERVING

1. Give the children a photograph of an animal (or have them observe the behavior of a pet, ants in an ant colony, worms in a wormarium, birds building a nest, or other live animals). Ask them to study the animals carefully and to record what they see.

2. Ask the students to observe the weather each hour on the hour, for the entire day. Have them record their findings and report their observations.

3. Select groups of children to plant some seeds. Ask them to observe daily what is seen and to record their observations.

4. Ask the pupils to observe what happens to plants that receive different kinds of treatment: sunlight, lack of sunlight; water, much water, little water. Ask the children to record their observations.

5. Place an onion (potato, sweet potato, lima bean, or other vegetable) in water. Ask the students to observe and record daily what they see.

6. In a walk around the outside of the school, taken at least once a month, have the pupils observe and record the changes that appear under different seasonal conditions.

7. Ask children to observe a parent at work preparing dinner. Ask them to record their observations and to report their findings.

8. Ask the pupils to observe the sky on a clear night. Ask them to record their observations and report their findings.

9. Ask the students to observe their shadows at different times of the day and under different light conditions. Ask them to record their findings and to report on what they observed.

10. Provide materials with different textures, such as silk, wool, velvet, burlap, muslin, or corduroy. Have children observe these materials and record what has been observed.

11. Ask the pupils to observe and describe the taste of certain foods such as lettuce, yogurt, apple, hard-cooked egg, peanuts, carrots, and celery.

12. If a trip can be taken to a construction site, have the children observe the construction and write about what was observed.

13. Ask the students to observe a photograph of a skeleton of an animal. Ask them to report on their observations.

COMPARING

Ask the children to compare

1. Two leaves, two plants, two flowers
2. A leaf and a flower
3. Winter and summer, spring and fall
4. A butterfly and a bird
5. Two tools, such as a pair of scissors and a saw, a pencil and a hammer, a pulley and an inclined plane
6. Two machines, such as a car and a truck, a toaster and a can opener, a jet airplane and a ferryboat, a cement mixer and a crane
7. A bird and an airplane
8. Water and air
9. Sand and water
10. A swimming pool and the ocean
11. A kite and a parachute
12. A frog and a butterfly
13. Reptiles and mammals
14. The eye and the ear
15. The respiratory system and the digestive system

CLASSIFYING

1. Invite the pupils to help in making a list of all the tools found in the classroom. Arrange the items on the list into groups. Ask the children to identify the attributes of each of the groups and to tell how each tool belongs to that group.

2. Have the students list all the vehicles they can think of that are used for transportation. Ask the pupils to classify the vehicles.

3. Ask the children to help in making a list of all the fur-bearing animals that they can think of. Then classify the animals.

4. Have the students help in making a list of all the animals they can think of that live in the ocean. Ask the pupils to classify the animals.

5. Invite the pupils to help in making a list of all the musical instruments they can think of. Ask them to classify the instruments. Then, see how many other ways these instruments can also be grouped.

6. Work together to make a list of all the toys owned by the children in the class. Then, ask the pupils to classify the toys. What discoveries can be made from this classification?

7. Have the students make a list of animals that are good pets. Ask the pupils to classify the animals.

8. As a class, make a list of some of the flowers that grow outdoors in your area. Ask the pupils to classify these flowers.

9. Work with the students to make a list of some of the birds that can be found in your region. Ask the pupils to classify the birds.

10. Gather a collection of rocks and stones. Ask the children to sort these into groups. Ask them to tell why each rock or stone belongs in that particular group.

11. Work with the pupils to create a list of things that need fuel in order to work. Ask the children to classify these.

EXAMINING ASSUMPTIONS

Present the following kinds of exercises to the pupils. Give them some time to talk together about the question raised. Then ask them to share their ideas.

1. When we observe how a soda straw works, what assumptions might we be making?

2. When we see two people pulling at a rope, one on each end, what assumptions might we be making?

3. When we see a lit candle going out, what assumptions do we make?

4. When we blow on food that is hot, what assumptions might we be making?

5. When we fill a thermos with hot soup and seal the thermos, what assumptions are being made?

6. When we see some mold on a piece of meat, what assumptions do we make?

7. When the seeds that we planted do not grow, what assumptions might we make?

8. When we make a paper airplane, what assumptions might we be making?

9. When we put a seashell to our ear, what assumptions might we be making?

10. When we turn on the water faucet in the kitchen, what assumptions might we make?

11. When we see objects in a mirror, what assumptions might we make?

SUGGESTING HYPOTHESES

Present the following inquiries to the students. Allow them to talk together about the question raised. Ask them to think of as many hypotheses as they can. Then ask them to share their ideas.

1. A plant kept in the classroom is bursting into flower. What might be some explanations for why this is happening?

2. The paint in this container has dried up. What might be some explanations for this?

3. Jack just came from the dentist, and he has five cavities. What might be some reasons for this?

4. It's harder to clean up an ink stain than it is to clean up a water stain. What might be some reasons for this?

5. Where does lightning come from? How do you explain it? What are some of your ideas?

6. The classroom clock is running ten minutes slow every hour. What might be some reasons for this?

7. One ice cube is melting faster than another. What might be some reasons that would explain it?

8. When plastic objects are placed in a tub of water, some sink and some float. What might be some explanations for this?

9. In which places can you hear an echo? In which places can you not hear an echo? How can you explain it? What are your ideas?

10. When you look into a mirror, you see things in reverse. How can you explain it? What are some ideas?

11. Arthur and Philip both visited Larry when Larry had the mumps. Arthur caught the mumps two weeks later, but Philip didn't. How do you explain it?

DESIGNING INVESTIGATIONS AND PROBLEM SOLVING

These activities are best carried out when small groups of children work together on the inquiry. Present the following types of tasks for group investigation.

1. Have the students design an investigation to change water into steam and another investigation to change the steam back into water.

2. Give each working group a container of water and some of the following implements: eye dropper, balloon, sponge, ball, paper cup, plastic bottle, thermometer, small bottle of food coloring. Instruct the groups to conduct investigations with the water and these implements. Ask them to record the observations of their investigations.

3. Give each working group several balloons. Ask the groups to conduct investigations with the balloons and try to find answers to these questions:

What are some good ways to get air into a balloon?

How do you know that there is air in the balloon?

Where does the air go when you let it out?

How do you get the air to stay in the balloon?

How long will the air stay in the balloon?

Why does the air stay in the balloon?

What other containers hold air? How do you know?

How can you get the air out of a milk carton?

How do you know the air is out?

How come the milk carton doesn't stay up in the air like the balloon?

4. Give the groups some pieces of cloth (an old bed sheet cut up into various-sized squares is excellent) and some string. Ask the groups to make some "parachutes." Ask each group to conduct investigations with the parachutes that will shed light on some of these questions:

How long does it take for a parachute of a certain size to float to the ground?

What is the relationship between the size of the parachute and the time it takes to fall?

What keeps the parachute from falling faster?

How do you know that?

Why do some parachutes fall faster than others?

Why does air catch inside the parachute?

How do you "catch" air?

What other articles make good parachutes? Why do you think so?

What articles do not make good parachutes? Why do you think so?

5. Give each group a balloon, a measuring cup, a ball, an empty milk container, a plastic bag, or other such containers. Ask the groups to conduct investigations with these items, to find out a little more about these questions:

How much does air weigh?

How can you weigh air?

Is air ever lighter? Heavier? How do you know?

6. Ask the groups to try to invent a way to lift a very large rock, cement block, or tree stump. (The item should weigh at least 200 pounds.)

7. Ask the groups to talk together and decide how they can find out the answers to these questions:

Where does rain come from?

Why does it rain hard sometimes?

Why does it rain more in Seattle than in Santa Fe?

Where does the rain go after it falls?

What is rain made of? What's in a raindrop?

What is rain good for? What is it bad for?

How do you measure rain?

What happens when there is too much rain?

What happens when there is too little rain?

8. Give each group a flashlight. Ask the children to design some investigations to show what they can find out about light.

9. Give each group a flat and a curved mirror. (A curved mirror may come from an automobile headlight, or flashlight.) Ask the children to conduct investigations to gather information on the following questions:

What do mirrors do?

How do they work?

In what other kinds of surfaces can we see reflections?

In what surfaces may reflections not be seen? How do you account for this?

How are the reflections from the curved and flat mirrors different? What accounts for these differences?

10. Ask the groups to conduct investigations to demonstrate how solar energy works. These are some questions that might focus their inquiries:

What does solar energy come from?

How may it be stored?

What is required in order for it to work for us?

What can it do for us?

11. Ask the groups to conduct investigations on insects.

What are insects?

What kinds of insects are there?

What are some of their distinguishing characteristics?

What foods do certain insects eat?

In what ways are they helpful or harmful to humankind?

What are their habitats like?

12. Ask the groups to conduct investigations that provide information on the following questions:

How can you measure the heartbeat of the pupils in your group?

What differences are found among different pupils' heartbeats?

How fast does each person's heart beat in one minute?

Under what conditions does your heart beat more slowly? List as many as you can.

Under what conditions does your heart beat faster? List as many as you can.

What makes your heart beat? What do you think?

Why can you feel your heart beat in the pulse of your wrist? What do you think?

IMAGINING AND CREATING

1. Ask the pupils to imagine what would it be like to

Live on another planet

Have your own space ship

Be lost in space
Have a pet tiger
Have a talking dog
Make yourself invisible
Be a scientist

2. Ask the pupils to participate in creating science by
Inventing a new toy
Inventing a way to get yourself to school on time
Inventing a rain-making machine
Inventing a rain-stopping machine
Inventing an apparatus to help you swim faster
Inventing a windup toy that takes out the garbage
Inventing a computer system that takes over most of the disliked chores in the house

DECISION MAKING

Present the following types of problem situations to the pupils. Have them work together in small groups and discuss the issues. Then ask them to share their ideas with the class.

1. We want to plant a garden in the back of the school. Some pupils want to plant vegetables. Some want it to be a flower garden. The principal says we have got to choose because we can't have both. What is the best thing to plant? How can we decide?

2. Fred's dog is pretty sick. He needs to have special vitamins. But he doesn't like the vitamins and won't eat his food when they are mixed in it. Should Fred forget about the vitamins? What do you think?

3. Amy hates bugs. Every time she sees an ant she stamps on it. Ruth says it's not nice to kill living things. Who is right? How do you know? What side are you on?

4. Arthur is terrified of snakes. But Allison wants to give her pet snake to the class as a gift. What should the class do? What's the right thing?

5. At 9:00 P.M., Martha's mother says, "Lights out!" but Martha wants to finish her book. She can read under the covers, with her flashlight, but her mother has told her it's bad for her eyes. What should Martha do? What's the right thing?

6. The people who live near the airport are complaining. The planes are too noisy when they are landing and taking off. The people in the neighborhood can't hear their TVs, and they can't hear each other. The airport people say, "That's the price we all have to pay for air travel: a little more noise." Who is right? What side are you on?

7. Claudia is a big fan of hot dogs. It's her favorite food. Her friend

Carolyn claims that hot dogs are junk food and that they contain chemical preservatives that are not good for you. Claudia says, "How can hot dogs be bad for you when they taste so good? Besides, they serve them in school for lunch!" Who is right? How can this be decided?

SUMMARIZING

Science studies present many opportunities for summarizing. For example, you can ask students to summarize
1. The results of a group's investigations
2. The way the human circulatory system works
3. The life cycle of a frog
4. How a pulley works
5. Why we have seasons
6. The process of photosynthesis

INTERPRETING DATA

Almost any paragraph or diagram with science information can be used to develop a set of questions to provide practice in extracting meaning from written material.

Present the following paragraph to the students. Ask them to respond to the statements that follow, using only the information in the paragraph. If a statement is true, that is, if the statement is clearly supported by data in the text, students should mark it with a *T*. If a statement is false, that is, if the statement is clearly refuted by data in the text, students should mark that with an *F*. If there is insufficient information in the text to determine if a statement is true or false, students should mark those statements with a question mark (*?*) to indicate that we can't tell if the statement is true or false.

VIBRATIONS

You can see vibrations by hitting a yardstick held over the edge of a table. You can feel vibrations by putting your hands on a radio or phonograph that is playing. You can also feel them by holding your hand lightly on your throat while you are talking. In each case, something is shaking back and forth very fast—vibrating—and making sound.[5]

1. It is hard to see vibrations. (*?*)
2. When you talk, your sounds are vibrating. (*?*)

3. Vibrations come from sounds. (*F*)
4. You can hit a ball and make vibrations. (*?*)
5. When you hit a yardstick, you make vibrations. (*T*)

CRITICIZING AND EVALUATING

Many scientific issues involve making judgments—from how we get rid of our industrial waste, to what life is. Science teaching becomes much richer and personally significant when these value issues may be examined in an intellectually responsible forum. Criticizing and evaluating activities should provide many opportunities for students to think responsibly and productively about the scientific issues that deeply affect our lives.

The ability of pupils to participate effectively in these activities is largely dependent upon the extent of their information base. It may be helpful, therefore, to encourage pupils to collect and organize information about these topics before engaging in criticizing and evaluating activities.

The following topics may lead to fruitful criticizing and evaluating opportunities.

1. What's wrong with our diet?
2. What does the research really tell us about smoking?
3. Can music turned up to full volume really hurt our ears?
4. Cleaning up industrial waste is expensive. Who's responsible for doing this? Is it worth doing?
5. Water birds die by the thousands from oil spills. Yet we've got to move that oil by tanker over the water if we are going to have gasoline. What's the answer?
6. They want to build another nuclear power plant close to the recreational facilities at Oregon Beach. Is it a good idea?
7. Some people claim there is no energy crisis; we don't have to worry about running out of oil. That's not likely to happen for at least another thousand years. Should we be conserving energy now?

Mathematics Activities

The children sit at their tables with their counting beads. "Eight divided by two," instructs the teacher. The children at the table get right to work. They make two groups and place four beads into each.

A visitor asks them, "Why do you put the beads into two groups?"

One boy responds, "Because it would be wrong if you didn't."

The visitor presses on, "What would happen if you had nine beads, then?"

They laugh. "You can't do it with nine beads. You've got to have eight to divide."

The visitor takes three beads and places each one at a different spot on the table. "Look at this," he says. "I've divided these three beads. I've divided them into three groups of one."

"No," the children tell him. "That's not dividing. You can't divide with three. You must have two beads in each group to divide."

The children have learned a rote system of dividing by two, and they know how to get the right answer. When they are asked to think about the mathematical process of division, they are stumped. Perhaps that is why so many of us have "mathaphobia." We have been taught rote formulas that we are unable to apply outside of a single context, instead of having been taught how to think mathematically.

Teaching for thinking in mathematics attempts to correct this malfunction. It shifts the emphasis from rote skills onto mathematical thinking. Can children learn to think mathematically? Can they learn to understand how mathematical systems work and how we can make numbers work for us? The exercises in this last section present examples of how this may be done. The activities should serve as further illustration of how teachers may aim for the development of concepts and skills, as well as the higher-order processes, this time in the curriculum area of mathematics. Once again, these activities are grouped by operation, with no distinction made for grade-level differences. Comparing rulers and measuring cups (and many other tasks) may be a fruitful exercise at several grade levels, and we believe that classroom teachers are the best judges of what may be appropriate for their particular classes.

COMPARING

Have the students compare:

1. A ruler and a measuring cup
2. Fractions and decimals
3. Hexagons and diamonds
4. The shape of a ball and the shape of a lemon
5. A pound of stones and a pound of rubber bands
6. Dominoes and marbles
7. A clock and a yardstick
8. A paper-towel cylinder and a cube of sugar
9. A calculator and your fingers
10. The schoolyard and the street

11. English pounds (currency) and dollars
12. Estimating amounts and measuring amounts
13. Two maps; a map and a globe

OBSERVING

Ask the pupils to observe the following and to record their findings, either in writing or by drawing.

1. The shape of the classroom.
2. The pattern of numbers in Figure 2.3.
3. This sequence of numbers:
     5,   10,   15,   20,   25,   30,   35,   40,   45,   50.
4. The objects in the classroom with respect to shape. What objects can be found that are round? What objects can be found that are square? What objects are triangular in shape? How do these shapes serve the purposes of the objects in terms of function?
5. The objects in the room with respect to size. What objects do the students estimate to be smaller than 5 inches (20 centimeters) long? What objects do they estimate to be larger than 5 inches long?
6. A student throwing a ball. How far can he or she throw it? How far can another pupil throw it?
7. One student throwing a ping pong ball; and the same pupil throwing a tennis ball; then a basketball.

FIGURE 2.3. Numbers Patterns

1	2	3	(4)	5	6	7	(8)	9	10
11	(12)	13	14	15	(16)	17	18	19	(20)
21	22	23	(24)	25	26	27	(28)	29	30
31	(32)	33	34	35	(36)	37	38	39	(40)
41	42	43	(44)	45	46	47	(48)	49	50
51	(52)	53	54	55	(56)	57	58	59	(60)
61	62	63	(64)	65	66	67	(68)	69	70
71	(72)	73	74	75	(76)	77	78	79	(80)
81	82	83	(84)	85	86	87	(88)	89	90
91	(92)	93	94	95	(96)	97	98	99	(100)

8. A Dienes cube.
9. A small-scale and a large-scale map.

CLASSIFYING

1. Make a list of the numbers from 1 to 50. Ask the pupils how these numbers can be classified. What does each different classification system tell you about these numbers?
2. Work with the class to make tracings of the footprints of all the pupils. Arrange these sets of footprints into groups. Ask the children to tell how each pair of footprints belongs in that particular group.
3. Ask the students to record the heights of everyone in the class. Ask them to classify these data in a graph.
4. Ask the pupils to make a list of all the tools they can think of that are used in measuring. Ask them to classify these tools.
5. Ask the children to make a list of all the things they can think of that are used to tell time. Ask them to classify these things.
6. Gather together a variety of containers of different sizes and shapes. Ask the students to arrange these in groups. How many different ways can they think of to group these containers?

SUGGESTING HYPOTHESES

Present the following situations and questions to the pupils for discussion. Invite as many hypotheses as they can think of for each situation.

1. Marti measured the length of the room. She found it was 22¼ feet (7 meters). Susan measured it too. She found it was exactly 21 feet (6½ meters). How do you explain this difference? What are some possible explanations you can think of? (After pupils have hypothesized, ask two students to measure the length of your classroom. Ask them to hypothesize once again about differences in measurements, if any.)
2. Bill weighed himself on the bathroom scale. He read his weight at 73 pounds (33 kilograms). When he got to school, he weighed himself on the scale in the nurse's office. Here he read his weight at 74½ pounds (34 kilograms). How do you explain this difference? What are some possible explanations you can think of?
3. Arlo counted all the children in the classroom. He counted 29. Frank counted them. He counted 28. How do you explain the different answers? What are some possible explanations?
4. "Bring me a large box, Leopold," said Miss Tate. Leopold went down to the basement and brought up a box that measured 24 inches by 18 inches

by 12 inches. "I said a *large* box," said his teacher. What went wrong? How can you explain it? Think of as many explanations as you can.

5. "I'll cut this apple in half, and we'll each have the same amount," said Ira. He carefully cut the apple right down the middle. Then he weighed the halves. One piece weighed 80 grams and the other weighed 100 grams. How did this happen? How do you explain it?

6. How come $\frac{3}{12}$ is the same amount as $\frac{1}{4}$? How do you explain it?

7. Louisa made this calculation. First she multiplied:

$$\begin{array}{r} 348 \\ \times\,236 \\ \hline 2,078 \end{array}$$

Then she added this total to two other figures:

$$\begin{array}{r} 2,078 \\ 10,440 \\ \underline{6,960} \\ 18,478 \end{array}$$

Her answer was incorrect. How can you explain how she got that answer?

IMAGINING AND CREATING

Present the following exercises to the students:

1. Think of as many ways as you can to use circles.

2. Work with one hundred toothpicks. Use them to make an imaginative design.

3. How can you measure a cat? Think of some imaginative ways to do it.

4. Invent a new way to tell time.

5. Cut out one hundred triangles of different colors. Use them to make a wonderful design.

6. What are some good ways to share one cupcake with three friends?

7. Use two pieces of construction paper of different colors. Use one piece for the mat. Cut the other piece into one-by-three-inch strips. Paste the strips on the mat to make a wonderful geometrical design.

8. Make up a game with numbers, using two pennies.

9. Invent a new way to add fractions.

EXAMINING ASSUMPTIONS

Present the following situations to the students and invite their responses to the questions:

1. When we divide a candy bar in half to share it with a friend, what assumptions might we be making?

2. When we count all the children present in the class today, what assumptions might we be making?

3. When we measure the length of the room, what assumptions might we be making?

4. When Robbie gets 8 out of 10 examples wrong on his arithmetic test, what assumptions might we make about his math skills?

5. When the clerk in the market weighs out two pounds of bananas, what assumptions might we make?

6. When the clock in the classroom reads 2:15, what assumptions might we make?

7. When the teacher says, "Bring me a large box," what assumptions might we make?

8. When we buy a package of cereal of a certain size, what assumptions might we be making about how much cereal is in the box?

9. When the teacher says, "Cut out a circle," what assumptions might we make?

10. When you think about five pounds, what assumptions might you make?

11. When the store advertises giant ice-cream cones for twenty-five cents, what assumptions might we make?

12. When Katie says, "If you leave here now, you should get to school in ten minutes," what assumptions might she be making?

DESIGNING PROJECTS, DOING INVESTIGATIONS, AND SOLVING PROBLEMS

Have the children work in small groups for the following activities:

1. Ask each group to work together to make a map of the school property.

2. Ask each group to design a plan for measuring each member's height accurately and then to carry out this investigation.

3. Using balance scales and a collection of miscellaneous items from the classroom (e.g., pencils, paper clips, chalk, erasers), ask each group to find out what items balance with a one-pound (or one-kilogram) weight. Ask the groups to record their findings.

4. Ask each group to find out who in the class is less than 3½ feet tall (or 1 meter tall) and who is taller than that height. Ask each group to record the findings on a graph. In what ways are the results of their studies different?

5. Ask the students in each group to talk together and figure out some good ways to weigh air. Then ask them to try out their ideas.

6. On a rainy day, ask each group to design an investigation to figure out how hard it has rained in a given amount of time.

7. Using a set of dominoes, ask each group to make up a game that would help pupils to practice their addition skills.

8. Using cuisenaire rods, ask each group to make up a system to help them multiply numbers accurately.

9. Ask each group to design an investigation to determine what is the shortest walking route from the school to a particular point.

10. Ask each group to design an investigation to determine to what extent January (or any other month) was colder (warmer) than February (or any other month).

11. Ask each group to design an investigation to determine whether liquids and solids of equal weight have the same bulk.

Have the students work in pairs to do the projects below:

1. Using scissors, glue, dowels, string, and pieces of colored construction paper, ask each pair to design and build a mobile.

2. Using toothpicks and glue, ask each pair to build a bridge.

3. Ask each pair to figure out a way to cut a pie in seven equal pieces.

CONCLUSION

Marilyn Ziti has "bitten the bullet." She has moved teaching for thinking into her classroom, and, after four months, the program is flourishing. There is a sense of exhilaration about her as she describes what the children are doing—how they have grown from uncertainty in their thinking to more inventiveness, more cognitive risk taking, more sophistication of ideas. She is incredulous at the range and depth of responses of her third graders, finding that they are capable of thinking about concepts and data far beyond her most hopeful expectations. What amazes her most is that even pupils who had been considered academically untalented can participate thoughtfully and intelligently on thinking tasks. She has by now woven teaching for thinking into all of her subject areas—language arts, science, social studies, and math—and is beginning to be aware of subtle changes in her pupils' behavior: less impulsiveness, less dogmatism, less underconfidence in expressing ideas, and considerably more independence.

A videotape of her work with the children shows the pupils working on a thinking task in science. They make observations about ice and about the conditions under which ice melts. They are working in small groups, cooperatively, but all the groups are working on the same activity. During the activity, Ziti is moving about the room, raising questions, reflecting ideas, and providing help with acquiring materials. She moves to Paul's group, and he tells her about the effect of coarse salt on his ice cubes. Ziti reflects his idea and asks him to suggest some hypotheses for why this might be happening.

He turns his face up to her and says, "Your questions! They really confuse me."

Ziti gently responds, "You're finding that my questions are troublesome for you."

"Yeh," Paul responds and turns away from her, back to his ice cubes. "I have to go down deep, deep inside of myself and find the answers."

"You have to do some really hard thinking," she reflects.

"Yeh," he sighs.

PART 3

Applications
in the Secondary School

Thinking operations, or if one prefers, reflective activities,* constitute a pedagogic method as well as an intellectual one—that is, they are as much a means of teaching as they are a mode of learning. There are schools of education, as well as colleges and universities, that have forcibly separated intellectual method (a means of acquiring knowledge) from pedagogic method (a means of communicating knowledge). In so doing, they have violently wrenched apart what is an organic and intellectual whole. Two centuries ago, Immanuel Kant recommended employing the *means* of acquiring particular knowledge (its internal epistemological method) as a natural way to teach and to learn it. To participate in the creation of knowledge or to see how it is created is an exciting experience, one that is self-justifying in that it is intrinsically motivating. The focus, then, in this section is on reestablishing the bond between intellectual and pedagogic method—a fostering not only of their juncture and intersection but of their amalgamation and coalescence.

In the material that follows, exercises and activities are offered to illustrate ways of providing opportunities for thinking. Initially, it is important to underscore that *thinking* is an omnibus term, a common label that includes several mental processes. Such processes have been categorized as "lower" and "higher" mental operations (see especially Charles H. Judd, *Education as Cultivation of the Higher Mental Processes*).[1] Those that are considered lowest include the functioning of the sense organs. Slightly higher, but still within the lower category, are those sense experiences that involve remembering, recognizing, and recalling. Still higher mental processes have been identified as comparing, classifying, interpreting, and evaluating.

---

*The terms *reflective activities* and *reflection* are used in order to suggest the delay or suspension of judgment between the simulus of a problem or issue and the response to it. This meaning is not ordinarily conveyed in its fullness by the omnibus term *thinking*.

...nations *higher* and *lower* have been used for several reasons.
...n suggests a distinction between mankind and the lower animals.
...gh animals perform lower mental operations such as recognizing and
...lling, as far as is now known they do not perform the higher ones. A
second reason for the distinction lower–higher relates to the amount of
contribution required. Recalling, for instance, requires no special contribution. The test of how well one can recall something may be seen in how
faithful one is to the original. On the other hand, the measure of quality of
a higher mental process is the amount of *change* that is introduced by the
individual, the nature of the contribution to the original.

A third reason for using the terms lower and higher has to do with
complexity. The lower processes are simple and unrefined; there is little
impingement on other processes, whereas in the higher processes impingement is unavoidable. In the lower processes memory furnishes the raw
material. However, when memory serves up such raw material or data, it
presents the several items in a very *loose* series, in what is no more than a
temporal sequence. It remains for a higher mental process to set up a connection between one loose item and another, to integrate and to link them
together into a new subjective entity.

Perhaps the matter of the impingement of one process on another, which
occurs only among the higher mental processes, may be viewed in yet
another light. As one engages in the mental process of evaluating, for example, it involves the operations of comparing, analyzing, criticizing, and judgment making. Similarly, the process of interpreting involves translating,
comparing, inferring, deducing, and predicting. These are complicated processes. In fact, lines between them become so blurred that it is difficult to
set up a classification scheme or taxonomy, simply because of their complex
interrelationship, the impingement of one process on another. The classification developed by B. S. Bloom, in his *Taxonomy of Educational Objectives, Cognitive Domain*, is a case in point.[2] Although it is a laudable attempt,
students are often troubled by the difficulty of fixing the lines of distinction
between processes. The very attempt to isolate one process from another—
that is, to abstract its pristine qualities—is almost an attempt to deny its
very nature, the fact of its *necessary* impingement on other processes.

This impingement of processes is even more sharply seen in the relation
between higher and lower processes. As one compares, analyzes, interprets,
and evaluates, the lower processes of recognition, recall, and association
must be involved. However, the reverse is *not* true: The lower processes
do not automatically envelop the higher ones. There is abundant research
evidence to indicate that the lower processes are engaged and strengthened
as the higher processes are given emphasis. Despite this, many teaching
practices seem to continue the emphasis on the lower processes. Judging

from tests that are administered from grade school through college, the lower processes of recall and recognition engage an entirely disproportionate amount of attention. As the philosopher Schopenhauer observed: "The majority of mankind . . . who study to fill their memory with facts, do not use the steps of the ladder to mount upward, but take them off and lay them on their shoulders in order that they may take them along, delighting in the weight of the burden they are carrying. They ever remain below because they carry what should carry them."[3]

It may be that some would analogize the slogan "Walk before you run" to the acquisition of facts first and *then* thinking about them. If the analogy is stretched in this way, it beclouds and obstructs the insight that thinking is a means of acquiring relevant facts. It has already been stated that it is erroneous to suppose that higher mental processes are by-products of an emphasis upon lower mental processes; just the reverse is the case. (As William James once said, "Science or rational order is the perfect mnemonic system.") Another reason for the visible emphasis upon the lower mental processes may be convenience and ease in constructing instructional materials or, perhaps, a paucity of materials that are directed to the higher mental processes. It is hoped that the illustrations included in this text may serve as inducement and stimulus to teachers in pointing out a direction toward which they can move.

One may ask, Why is a pointed emphasis upon thinking (and associated operations) necessary in the first place? The goal and ideal is to encourage criticism, for without criticism there is no life of science or life of art; in a real sense, criticism is the life of life itself. By this is meant that the course of criticism has to be kept steady and firm—that is, directed *inward*, to hold suspect that which the mind seizes and dwells upon with particular delight. It is frightfully easy to point criticism outward; in fact, it is most often regarded as the "thing to do." "State *your* case; let others state theirs." (Perhaps life in a fundamentally adversarial culture has something to do with this.) This means that we tend to guard our hoarded wisdom as if it were a veritable treasure trove whose grounds are off limits to would-be missionaries and proselytizers. Now, it has been said that absolute certainty is the privilege of the uneducated and the fanatic, and that education involves the loosening of such certainty. If there is any value and truth in this prescription, the criticism sought after here is primarily criticism of the self and its ideas, not of the other fellow and the "other" idea. In fact, it involves cultivating a search for the elements that make an argument strong, precisely in those particular positions with which we are in fundamental disagreement. (By "strength" of argument is meant its substance and soundness, not the manner or style of its presentation or expression.) One has to guard against seeing the goal as learning tricks and stunts to use as a means for winning an argument at all costs or for showing someone up. A higher morality may prevail: that of facilitating understanding leading to self-understanding. Practices such as debating or arguing for the sake of winning, or learning tricks wherewith to demolish an opponent, would then be seen as monstrous caricatures. Thus, it is hoped that one will begin to foster the habit of not lavishing too much affection on one's own conclusions. Doubt is to become the handmaiden to ongoing inquiry.

In the ensuing sections of this part, eight operations relating to thinking are identified. The operations that have been selected are reacting to coding, comparing, classifying, summarizing, observing and reporting, interpreting evidence, finding assumptions, and inquiring. This listing is not the only possible way of describing the operations. Furthermore, the order in which the operations are presented represents a convenience. Elsewhere in this book (in Part 1, for example), the reader will have encountered different listings. The examination of differences and similarities may be of interest. (It may also be instructive to compare the terminology and nomenclature employed here with that used in other texts.)

Each of the following sections on thinking operations begins with introductory material in which an attempt is made to illuminate dimensions of the operations as they are applied to classroom practice. These introductions offer direction to the various illustrative exercises for each operation. Thoughtful consideration of the introductions is urged, for one cannot teach what one does not know or understand. One exemplifies or becomes capable of instructing what one *does* understand. If there is insufficient comprehension of the structural characteristics of the operations, there is danger of the operations' being used as mere artifices or mechanical devices. For this reason it is recommended that the introductions be studied before attempting to work on the exercises themselves.

It is strongly urged that the exercises given in the following sections of this part not be considered a syllabus to be covered, a workbook to be given to students, or as examples *of* thinking. They are, rather, examples designed to *elicit* thinking. It is hoped that the teacher will first gain proficiency in carrying out the thinking operation before introducing it to students. Then the teacher will comprehend it more fully and will understand what is required in order to construct instructional materials. Some of the exercises show responses that were given by students; they are presented as illustrations only and are not intended as a pattern that must be slavishly followed in developing new materials. The operations may be applied within the framework of an existing curriculum, but they do require the teacher to develop the potential of that curriculum more fully. For instance, although most exercises have been grouped according to the usual headings of secondary school subjects, it may be seen that applications will cross over those lines and extend beyond them. It is hoped that the pages that follow will provide illustrations sufficient to guide teachers toward invention and construction of their own materials in teaching for thinking.

REACTING TO CODING

Very often, the content of *what* we think and the manner or progression of our thinking patterns is revealed in the way we speak and write. It would seem worthwhile, then, to help students analyze patterns of expression that relate to thinking processes. This can be done by having them analyze and code passages from books, editorials, letters to the editor, and foremost, their own writings, particularly if done on an ongoing basis. A coding scheme is set forth in the paragraphs below, along with some justifications for its presentation. It is followed by some suggestions for implementation in a classroom.

It may be supposed that practice in differentiating between the observational and the inferential, and between description and ascription, is to be reserved for the uneducated. Yet who can fail to note that the tendency to attribution and imputation is so bound up in the psyche of the human being that, unless one is on guard, attribution of feelings and motives to others falls from our lips routinely, "as a manner of speaking." We may note the grace and ease by which internal feeling is fused to external fact in the following casual expression: "*It* was a good play." Of course, the more precise and more difficult statement would be: "*I* liked the play." Or, we may reflect on how easily we slip into exaggeration and overstatement in order to make a modest observation. In this, business enterprises and the selling ethic itself have helped to condition and shape our linguistic patterns with such "manners" of speaking as: *singularly unique* concepts, *new innovations,* and *free gifts.* In what surely is something akin to bitter irony, it is because such gifts are, indeed, free that the recommendations to follow are made. It is necessary to state at the outset that the scheme below is only one of several possibilities, and it is intended to be neither limiting nor exhaustive. Variations in order and treatment are found elsewhere in the text.

A Coding System

ATTRIBUTIONS: CODE A

These are statements that are ascriptive rather than descriptive. Usually they impute feeling to someone else. They also commonly ascribe causation or motivation to a person or, in some cases, to an idea. In the typical context, the word *because* is the signal for a possible attribution: "The reason they are poor is *because* they don't want to work." Here, motivation and causation are being attributed. Or, "If they were not so lazy, they might get somewhere." Here, a feeling or temperamental outlook is being ascribed. Some see the confusion between description and ascription essentially as the confusion between observational and inferential terms. That is, instead of using terms that are "cameralike" in their objectivity in that they point to matters that others can verify, very often individuals will substitute an inference in the honest but mistaken belief that it is observation. For example, upon noticing a man staggering, some will say, "That man is drunk!" They will be fully satisfied that the statement is indeed an observational one. The fact of the matter is that it is clearly an inference, despite the form and even the sound of factuality. As an inference, it may or may not be true; hence, a qualification ("probably") is in order.

EXTREMES: CODE X

Extreme terms permit no exceptions: *all, none, always, never, ever, no difference, the same, completely, entirely.* In a sense, they are usually exaggerations and overstatements; they bespeak a redundancy despite their frequent use for color and emphasis.

> *Nothing* is *ever* learned.
> This has *no* value *whatsoever*.
> This method is *identical* with the other. It is *exactly* the *same*.
> He does it *constantly*.
> That's what it's *all* about.
> This is the *only* way to do it.
> I *never* generalize.
> There are *no* absolute truths.
> Trust *no one*.

It will be recognized that these statements are absolute in their sweeping inclusiveness. Sometimes the absolutes take the form of paradox, as in the last three examples. Very often, where one finds extremes on display, one also finds attributions.

EITHER–OR'S: CODE E-O

In one sense, the *either-or* may be viewed as a subcategory of the extreme statement. There is an erection of absolutes, a polarization of possibilities and alternatives that circumscribe the area of choice. In logic, this is known as the fallacy of *accent*—that is, one accents only two possibilities, thus forcing someone else to accept the accentuation. As a manipulative and argumentative device, it may be seen as supremely helpful in invoking the combative spirit: "You're either for us or against us." The usage, of course, reveals a two-valued orientation: "we or they," "good or bad." In situations calling for the competitive and combative spirit and for delimitations of the areas of choice—for example, games, wars, political campaigns—the *either-or* serves as a powerful underpinning and spur to action. In situations calling for the study of a problem and the consideration of views, *either-or* tends to interfere with reflection; often it is used to intimidate. Moreover, the narrowing of solutions to problems to only two alternatives is typically found in speech patterns given to the frequent use of extremes. The word *problem*, by definition, suggests alternatives. With only one course of action open, there can hardly be a problem. In proportion to the number of alternatives that are available as solutions to a problem, possibilities for reflection are increased.

Perhaps the persistence with which we are prone to express ourselves in two-value terms is a carryover from the world of prescience. Upon careful analysis, opposing terms like *up* and *down*, and *healthy* and *sick*, reveal their historic past. These simple polarizations often incapacitate us because of the way they restrict and rigidify our thinking. One is reminded of the honest man who divided humanity into two classes: lawbreakers and law-abiders. When asked what a law-abider was, he replied, "Someone who keeps *the* [one, some, most, all?] law." When asked what a lawbreaker was, he replied, "Someone who breaks *the* [one, some, most, all?] law." No matter which he chooses—one law, some laws, most laws, all laws—our honest man is in trouble logically and is in an indefensible position. Now it is probably clear that all of us are in some sense law-abiders *and* lawbreakers. Fortunately (unlike our honest man), our legal code recognizes multiple values. It has multiple categories for lawbreaking (misdemeanor, offense, felony) and degrees of violation within each type (e.g., burglary, petty larceny, grand larceny, embezzlement, and armed robbery). Yet some of us prefer simplicity: "They're all crooks." Perhaps it makes it easier to deal with the matter.

QUALIFICATIONS: CODE Q

Expressions in this grouping may be thought of as suggesting caution. (They are also frequently intended to hedge in or restrict the scope of a statement, as when terms of rough quantity or quality are employed.) Colloquially, they have been referred to as *weasel* words that cast doubt on a proposition: *perhaps, it seems, apparently, might, probably.* It is something of an irony that when these are used ironically, they suggest certitude rather than doubt.

ANALOGIES: CODE An.

Analogies express a relationship. Though properly used for color and for illustrative purposes, they are often misused as demonstrative proofs. In a sense, analogical words—*like, same as, you might as well say, just like*—are forms of the extreme statement. "This is the same as that" permits no exception. "This is similar to that" (a qualification) does permit an area of difference. Since an analogy is illustrative only of an approximation with a difference built in, the user is asked to reflect on the point of difference (along with the accentuation of the similarities).

IF-THEN'S: CODE I-T

Here, too, a causal relationship is being expressed. In typical hypothetical statements, sometimes the *then* is omitted but is understood. Sometimes the *if* is omitted, as in "Had the nation not permitted this, the results would have been different." Some examples are

> If he weren't what he is, this wouldn't have happened.
> How could it be there if I didn't see it?
> How could it be any good if it's not advertised?
> If you're so smart, why ain't you rich?
> If the good Lord wanted us to fly, he would have given us wings.

The task of the teacher is to help the student see whether or not the *then* follows from the *if*. It will be seen that the above statements and questions are non sequiturs in which the conclusion is actually unrelated to the conditional premise. In logic this has been labeled *false cause.*

EVALUATIVE STATEMENTS: CODE +/−

These are the *like* and *dislike* terms in which we give clues to our feelings and preferences and, sometimes, our behavior. As was indicated earlier, they often involve substitution of an attitudinal statement for a descriptive statement. As a matter of common idiom, this substitution is warrantable if justifiable criteria are offered for evaluations and the evaluations are set forth in the light of those criteria: "The play was *bad*"; "This is an excellent book"; "The ideas expressed are positively abominable." However, simply to ascribe our preferences to matters outside us is intellectually immature.

Using Coding in the Classroom

In using the coding system, it is perhaps best for the teacher not to introduce the entire system at one time nor to present any part of it didactically. Instead, one may proceed as follows. When looking at written assignments, the teacher puts an X over all extreme words. Papers are returned to students, who are asked to copy out the sentences where words have been marked. They are instructed to note how the words or sentences are similar, on the assumption that they will discover ways in which the words are all-inclusive. (It is much better if the students themselves arrive at this, and somewhat less effective if they are told.) The act of copying out the words and sentences permits them to see what the sentences have in common and to react to the coded words.

On a later assignment, the teacher continues to use the code X and introduces another symbol. Again the students are asked to react and are led to discover and discern the similarities between the words that have been coded. The system is introduced in this fashion, one part at a time, with allowance for several weeks of assimilation of the old before the new is presented.

In the illustration of a coded paper that follows, it may be seen that several code symbols might be used for the same sentence (and this has been deliberately indicated here). Where this is so, it suffices to select what appears to be dominant in the sentence *as a unit*. It is neither necessary nor desirable to lift each individual word out of the sentence and, by overanalysis, to destroy contextual meaning.

+

I-T

I am writing about the letter you received on December 31st from Sidney F. He is entirely correct in saying that people of foreign countries have a poor concept of Americans. I happen to know this for a fact.

Last year, I spent a school year in Puerto Rico. While I was there, I met many people in school and out. I can safely say that I found a basic fault in most of them.

This fault was that they generalize too much. If they saw an American sailor drunk, they would say that Americans are drunks. If they read in a newspaper that a restaurant refused to serve a Negro, they say that Americans are prejudiced.

Q

Don't misunderstand me. I'm <u>not saying</u> that all Puerto Ricans

X   Q

are this way—just too many of them. But these people aren't the only ones. I have found <u>this fault</u> in too many people of too many nationalities. In my opinion, Americans also have this fault. If

>   X
> Americans hear of a revolution in any part of the world, <u>the very</u>
>   X   A   Q
> <u>first thing</u> <u>you hear</u> is <u>that those involved in the revolution</u> are all
> troublemakers.
>   X and A   X
> The <u>only reason</u> for this fault in many people is <u>just plain sim-</u>
>   –   X
> <u>ple ignorance</u>. People don't know all of the reasons or facts for
>   A
> things happening. As a result, the people comment on the small
>   X
> part they know. If they would wait, gather all the information,
>   X

I-T   study it and then, and only then, comment on things, the people
>   A   X   X
> of the world would all understand everything and each other bet-
>   Q

\+   ter <u>and I think</u> this would result in more unity.

The teacher's duty has not been discharged with the mere presentation of the coding system. Consistent instruction takes place during the year. To be sure, this type of analysis is time-consuming, but students may participate in the analysis by coding each other's papers as well as their own.

Teachers may also use coding as a diagnostic instrument. The dogmatism and absolutism, the confusion of evaluations with description, the illogicality of the *if-thens* are not marked wrong; the student is not scored by having to pay penalty points. Instead, a sample of writing is taken at the beginning of the term and marked, perhaps, on a five-point scale as to its appropriateness and restraint. How sweeping are the student's assertions? Are evaluations keyed to a criterial system? Do the expressions of certitude match the data gathered? A sample of writing taken at the end of the term is similarly treated, and the amount of growth, as a result of consistent instruction, may then be noted.

COMPARING

Comprehending and Applying the Operation

A very basic form of description is to tell what something *is* or to tell what it is *like*. These two forms constitute the largest percentage of our daily observations. A being who could not discern likeness and difference could not think, since classes or classifications—that is, conceptualizations—are based on determinations of similarity. This discerning or discriminating capacity is the core of what may be termed *rational processes.* "Strictly single-item information cannot initiate a thought process" (Sir Frederic Bartlett).

Some things that are similar are also different: That is, "similar to" and "different from" are relational terms. It is probably impossible to conceptualize complete and total difference between two items, ideas, situations, or events. Where the extreme condition of similarity in which all difference is excluded prevails, it is seen as one of identity or sameness. When looking for similiarities, one is distinguishing the items to be compared, *as a unit*, from the universe of things (or the general). Then one has to distinguish them from each other (or the particular).

In comparing, to decide whether the point of similarity or difference is critical depends upon the purpose to be served. If our purpose is to distinguish or delimit, then the point of distinction becomes critical. (For example, what are the critical distinctions between a craft and a profession or between education and training? This is not a simple matter of adding up similarities or differences, as one might do when comparing apples in size, color, shape, and taste.) If, on the other hand, our purpose is assimilative, then we tend to ignore or at least to minimize distinctions. Then, too, there are times when we make distinctions that are minute or insubstantial; for instance, the seemingly comparative designations "new and old methods of teaching" actually conceal important similarities, as do the simple terms *new* and *old* in general use. At other times, we create empty and artificial categories that stand for little that is actual: for example, "traditional" and "progressive." These are then stuffed with miscellany and loose trash lying about; hence, confusion is inevitable.

Comparing skills tend to forestall the tendency to polarize with either-or choices, since they foster the tendency to search for similarities. Finding similarities may be a higher-order mental process than finding differences, in that it requires a linking and synthesizing. In order for there to be differences between "things," there first have to be similarities. Therefore, the place to search for differences is right within the similarities. Moreover, since there seems to be a tendency to focus initially on differences, it may be countered by the insistence that differences finding be deferred until similarities have been listed.

Comparing styles themselves can be differentiated. For instance, some focus on the totality and others on the partiality of the matters to be compared. Then, too, the subject content of the matters to be compared influences and may determine whether they will be seen in the totality or the

partiality. Differences in approach will be noted if sets of comparisons themselves are compared.

Exercises in Comparing

Ask the students to compare the items in each pair in the following list:

1. Fog and dew
2. Frost and rain
3. Snow and hail
4. Drizzle and sleet
5. Mist and glaze
6. Whirlwind and monsoon
7. Cyclone and hurricane
8. Tornado and typhoon
9. Fingers and toes
10. Skin and fruit peel
11. White blood cell and red blood cell
12. Earthquake and volcano
13. Halo and rainbow
14. Harmony and discord
15. Echo and reflection
16. Solar year and lunar year
17. Julian calendar and Gregorian calendar
18. French Revolutionary calendar and Gregorian calendar
19. Pressure and force
20. Weight and height
21. Flower and vegetable
22. Sponge and clam
23. Fruits and nuts
24. Digestive system and circulatory system
25. Lord Kelvin's cosmozoic theory of life with Ernst Haeckel's primeval-sea hypothesis
26. Darwin's and Lamarck's theories
27. Latitude and longitude
28. Northern Hemisphere and Southern Hemisphere
29. Torrid zone and temperate zone
30. Continent and island
31. Country and nation
32. Political and geographic
33. Economic and social
34. Chemical and biological
35. Physical and geologic
36. Geometric and arithmetic
37. Artistic and scientific
38. Beethoven and Strauss
39. Bach and Mahler
40. Harmony and counterpoint
41. Form and content
42. Vibrato and staccato
43. Trumpet and violin
44. Harp and piano
45. Velazquez and van Gogh
46. Picasso and Rembrandt
47. Shellac and varnish
48. Addition and multiplication
49. Fractions and integers
50. The *Odyssey* and *Robin Hood*
51. Peter the Great and Charles Stuart I
52. *A Tale of Two Cities* and *Julius Caesar*
53. Oliver Cromwell and Robespierre
54. Vowel and consonant
55. Comma and period
56. Number and numeral

57. Mean and median	67. Serf and slave
58. Circle graph and bar graph	68. Peasant and proletarian
59. Circle and oval	69. Television and cinema
60. Rectangle and square	70. Typewriting and word
61. Area and perimeter	processing
62. Interest and dividend	71. FORTRAN and LOGO
63. Salary and wage	72. Music and noise
64. Profit and rent	73. Two problem solutions
65. Fee and royalty	74. Two translations
66. King and dictator	75. Two comparisons

LANGUAGE

Ask the students to compare the words in the two columns below. How are these words alike, and how are they different?

dancer	Tanzer
devil	Teufel
door	Tür
drink	trunk
father	Vater
God	Gott
knead	Kneten
knee	Knie
knob	Knopf
boy (knave)	Knabe
knuckle	knöchel
thick	dick
thief	Dieb
thing	Ding
this	dies
thistle	Distel
thunder	Donner
*	*
forest	forêt
festival	fête
priest	le prêtre
school	école
stamen	étamine
state	état
stole	étole
stranger	étranger

strangler	étrangler
strap	étrape
stop	s'arrêter
study	étudier
stuff	étoffes

SOCIAL STUDIES

1. Have the students read the following two newspaper stories reporting the same event:

LONDON TIMES, OCTOBER 19, 1959

Clashes occurred during celebrations in honor of the poet Schiller, which took place in Vienna last night. About 2000 neo-Nazi organizers and participants of the freedom torch procession were attacked by members of the *Bundesjugendring*, which includes about 400,000 members of different creeds and from all walks of life. The police, who appeared in considerable force, could not prevent serious disturbances, which resulted in a number of arrests and some injuries on both sides. The *Bundesjugendring* protested several days ago against the Schiller freedom celebrations by the "gravediggers of freedom" and announced there would be counterdemonstrations against the neo-Nazis if the Government did not prohibit the torch parade.[4]

NEW YORK TIMES, OCTOBER 19, 1959

About twenty-five persons, some demonstrators wearing illegal swastika badges, and other "anti-Fascists," were arrested here last night when the police broke up fighting between Communists and youths who staged a torchlight procession.[5]

Ask the students to compare the accounts and list the similarities; then list the differences. Next have them consider:

Are the similarities more significant than the differences? Why?
Are the differences more significant than the similarities? Why?
How do you account for the differences that exist?
Follow the same procedure for the next two newspaper articles:

NEW YORK TIMES, JUNE 6, 1960

Windsheim, Germany: SEPP DIETRICH, former commander of Hitler's bodyguard and ranking officer in the Nazi Elite Guard, was present, uninvited, at a reunion of 1,500 men of the unit here today.[6]

ASSOCIATED PRESS, JUNE 6, 1960

Windsheim, Germany: About 1,200 diehard SS (Nazi Elite Guard) men marched through this old Franconian town Sunday night singing Nazi songs. And yesterday police said they had no grounds to stop them.

"We are the Black Guards that Adolf Hitler loved so much," the former black-uniformed SS men roared. They then sang another song: "If all become unfaithful, we'll stand by you."

Many observers thought that by singing the latter song, the old ex-SS men wanted to show their allegiance is still with Hitler and his Nazi ideologies. Police didn't think so. They said that the former SS men, all members of the Sixth Mountain Division, were drunk when they sang the songs. "Under the influence of alcohol, they may have thought they were back 20 years in their lives," a police official explained.

Officially, the meeting was aimed at finding SS men still missing. World War II SS Gen. SEPP DIETRICH, the man who commanded Hitler's bodyguards and later the Leibstandarte Division, a crack SS unit, presided over the meeting as honorary guest.[7]

2. Ask the students to read the following quotations from two famous documents from the presidency of Abraham Lincoln.

FROM LINCOLN'S *FIRST INAUGURAL ADDRESS*, MARCH 4, 1861

Apprehensions seem to exist among the people of the Southern States that by the accession of a Republican administration their property and their peace and personal security are to be endangered. There has never been any reasonable cause for such apprehension. Indeed, the most ample evidence to the contrary has all the while existed and been open to their inspection. It is found in nearly all the published speeches of him who now addresses you. I do but quote from one of those speeches when I declare that "I have no purposes, directly or indirectly, to interfere with the institution of slavery in the States where it exists. I believe I have no lawful right to do so and I have no inclination to do so."

FROM LINCOLN'S *EMANCIPATION PROCLAMATION*, JANUARY 1, 1863

That on the first day of January, . . . [1863], all persons held as slaves within any State, or designated part of a State, the people whereof shall then be in rebellion against the United States, shall be then, thenceforward, and forever free; and the Executive Government of the United States, including the military and naval authority thereof, will recognize and maintain the freedom of such persons, and will do no act or acts to repress such per-

sons, or any of them, in any efforts they may make for their
actual freedom.

Have the students list the differences between the two statements. Are they
significant differences? Why? Then ask the students to find out the circumstances surrounding the *Inaugural Address* and the *Emancipation Proclamation*. In what way were these circumstances similar? Different? How do
the pupils account for the seeming change in viewpoint evidenced in the
two documents?

   3. As the students read the following accounts, ask them to consider what
similarities can be found in them. Are the similiarities or the differences
more critical? Have them give reasons for their answers.

     A. While the famous regiments of Charles V triumphantly overran
       Europe, off in the New World Spanish soldiers and sailors were
       discovering and conquering vast regions. Our country dedicated
       itself solely to the great task of Christianizing the trans-Atlantic
       world, sacrificing to this lofty historical end the ideals of political
       and religious liberty which the spirit of the times called for. To
       fulfill this civilizing mission, it was necessary to maintain the tra-
       ditional monarchy and the Catholic Church as centers of power
       and guidance. Consequently the soldier who acclaimed the king
       and enlarged the fatherland was accompanied by the missionary
       who proclaimed his God and spread the Gospel. . . .
         If we compared the scanty means of those explorers with the
       immense resources which Stanley, Brazza, and the rest of the
       African explorers had at their disposal, we should see how illus-
       trious our magnificent forbears appear. For they were inspired
       not so much by desire for gold as by a noble yearning for fame
       and by a generous aspiration to carry the Cross in triumph over
       all the world. A race of sublime Quixotes, consumed by a passion
       for the unknown and the great, which made of the 16th century a
       poem of action, eclipsing the most exalted figures of ancient his-
       tory, Greece would have ranked them among her demigods. . . .[8]

     B. It was the lust for gold that led on the Spanish adventurers. . . .
       It was the immense treasure from the New World that became
       the foundation stone of the great Spanish character and
       industry. . . .[9]

     C. The Inca, as the ruler of these Indians was known, was taken
       prisoner and cruelly murdered even though he paid as ransom for
       his freedom a roomful of gold worth about $15,000,000.[10]

D. For all their expenditures of money and lives, the Spaniards, seventy years after Columbus' great voyage, had not a single settlement in America north of the Gulf of Mexico. . . . They did not colonize this region as they did the West Indies, Mexico, and Central and South America. The provinces, or vice-royalties, which they set up in New Spain were governed quite despotically. All the trade was regulated by the "India House" at Seville and forbidden to foreigners. The Roman Catholic religion was the only one allowed. The native Indians and imported Negroes were frightfully treated under the lash of the slave drivers. The land was in the hands of a few wealthy proprietors. There were no representative assemblies.[11]

E. Accomplished during a century that was as brilliant and hard as the steel of Toledo, the conquest of America lost its adventurous aspect when the clamor of arms ceased. The man to use the most somber colors in painting the violence and excesses inherent in that kind of conquest is Father Las Casas, a priest of Seville.

Foreign authors have depended upon his testimony to loosen their tongues in insults against our country, without considering the fact that similar deeds were committed by the Portugese in the conquest of the Indies, and by the Englishmen, Frenchmen and other European peoples in the American colonization. In the discovery and conquest of the New World, Spain showed herself as she was at the time, a nation with deplorable faults but also great virtues; and thanks to the latter, that continent came soon into the bosom of civilization. If there were crimes, "the crimes were of the times and not Spain's," as the poet said. To expect the discovery and conquest of America without war—and war without violence, ravages, and desolation—is the same as expecting parting without sorrow and life without death. Only the nation that has fought with tactics different from those practiced by Spain is privileged to throw the first stone at Spain.[12]

F. After the taking of Mexico, Cortez divided the land among the conquerors, and on the ruins of the Aztec city he began to build the Spanish city of Mexico, proclaiming its future greatness. He organized a city corporation, established markets, repaired the aqueduct of Chapultepec, which had been cut during the siege, laid down moral laws, thus beginning the government of the colony whose wealth he protected by wise measures. . . .

Then Pizarro showed his admirable gifts as organizer and colonizer; he divided the land into districts, he organized the administration of justice and the working of the mines . . . and in a

short time, thanks to his energy and will, the church, town hall,
palaces, and houses formed a beautiful city (Lima) which grew
and prospered.[13]

G. Pizarro, in imitation of Cortes, laid hands on the Inca, Atahualpe,
and held him as security for the good behavior of his people. In
return for his freedom the Inca promised to fill a large room with
objects of gold to a depth of nine feet. Almost immediately por-
ters began to come in bearing golden vases, goblets, and jars;
miniature gold birds and beasts, golden leaves, flowers, beads,
roots. Melted down, this mass yielded 1,326,539 pesos de oro,
the equivalent of $15,550,000 in American money. Having
secured this treasure, the Spaniards treacherously led their pris-
oner out to the plaza of Caxamarca and strangled him with a
bowstring.[14]

H. In order to govern such distant colonies, the mother country laid
down the wise laws of the Indies, a code that gives us a claim to
glory because of the noble humanitarian impulse by which it was
inspired.

Thanks to the laws of the Indies, all Spanish America was covered with universities and other centers of learning which spread
culture among all those peoples, stimulating in some—Mexico
and Peru for instance—a great flowering of literature.

While the colonial systems of other countries are concerned
solely with material exploitation of the colonies, ours always was
preoccupied especially with moral purposes. We strove to propa-
gate learning in such a way that within a few years of its conquest
all Spanish America was covered with universities and other institutions of learning. In this respect no other colonizing has out-
done Spain's; and perhaps this explains why, the culture of the
natives having been raised so considerably, Spanish America was
soon able to free herself from our dominion and rule her own
destiny. For this reason Señor Barrantes called our colonial system "Generous and Christian, without doubt, but also suicidal."
Therefore, today, now that the old hates are dying out, all Americans of Latin blood are stretching their arms toward the mother
country, proud to feel the noble blood of Spain coursing through
their veins. . . .

The discovery of America is the most transcendent episode of
secular history since in a way it completed the work of God making contracts between bands and peoples separated by force of
geological cataclysms, and triumphantly carrying them the Gospel
of Christ and the word of Spain. . . .[15]

After the pupils have read the accounts, ask them:

> Which accounts present Spain in the role of a civilizing mission?
> Which accounts look upon the conquistadores as scourges of the devil rather than as emissaries of the Christian God?
> The differences in the accounts appear to be crucial. Why do the accounts differ so much?
> Which account is correct?

SCIENCE

Have the students compare the heart and the lungs. Below are some sample student responses.

SIMILARITIES
Body organs
Necessary to keep body alive
Located in upper half of body
Expand and contract
Made up of cells
Contain compartments
Have openings into tubes

DIFFERENCES

Heart	*Lungs*
One organ	Paired organ
Contains blood	Contain air
Contracts itself	Forced to contract by pressure of diaphragm
No opening to outside of body	Open to outside of body
Made of muscles	Made of elastic tissue
Contains valves	No valves
Four compartments	Many compartments
Eight openings into tubes	Two openings into tubes

SUMMARY

If either organ stopped functioning, the body would not survive. A critical difference lies in the material used by each organ to perform its life-maintaining function, the heart containing blood and the lungs containing air.

INDUSTRIAL ARTS

Ask the students to compare paint and wood stain by listing the similarities and the differences. An example of student responses follow:

SIMILARITIES

They are liquids.
They impart color to wood.
They come in a variety of colors.
They are applied with a brush or applicator.
They are stored in airtight containers.
They may be used decoratively.
Pigment in each determines the color.

DIFFERENCES

	How Applied	*Coverage*	*Result*
Paint	Allowed to dry	Forms protective coat	Hides the wood
Stain	Excess wiped off	Penetrates into grain	Changes color of wood

CLASSIFYING

Comprehending and Applying the Operation

Classifying is an extension of comparing and involves the noting of similarities or differences in the items being compared, which are then assigned to groups on the basis of size, form, structure, effect, or some other criterion that has been predetermined. Essentially, classifying (categorizing) is the basis of conceptualization or the creation of concepts. Groups or classifications may themselves be expanded into ever larger systems to become a taxonomy. Subjects such as botany and natural science are fundamentally huge taxonomic systems.

A being who could not classify could not think, since it involves discernment of similarities and differences. Although a concept is a verbal form (of classifying), classifying or categorizing occur through immediate apprehension of the senses alone—for example, colors, odors, tastes, textures, and qualities of objects felt. Such immediate apprehension makes it difficult (if not impossible) for us *not* to classify phenomena such as odors and colors. From early childhood, it is the way in which we begin to make sense of the outside world, and we continue to receive the outside world into ourselves (as it were) through continually expanding our conceptualizations.

Classifications are correct if they are appropriate—that is, to the extent that they serve the purpose of the grouping. Therefore, judgment as to the appropriateness of the items within a given group should not be made from a scheme structured on a differing classifying principle or purpose. (Since such judgments are, in fact, frequent daily occurrences, they cause what has been loosely labeled "communication breakdowns.")

In order to create groups or subdivisions from a larger mass, the basis or purpose of the subdivision has to be significant. There are different bases or purposes on which to subdivide and classify; for example, a safe driving council will classify automobiles on a basis other than color, price, or styling.

The weakest classification schemes are identifiable by the lack of a sorting principle or the operation of more than one sorting or grouping principle at a given time. Slightly less weak are those classification schemes with too great an overlap between groups or categories, resulting in a residue of items that do not fit.

The process of abstracting is basic to the processes of thought. In extracting or abstracting a single characteristic as the basis of classifying, one has to be aware that one is *necessarily* omitting. Classifying or categorizing cannot be done without such omission. There is no possible way for experience to be abstracted and characterized *perfectly*. If this principle is grasped, it helps us to comprehend the science and theory of law (jurisprudence) as a mammoth classification scheme. We then begin to see why lawyers can spend days disputing the details of a contract ("Is it a wage, a salary, or a fee?") and why conflicts can develop over the interpretation of tax laws and the meanings of legislative statutes. It should also help us to see why wars can be, and are, fought over such classifications as imperialist/nonimperialist; Communist/non-Communist; republican/monarchist; elitist/nonelitist; sexist/nonsexist; democratic/undemocratic.

Although a classification is a convenience (and although there can be considerable variation among classification schemes), it is not, in most cases, arbitrary, nor is it an indestructible truth. Yet some of the greatest conflicts have arisen in connection with classifications of human beings that have hardened into rigidity. As suggested above, *any* political, racial, religious, national, geographic, social, generational, sex, or physical-characteristic grouping can be a force for ill will if its stance is primarily adversarial.

Classifications can be created by focussing either on the similarities between items or on their differences. If we focus on the similarities, say, among a carrot, beet, radish, turnip, parsnip, and potato, as we omit or erase the differences between them, we have moved *up* an abstraction ladder to the concept "vegetable." If we focus on the differences between a carrot and a radish (or between carrots themselves) and thereby omit the similarities between them, we have moved *down* an abstraction ladder to create a subgroup. In a real sense, then, it can be seen that the *more* we talk about, the *less* we are saying (referring to), and the *less* we talk about, the *more* we are saying (referring to).

A class cannot be a member of itself. It *is* in a class by itself. (This is the principle of sui generis.) Once we have created a concept through abstraction of differences—that is, by omitting them—we cannot then include this class as one of the members of the original group. For instance, if "school" is a category we have created to group such units as laboratory, gymnasium, library, classroom, music room, art center, and study hall, the category "school" must remain outside the grouped units themselves. This is one of the hardest principles for human beings to practice consistently. Although it can be understood cognitively as an abstraction, in daily living it is rarely remembered, and it fuels communication breakdowns, quarrels, and conflicts.

There *are* well-established classification schemes, as in law (felony, offense, misdemeanor); parts of speech (noun, verb, adjective); and the biological distinctions (animal, plant, mineral). It is necessary, at times, to be able to put the parts where they belong in these well-established classification schemes. However, this is not what is intended here. The emphasis is on the *development* of groups and categories on the basis of some principle of similarity or difference.

Being aware of shifts from the general to the particular (sometimes referring to what is genus and then to what is species) is, perhaps, the central task in achieving clarity in thought or conceptualization.

Exercises in Classifying

Ask the students to classify the items within each of the following entries:

1. 1776, 1941, 1812, 1839, 1861, 1898
2. Prokofiev, Beethoven, Tchaikovsky, Schubert, Verdi, Mendelssohn, Brahms, Schumann, Scarlatti, Rossini, Purcell, Haydn, Shostakovich, Mozart, Gounod, Vivaldi, Wagner, Smetana, Bach, Dvorak
3. Tennis, pool, golf, hockey, jai alai, Ping-Pong, volleyball, basketball, baseball, lacrosse, polo, football, soccer, badminton
4. Matisse, Renoir, Picasso, Gainesborough, Dürer, Holbein, Vermeer, Rembrandt, Degas, Modigliani, Lautrec, Goya, Velasquez, Turner, Cezanne, Manet, Monet

5. Meager, menial, mortify, demonic, domicile, needless, noctur-
   nal, destitute, denounce, depradation, decry, mutual, mystify,
   negligent, nimble, monster
6. Flute, violin, cymbals, tambourine, trumpet, harp, lute, clarinet,
   English horn, triangle, cello, viola, French horn, trombone
7. The parts of the body
8. The countries of the world

LANGUAGE

1. Have students examine the list of words below. They have been selected
because they contain all the simple vowel sounds of present-day English.
The best way to find out what these sounds are is to pronounce the words
aloud many times to determine which sounds are alike and which differ from
one another. Remember that speech cannot be studied in silence; your
students can learn more about the English language from their own observations than from what an author can tell them because they are in a better
position to examine their own speech. Help the students determine how
many stressed vowel sounds there are in modern English as it is spoken in
your locality. Ask the students to rearrange the list, putting words of similar
vowel sounds together. For example, although *soul* and *boat* are spelled
differently, they have the same vowel sound, and hence belong together.

Soul	Gnaw	Full	Sham	Which
Good	Bid	Cough	Measure	Cube
Great	Book	Leave	Think	Ask
Pass	Word	Bird	Boat	Ale
Calm	Top	Bathe	Chews	Farther
Nut	Jerk	Feed	Hand	Frost
Let	Son	Rude	Zinc	Bead
Long	Heard	Turn	Yet	Quay
Tall	Many	Nap	Take	Bath
Water	Drawn	Balk	Use	Of
Golf	Bade	Have	Just	None
Palm	Glass	Branch	Shoe	Foot
Heir	Learn	Fir	Air	Basket
Song	Wear	Path	Psalm	Wool

Ask the students: How many vowel characters does the English alphabet
provide for these vowel sounds? What vowel characters do not always represent the same sound? Next have the students consult the dictionary to
discover the symbols that are employed in indicating the vowel sounds in
the list.

The foregoing exercise was tried with students who grouped the words according to the way *they* made the particular sounds. Despite "wrong" answers, the students had to listen to themselves and to others acutely. On the basis of dictionary investigation, they also discovered that there was not only one way to make sounds; there were certain accepted "groupings," each of which had its internal standards. When these standards are accepted in a particular locality, they are adhered to in the interests of intracommunication.

2. Ask the students to group the following French pronouns:

      elle   elles   vous   tu   nous   me   les   le   ils   il

Some students who tried this exercise developed four groupings: *voice* (first, second, third); *gender*; *case*; and *number*. By case, for example, they grouped the pronouns as follows: *subjective*—elle, elles, il, ils, tu; *objective*—le, les; *both subjective and objective*—nous, vous. By number the pronouns were grouped into *singular*—elle, il, le, me, tu—and *plural*—elles, ils, nous, vous.

3. To help students understand classifications, present the following list, and ask them to consider whether the items in each pair are opposites.

Riches and poverty	Heads and tails
Red and blue	Fat and slim
Republican and Democrat	Round and square
Protestant and Catholic	Tall and short
Soft and hard	Fever and chills

Have students examine the grouping in the diagram below. Ask them how the diagram shows opposites in the last item in the list above. How can they tell whether the other pairs in the list are opposites?

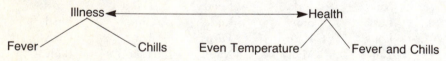

SOCIAL STUDIES

Ask the pupils to group the following states any way they think appropriate:

Connecticut	New York
Delaware	North Carolina
Georgia	Pennsylvania
Maryland	Rhode Island
Massachusetts	South Carolina
New Hampshire	Virginia
New Jersey	

A sample student response is shown below:

Geographical locations

Agricultural states, industrial states

Northern states, southern states

Union states, Confederate states

States named after a monarch or a lord

States with Indian names

States with the word *new* in them and states without *new*

Size or population

Number of rivers and number of mountains

SCIENCE

1. Have the students classify the following:

Lion	Frog	Codfish
Whale	Horse	Rattlesnake
Eagle	Canary	Lizard

Some students who tried the exercise developed these categories:

Air-breathing	Terrestrial
Warm-blooded	Meat-eating
Four-legged	Egg-laying

The lists that follow show how the animals were grouped in two pairs of categories:

Egg-laying	*Non–egg-laying*
Codfish	Lion
Eagle	Whale
Rattlesnake	Horse
Frog	
Canary	
Lizard	

Warm-blooded	*Cold-blooded*
Lion	Codfish
Whale	Rattlesnake
Eagle	Frog
Horse	Lizard
Canary	

2. Ask the students to figure out how many different ways they can group the following:

Sea horse	Giraffe	Common water snake
Penguin	Mud puppy	Ring-necked pheasant
Bat	Cardinal	Hippopotamus

Moray eel	Shrew	Common toad	Turtle
Flounder	Sailfish	Leopard frog	Python
Alligator	Mouse	Collard lizard	
Whale	Ostrich	Tortoise	

Some students responded with these categories:

Size

Mating habits

What it eats

Where it lives

How it protects itself

Fish, animal, bird, reptile

Mammal, egg laying

After the pupils have decided on a principle for classifying, have them work out the actual grouping. They can then evaluate the grouping system.

3. Present the following for students to classify:

Light bulb	Ammeter
Dry cell	Voltmeter
Generator	Storage battery

Some category responses from students follow:

Producer or user of electricity

Containing glass in its makeup

Containing a permanent or electromagnet

Containing movable parts

Presence of chemical action in its operation

These lists show how the items were grouped into two pairs of categories:

Chemical Action	*No Chemical Action*
Dry cell	Light bulb
Storage battery	Generator
	Ammeter
	Voltmeter

Producer of Electricity	*User of Electricity*
Dry cell	Light bulb
Storage battery	Ammeter
Generator	Voltmeter

4. Present this list of elements to the pupils, and have them name as many categories as they can under which the elements can be classified.

Hydrogen	Bromine	Potassium	Carbon
Uranium	Sulfur	Oxygen	Cadmium
Lithium	Chlorine	Aluminum	Radon
Magnesium	Argon	Mercury	Neon

The categories that follow were suggested by some students working on this exercise:

> Solid, liquid, or gas, at room temperature
> Solubility in water at room temperature
> Metals, nonmetals
> Ionic, covalent
> Density compared to water
> Ability to form isotopes
> Active, inert
> Electron donor, electron receiver
> Positive valence, negative valence
> Ph value
> Flame tests
> Sulfide precipitates
> Radioactivity
> Supports combustion, does not support combustion
> Flammable, nonflammable
> Colorless, colored
> Occurrence: free or combined
> Odor, odorless, characteristic odor
> Reducing agent, oxidizing agent
> Found in organic compounds, not found in organic compounds

MATHEMATICS

1. A "set" is a collection of objects containing a common factor or element. Have the students group the set in Figure 3.1 into as many of the subsets as they can. They should place an X next to the number that would fit into the particular grouping, as has been done for the prime numbers.

FIGURE 3.1. Set of Numbers for Grouping into Subsets

	20	21	22	23	24	25	26	27	28	29	30	31	32	33	34	35	36	37	38	39	40
Integers																					
Real numbers																					
Natural numbers																					
Rational numbers																					
Irrational numbers																					
Even numbers																					
Odd numbers																					
Prime numbers				X						X	X							X			
Negative numbers																					
Positive numbers																					
Cardinal numbers																					
Ordinal numbers																					

2. Ask the pupils to group the following shapes:

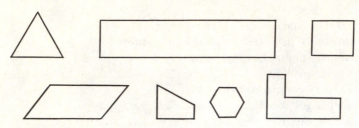

Some students responded with these categories:

    Quadrilaterals and polygons

    Parallelograms and nonparallelograms

    Regular polygons and irregular polygons

    Rectangles and nonrectangles

    Odd number of sides and angles and even number of sides and angles

    Those containing only right angles and those with various-sized angles

Within the categories, the students grouped the shapes as shown in Figure 3.2.

FIGURE 3.2. Student Groupings of Shapes Within Categories

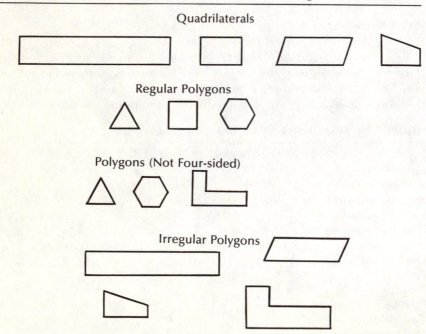

3. Have the students classify the following numbers: 1, 2, 3, 4, 5, 6, 7, 8, 9, 10. The categories below were suggested by some students:

Odd numbers, even numbers

Prime numbers

Numbers evenly divisible by 4 and those not

Numbers with factors of 3 and 1 only, and numbers with factors other than 3 and 1

Two-digit numbers, one digit numbers

Numbers greater than or equal to 7 and numbers less than 7

Within two pairs of categories, they grouped the numbers as follows: prime numbers—2, 3, 5, 7— and nonprime numbers—1, 4, 6, 8, 9, 10; numbers with factors of 3 and 1 only—3, 9—and numbers without factors of 3 and 1—1, 2, 4, 5, 6, 7, 8, 10.

BUSINESS MANAGEMENT

1. Present the following list of businesses for your students to classify:

Farmers' Cooperative Association

M. Johnson, Groceries

United States Post Office

Black and Grey Manufacturing Company

Z and B Trucking

Tennessee Valley Authority

Great Lakes Lighting Company

Minnesota Mining Corporation

An example of categories developed by students follows:

Ownership (public or private)

Organization (sole owner, partnership, corporation, cooperative)

Function (producer, manufacturer, wholesale, retailer, distributor, public utility)

Profit-making or non–profit-making

Supplier of goods or services

Interstate or intrastate

Businesses they listed under sample categories are shown below:

Supplier of Goods	*Supplier of Services*
Minnesota Mining Corporation	Great Lakes Lighting Company
Farmers' Cooperative Association	United States Post Office
M. Johnson, Groceries	Tennessee Valley Authority
Black and Grey Manufacturing Company	
Z and B Trucking	

Profit-Making	*Non–Profit-Making*
Minnesota Mining	Tennessee Valley Authority
Corporation	United States Post Office
Z and B Trucking	Farmers' Cooperative
M. Johnson, Groceries	Association
Black and Grey Manufacturing	
Company	
Great Lakes Lighting Company	

2. Listed below are some types of stores.

General store	Mail-order house
Discount house	Neighborhood store
Specialty store	Automatic vending
Department store	Roadside stand
Variety store	Pushcart
Supermarket	Flea market

Ask the students: On what bases have such groupings emerged? In what ways are all these stores alike? What are some ways you could distinguish between them? An example of a student response to the last question follows:

How goods are sold
How goods are displayed
What services are offered
How the store is owned
What kind of ownership it is
Where the store is located
How the working personnel are organized
How goods are distributed

HOME ECONOMICS

Below are listed some foods. Ask the students to group them in a way they believe to be proper.

Applesauce	Chocolate cream pudding
Baked apple	Cranberry jelly sauce
Muffins	Oven-fried chicken
Omelet	Cinnamon toast
Steak	Hot chocolate
Leafy salad	Vegetable-oil pastry
Waffles	Cream of tomato soup
Biscuits	Creamed dried chipped-beef
Custard	Fruit-jello mold
Popcorn balls	Macaroni-salad supreme

Some students developed the following groupings:
1. Fruits, breads, meats, dairy products, vegetables
2. Fruits, desserts, breads, meats, eggs, soups, salads
3. Foods I like and foods I dislike
4. Desserts, beverages, breads, proteins, and vegetables
5. Fattening foods and nonfattening foods
6. Breakfast, lunch, dinner, and snack foods
7. Solids and liquids
8. Foods that require cooking and foods that can be eaten uncooked
9. Foods that are cooked on top of the stove and foods that are cooked in the oven
10. Foods served cold and foods served hot
11. The basic four: breads and cereal, meat, dairy products, fruits and vegetables

Have the students in your class analyze each of the groupings listed above and try to determine on what basis or principle each was selected. Next ask the students to look carefully at the eleven groups themselves and try to figure out a way of grouping *them*.

SUMMARIZING

Comprehending and Applying the Operation

Summarizing involves a selecting of "what counts"—an ability to find the essence, to abstract out, to grasp the central idea and to express this essentiality succinctly. It is probably apparent that the operation impinges directly on translating and interpreting. It reads between lines and moves beyond the given to abstract and filter out, to integrate and synthesize salient points.

There is a distinction between the summary as *product* and summarizing as *process*. The former is a synthesis, the latter requires analysis. The summary as product may be deemed an interpretation; the act of summarizing extends beyond interpretation in that a decision has to be made about what to include and what to omit (and in what order); an evaluation of the significant and the insignificant is required.

A critical difference between summarizing and reporting is that in the former, omission is a creative act, requiring the determination and extraction from the whole of what is essential. In the latter, omission is a *defect*. Chronology and sequence tend to be structural props of an operation that is essentially reproductive. Summarizing and reporting are *not* to be equated. The deficit of the one is the asset of the other.

The skills of summarizing are acquired through repeated practice in abstracting and extracting the essence (or kernel) from larger material. Since comprehension and translation are intertwined in the process of summarizing, they need not be separated out and dealt with *prior* to the act of summarizing. (One process subsumes and engages the other.)

Eliciting one summary of material is less instructive than eliciting several for comparison of the bases upon which a determination of essentiality rests. Moreover, since there are many styles of summarizing, exposure to this variety of styles forestalls repetitiveness and mechanization of approach.

Exercises in Summarizing

Ask the students to summarize

1. The most important rules of a particular subject: geometry, biology, bookkeeping, poetry
2. Accounts of a series of experiments; for example, famous experiments by Galileo, Lavoisier, Faraday, Pasteur
3. Excerpts of a log or diary from the records of Columbus, Magellan, Lewis and Clark
4. Their biographies
5. The story of the United States
6. Frequently mentioned theories; for example, germ theory of disease, Locke's theory of government, Darwin's theory of evolution, Marxist theory, heliocentric theory, genetic theory

Titling, subtitling, retitling, or captioning are forms of summarizing. Have the students practice these forms using pictures, diagrams, charts, graphs, cartoons, problems, experiments, processes, and chapters and sections in books.

Another form of summarizing is data organization such as mapping, diagramming, charting, and preparing headings, indexes, tables of contents, and keys to charts. Preparing initial outlines and abstracts for term papers also gives pupils practice in summarizing.

LANGUAGE

1. Have the students read the following poem and retitle it to express the central idea. Ask them to make a listing of what may be omitted from a summary.

THE BLIND MEN AND THE ELEPHANT
It was six men of Indostan
 To learning much inclined
Who went to see the elephant
 (Though each of them was blind,)
That each by observation
 Might satisfy his mind.

The first approached the elephant
 And happening to fall
Against his broad and sturdy side
 At once began to bawl:
"God bless me, but the elephant
 Is very much like a wall."

The second, feeling of the tusk,
 Cried: "Ho, what have we here
So round and smooth and sharp?
 To me, 'tis very clear
This wonder of an elephant
 Is very like a spear."

The third approached the animal
 And happening to take
The squirming trunk with his hands,
 Thus boldly up he spake:
"I see," quote he, "the elephant
 Is very much like a snake."

The fourth reached out his eager hand,
 And fell upon the knee:
"What most this wondrous beast is like,
 Is very plain," quoth he;
" 'Tis clear enough, the elephant
 Is very like a tree."

The fifth who chanced to touch the ear,
 Said: "Even the blindest man
Can tell what this resembles most.
 Deny the fact who can,
This marvel of an elephant
 Is very like a fan."

The sixth no sooner had begun
 About the beast to grope

Then seizing on the swinging tail
   That fell within his scope,
"I see," quoth he, "the elephant
   Is very like a rope."

And so the men of Indostan
   Disputed loud and long,
Each in his own opinion
   Exceeding stiff and strong
Though each was partly in the right
And all were in the wrong.[16]

2. Select a series of ten famous novels, such as *Moby Dick, Huckleberry Finn, The Red Badge of Courage, The Last of the Mohicans*—that is, books that most students have read. Ask the students to retitle the novels and present justifications for the titles.

3. Present the following two selections and ask the students to make a listing of what may be omitted from a summary of each of them; to provide at least two titles for each selection; and to provide a single title for both selections *taken as a unit*.

  A. Discussion in the U.S. Senate of 13 billion dollars appropriated for the War Department and returned unused.

    Senator Barkley: It is always impossible to sit down at a table and calculate to the fineness of a bat's eye just how much is going to be needed everywhere.

    Senator Wheeler: Mr. President, I do not wish to be understood as criticizing the War Department for turning back the money; but when the Senator talks about 13 billion dollars being what can be put in a bat's eye . . .

    Senator Barkley: The Senator knows that I was not talking about putting 13 billion dollars in a bat's eye. I was talking about Army officers sitting down at a table and working out to the fineness of a bat's eye everything they needed in the way of supplies and equipment.

    Senator Wheeler: The Senator was talking about a bat's eye, and I say he was talking about putting 13 billion dollars in a bat's eye.

    Senator Barkley: I think the Senator is playing on words.

    Senator Wheeler: The Senator from Kentucky was playing on words.

Senator Barkley: I do not understand that even the Senator from
    Montana thinks that 13 billion dollars can be put into a bat's
    eye.
Senator Wheeler: The Senator was playing on words when he was
    talking about the 13 billion dollars which I mentioned. He
    said that Army officers could not sit down and work it out to
    the fineness of a bat's eye. I said that 13 billion dollars could
    not be put in a bat's eye.
Senator Barkley: For once, the Senator and I agree. Thirteen billion
    dollars cannot be put in a bat's eye. That is settled. (Laughter)
Senator Wheeler: I am glad to have the Senator agree with me once
    in a while.[17]

B.   "In your country, brother, what is the wage of a master bailiff,
master hind, carter, shepherd, swineherd?"
    "Twenty-five milrays a day; that is to say, a quarter of a cent."
    The Smith's face beamed with joy. He said:
    "With us they are allowed the double of it! And what may a
mechanic get—carpenter, dauber, mason, painter, blacksmith,
wheelwright, and the like?"
    "On the average, fifty milrays; half a cent a day."
    "Ho-ho! With us they are allowed a hundred! With us any
good mechanic is allowed a cent a day! I count out the tailor, but
not the others—they are all allowed a cent a day, and in driving
times they get more—yes, up to a hundred and ten and even fifteen milrays a day. I've paid a hundred and fifteen myself, within
the week. 'Rah for protection—to Sheol with free trade!' "
    And his face shone upon the company like a sunburst. But I
didn't scare at all. I rigged up my pile driver, and allowed myself
fifteen minutes to drive him into the earth—drive him *all* in—till
not even the curve of his skull should show above the ground.
Here is the way I started in on him. I asked:
    "What do you pay for a pound for salt?"
    "A hundred milrays."
    "We pay forty. What do you pay for beef and mutton—when
you buy it?" That was a neat hit; it made the color come.
    "It varieth somewhat, but not much; one may say seventy-five
milrays the pound."
    "*We* pay thirty-three. What do you pay for eggs?"
    "Fifty milrays the dozen."
    "We pay twenty. What do you pay for beer?"
    "It costeth us eight and one-half milrays the pint."
    "We get it for four; twenty-five bottles for a cent. What do you
pay for wheat?"
    "At the rate of nine hundred milrays the bushel."

"We pay four hundred. What do you pay for a man's tow linen suit?"

"Thirteen cents."

"We pay six. What do you pay for a stuff gown for the wife of the laborer or the mechanic?"

"We pay eight cents, four mills."

"Well, observe the difference: You pay eight cents and four mills, we pay only four cents." I prepared now to sock it to him. I said: "Look here, dear friend, *what's become of your high wages you were bragging so about a few minutes ago?*"—and I looked around on the company with placid satisfaction, for I had slipped up on him gradually and tied him hand and foot, you see, without his ever noticing that he was being tied at all. "What's become of those noble high wages of yours?—I seem to have knocked the stuffing all out of them, it appears to me."

But if you will believe me, he merely looked surprised, that is all! He didn't grasp the situation at all, didn't know he had walked into a trap, didn't discover that he was *in* a trap. I could have shot him, from sheer vexation. With cloudy eye and a struggling intellect he fetched this out:

"Marry I seem not to understand. It is *proved* that our wages be double thine; how then may it be that thou'st knocked therefrom the stuffing?—and I miscall not the wonderly word, this being the first time under grace and providence of God it hath been granted to me to hear it."

Well, I was stunned; partly with this unlooked-for stupidity on his part, and partly because his fellows so manifestly sided with him and were of his mind—if you might call it mind. My position was simple enough, plain enough; how could it ever be simplified more? However I must try:

"Why look here, brother Dowley, don't you see? Your wages are merely higher than ours in *name*, not in *fact*."

"Hear him! They are the *double*—ye have confessed it yourself."

"Yes-yes, I don't deny that at all. But that's got nothing to do with it; the *amount* of the wages in mere coins, with meaning-less names attached to them to know them by, has got nothing to do with it. The thing is, how much can you *buy* with your wages?—that's the idea. While it is true that with you a good mechanic is allowed about three dollars and a half a year, and with us only about a dollar and seventy five—"

"There—ye're confessing it again, ye're confessing it again!"

"Confound it, I've never denied it, I tell you! What I say is this. With us *half* a dollar buys more than a *dollar* buys with you—and *therefore* it stands to reason and the commonest kind of common sense, that our wages are *higher* than yours."

He looked dazed and said despairingly:
"Verily I cannot make it out. Ye've just *said* ours are the higher, and with the same breath ye take it back."[18]

4. Have the students read the following statements. Ask them what connection they see between them.

General education is basic to the proper development of a person's capacities.

Herman Melville was the first important naturalist in the mainstream of American fiction.

Society has robbed man of his economic independence.

Effective communication is necessary in labor-management disputes.

California produces more oranges than Texas.

The American way of life is the result of interaction of both the Puritan and frontier influences.

Effective communication is important in maintaining family unity.

Using these statements as examples of central ideas or themes, have the students extract some rules that might help them in formulating a central idea or theme.

SOCIAL STUDIES

1. Present the following selection and ask the students to provide a title that expresses the central idea:

Twelve years passed before Harvey was ready to publish his findings. Harvey had this to say: "[The theory of circulation of the blood] is of so novel and unheard of character, that I not only fear injury to myself from the envy of a few, but I tremble lest I have mankind at large for my enemies." Sir William Osler suggested that "perhaps it was the motive of Copernicus who so dreaded the prejudices of mankind that for thirty years he is said to have detained in his closet the Treatise of Revolutions."[19]

2. Have the students provide four subheadings and one all-inclusive heading for the following passage:

At the end of the sixteenth century, the accepted theory of the earth in its relationship to the universe was known as the Ptolemaic theory, named after the philosopher Ptolemy, who lived 1,500 years earlier. Briefly, this theory suggested that the earth was stationary, for if it turned, it would break into pieces and fly off into space. Moreover, anything floating in the air, such as a cloud or a bird, would be left behind, and an object tossed into the air would descend a considerable distance westward.

In the sixteenth century, the philosopher Copernicus maintained that it was more logical to assume that the earth turned, instead of the entire universe, for if the earth did not rotate, the sky would have to revolve to produce day and night.

With few exceptions, this idea was violently opposed by the general public and by scientists alike. According to one story, the printer's shop where Copernicus's book was being printed was attacked by university students who tried to destroy the press and the manuscript. The printers had to barricade themselves to finish the job. A burlesque play that depicted Copernicus as having given his soul to Satan was produced by a group of players. Below are some selections that may help to indicate how the Copernican system was received:

- "The new astronomer . . . wants to prove that the Earth goes round, and not the Heavens, the Sun, and the Moon; just as if someone sitting in a moving wagon or ship were to suppose that he was at rest, and that the Earth and the trees were moving past him. But that is the way nowadays; whoever wants to be clever must needs produce something of his own, which is bound to be the best since he has produced it! The fool will turn the whole science of astronomy upside down. But, as Holy Writ declares, it was the sun and not the Earth which Joshua commanded to stand still" (Martin Luther).
- "The world also is established, that it cannot be moved" (Psalm 93). "Who will venture to place the authority of a Copernicus above that of the Holy Spirit?" (John Calvin).
- "He stopped the sun and set the earth in motion" (Philip Melancthon).
- "The first proposition, that the sun is the center and does not revolve about the earth, is foolish, absurd, false in theology, and heretical, because expressly contrary to Holy Scripture. The second proposition, that the earth revolves about the sun and is not the center, is absurd, false in philosophy and from a theological point of view at least, opposed to the true faith" (Roman Catholic Church).
- Francis Bacon, one of the leaders of the scientific movement, argued against the idea that the earth rotated on its axis and circled in an orbit around the sun.
- In 1616, the writings of Copernicus were placed on the Index of prohibited books "until they should be corrected," and "all writings which affirm the motion of the Earth" were condemned.
- Giordano Bruno, a follower of Copernicus, suggested the theory that space was boundless and that the sun and its planets were but one of many similar systems. He also suggested that there

might be other inhabited worlds with rational beings equal or superior to ourselves. Bruno was tried before the Inquisition for blasphemy; condemned; and burned at the stake in 1600.

- In 1633, the astronomer Galileo, under threat of torture and death from the Inquisition, was forced on his knees to give up his belief that Copernicus's theories might be sound. He was sentenced to imprisonment for the remainder of his days.

MATHEMATICS

For this exercise, give students or have them obtain some data with which to work on subjects such as drug or alcohol abuse, suicide rates, car deaths, birth rates, technological dispacement of workers, school populations, and political preferences. Ask the students to prepare charts or graphs with keys and titles from the data. In a variant of this exercise, have students chart food prices at the local supermarket over a period of weeks. They should prepare keys and captions to explain the charts.

OBSERVING AND REPORTING

Comprehending and Applying the Operation

Observing and reporting are a basic means of learning. Secondary accounts of an event or phenomenon, such as are contained in books or reports, *may* be more refined and accurate, but they tend to be less absorbing. Sense perception is a primary source of our knowledge, but it is imperfect. Thought or reflection is the check on imperfect perception and perceptual bias. Since we are driven by passion, impulse, and routine to obtain satisfaction of our physical needs, on such occasions we have a tendency to overestimate our capabilities in perception and to underestimate our limitations. Indeed, we have a tendency to laugh at suggestibility and credulity in others while disclaiming such characteristics in ourselves.

What we call primary (eyewitness) evidence, as distinguished from a secondary accounting, is essentially a chronological claim. It is not to be taken as a claim to freedom from distortion. Moreover, as a check on the accuracy of sense evidence, thought or reflection is hardly sufficient, if unaccompanied by the initial presumption that sense perception has inaccuracy built in.

Observing is different from mere seeing and hearing. It involves noting and discerning similarity within difference, and the reverse, as well as determining *which* is critical. Sometimes, acrostics and personal mnemonic devices are effective tools for fixing or connecting details that might otherwise remain unconnected.

Reporting is a recounting of our observing(s)—our sense experiences. There can be an error in the observation itself or in the recounting of that observation, or in both. Often it is the inaccurate observation that leads to misinterpretation and false inference in reporting. At other times it is the confusion of fact with inference that leads to a misreporting. Then, too, with the passage of time (sometimes even minutes), recollections of occurrences and events often blend in with imagination and fanciful invention. This is the basis of folklore.

Personal experiences have to be evaluated with caution. They are not identical with universal proofs. "I know—from experience . . ." is of a different epistemological order than developed theory subject to controlled test.

The primary function of memory is to aid us in the attainment of a present goal. Hence, accurate recall of details is not always necessary. In some instances, checking perceptions is much easier than checking recollections (rememberings)—for example, as in checking the number of spokes in an umbrella or bicycle wheel. (Here it is probably impractical, as well as unreliable, even to try to recall.) However, when we do have to remember details, as when we are witnesses to an accident or crime, how reliable is our testimony in the light of the passage of time, the effect of our talking to others, a gallery full of people?

The operation of observing and reporting tends to provide a natural mechanism for the unification of intellectual and pedagogic method; that is, it is a means of coming to know, and also a means of teaching and learning. To disconnect observing from reporting is to interrupt and interfere with the processing of knowledge. The closer the reporting operation is to the act of observing, the better.

Exercises in Observing and Reporting

LANGUAGE

1. Have one student study the following newspaper story, write it out from memory, and then read it out loud in the style of a police report to three other students. Then ask them to write out from memory what they have heard. Have the students compare inclusions and omissions in the various reports.

April 19, [1906]—Earthquake and fire yesterday laid nearly half of San Francisco in ruins. The fire is not yet under control. More than two hundred people were killed, one thousand injured, and the property loss, so far, is estimated at $200,000,000. Practically the entire business district was burned. Dynamite was used to check the progress of the flames.

The sweep of the earthquake was wide, deaths and large property losses marking its track in several cities to the north of San Francisco. Shocks were felt in the Far West, New York State, and Washington, D.C., and at the same time San Francisco quaked, a shock was felt in Austria.

Messages of sympathy and offers of aid were sent from all over the country immediately on receipt of the news, President Roosevelt and Congress sending messages and Boston subscribing $25,000 at once.[20]

2. Give students a list such as the following. Tell them to study it for a few minutes and then recall what they have "seen":

Voice	Choppy	Low
Singing	Soprano	Happy
Short	Smooth	Music
Full	Alto	Sad
Light	Ugly	Beautiful
Body	Words	Long
Breath	High	Slow
Raucous	Fast	Pleasant

3. Write out a message for one student to see. The message should then be passed on orally, in succession, to half a dozen others. Each one repeats the message aloud so that the rest of the class may "observe" the kinds of changes that inevitably occur.

4. Present the story below. Then ask students to make up a series of statements from memory, some of which are factual and some inferential, and label them accordingly. Some examples are, "The man was suffering from insulin shock"; "The man was walking unsteadily"; "Something was apparently wrong with the man."

A man staggered into a drug store gesturing unsteadily. His speech was incoherent and his gait very erratic. A woman customer, in irate fashion, said to the clerk, "Jim, that man is drunk! Throw him out of here!" As the clerk responded, he noticed that the man was pointing to his pocket. He put his hand into the man's pocket and took out some chocolate cubes and put one into the man's mouth. The man later returned to the drug store; his speech was coherent and his gait steady.

SOCIAL STUDIES

1. In the following passage, each phrase between the slanted lines represents a single place, person, date, or occurrence, and there are twenty-four phrases in the selection. Present the passage to the students, and after two minutes of study, have them write from memory a brief news story incorporating as many facts as possible. (Eighteen facts would be a good score.)

> Shortly before noon/Sunday/June/28,/1914,/Archduke/Francis Ferdinand,/heir-presumptive/to the thrones of Austria-Hungary,/and his wife,/Sophie,/were assassinated/by Gavrilo Printsip/in the Bosnian city/of Sarajevo./ Six weeks later/Austria-Hungary/and Germany/were involved in an armed struggle/with Serbia,/Russia,/France,/Belgium,/and Great Britain./

2. Present the following chronology, and point out to the students that some statements are of a factual type and others are interpretations (inferences) drawn from facts. Have students distinguish between the two by marking those that they believe to be factual with an *F* and those that they believe to be interpretations with an *I*.

1776: John Hancock, Thomas Jefferson, Benjamin Franklin, and other delegates from the thirteen American colonies sign the Declaration of Independence.

1776: By their victory at Trenton, the Americans prove to be better soldiers than the British.

1781: The Articles of Confederation create a tie among the colonies.

1787: Members of the Constitutional Convention draft a constitution in secret session.

1791: The Bill of Rights is ratified and becomes a part of the Constitution.

1793: Eli Whitney's cotton gin makes southern agriculture more productive and creates a boom in the slave market.

1798: Adams uses the Alien and Sedition Acts for the sole purpose of taking the vote away from his opponents.

1803: Chief Justice Marshall's rulings in *Marbury* vs. *Madison* show that he intends to make the Supreme Court more powerful than the drafters of the Constitution intended it to be.

1804: The Twelfth Amendment requires that the President and Vice-President be elected separately.

1829: As the first popularly elected President, Jackson succeeds in making the government more democratic.

1837: Van Buren defeats several Whig opponents and becomes President.

1852: *Uncle Tom's Cabin* brings violent reactions in the South and moves the South closer to secession.

1861: The Civil War in the United States begins with the Battle of Fort Sumter.

1862: The battle between the *Monitor* and the *Virginia* shows that the North has better ship-building facilities than the South.

1215: This is the date on which the Magna Charta was signed. The Magna Charta is the basis of democracy.

Fifteenth and sixteenth centuries: The Renaissance occurred during this time.

500–1000: These were the Dark Ages.

1789: This marks the beginning of freedom and nationalism in France.

1781–89: This was the critical period in the United States.

1500: This was the beginning of the modern period of history.

3. Tell the students: In the following exercise, it is *you* who are the object of observation. Observe your own reactions, your feelings and thoughts, as accurately as you can as you read each of the following excerpts. Report fully and accurately in writing on what you observe (i.e., sense, feel) taking place in yourself as you read. Report on each selection separately before proceeding to the next. As a further test of your observational and reporting powers, you will not be told what the source of the excerpt is yet. Write your report. Then, when the source has been revealed, write another report on your second "observation."

   A. It is the Anglo-Saxon manifest destiny to go forth as a world conqueror. He will take possession of all the islands of the sea. He will exterminate the people he cannot subjugate. That is what fate holds for the chosen people.[21]

   B. The struggle is not alone for civil rights and property and home but for religion, for the church, and the gospel.[22]

   C. A solemn crisis is at length upon us. The issue is not merely war or peace. It is one far more momentous and alarming than all these—the very existence of liberty itself—the continuance or the disastrous overthrow of the great principles of popular rights, constitutional authority, and genuine liberty for which our fathers bled on the battlefield, and which has been the pride and glory of

all American hearts. . . . We repeat, the real and vital issue
before our country is the existence or annihilation of freedom.[23]

D. That the synod regards the present war on our part as a war of
defense commending itself to our people's efforts, prayer and
hearts as a hallowed though stern contest for sacred rights involving our homes and altars, liberty and religion, and to it we sol-
emnly, prayerfully commit our persons and efforts, our energies
and property, our sons and lives.[24]

E. Only if we exert all of our strength can we beg the Lord to afford
us His aid, as he has done hitherto. We had harmed neither Brit-
ain nor France nor the United States; we had made no demands
which might have caused enemies to declare war on us.[25]

F. The year 1942—and we pray to God, all of us, that it may—
should bring the decision which will save our people and with
them our allied nations.[26]

SCIENCE

Have the students engage in the following observations not requiring the
use of the eyes:

       Touching—qualities (soft, hard, furry, silky, scratchy)
                 shapes (round, square, pointed, tubular)
                 fabrics (wool, cotton, linen, corduroy, velvet)
                 objects (glass, leather, paper, metal)
       Tasting—sweet, salty, sour, bitter
       Smelling—odors, spices, fragrances, smoke
       Listening to sounds—pitch, volume, duration, intensity, qualities

Next have the students observe the following using their eyes:

       Fire, rock, leaf, tree, drop of water, hail, ice, snowflake
       Plants, laboratory animals, models, the sky
       Pictures, diagrams, charts, drawings (shown fleetingly)
       Classmates who stand briefly in front of the room
       The scene out a window

Then have students practice nonverbal reporting:

       Mapping the neighborhood or city
       Drawing or sketching the classroom or school grounds
       Gestural descriptions (which then become the source of new
           observations)

As a further exercise, show students the diagrams in Figure 3.3 briefly. For
each, after a one-second exposure, students should indicate how many dots
they saw. Then have them consider in what ways the observations of the
two differ.

FIGURE 3.3. Diagrams to Show Fleetingly

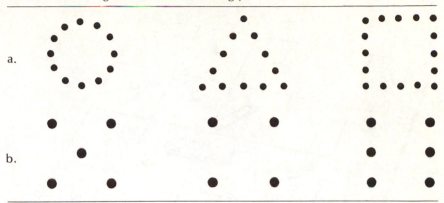

MATHEMATICS

Have students engage in construction of a form such as a carving, a model, a resonating box, or a geoboard (see Figure 3.4). Other students may make observations of the process of construction, as well as the product.

It is easy to construct a geoboard. On a piece of ⅜-inch plywood, 11¼ inches square, draw a series of horizontal and vertical lines 2¼ inches apart to form a grid on the surface of the plywood. The grid will be five squares long and five squares wide. In the center of each square put in a nail. The only additional equipment needed is a box of differently colored elastic bands. Students may be left to their own devices with the rubber bands and the board for a length of time. (Some discoveries such as the following may ensue: by stretching a rubber band around four adjacent pegs, a square of the unit can be formed; by stretching a second rubber band between the diagonal of this unit square, the figure will be divided into two triangles.)

INTERPRETING EVIDENCE

Comprehending and Applying the Operation

"The great business of life is in drawing inferences" (J. S. Mill). To interpret or extend on this statement, one may find that the areas, and kinds, of human disagreement and conflict offer worthwhile instructional material. From such study of the nature of disagreements, it may be noted that there

FIGURE 3.4. Geoboard

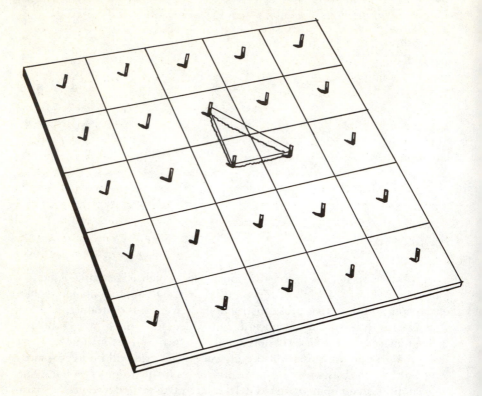

tends to be less dispute over what the facts *are* and more over what they mean or signify. Two newspaper accounts of the same incident are sufficient to exemplify this. The classic witness stories in which several people viewing the same event dispute loud and long are also a case in point. (In the arts, the theme of the Japanese film *Rashomon* exemplifies this poignantly.)

Interpreting means to bring meaning *to* material, situation, or event and to extract meaning *from* it. It involves gap filling or extending on given material, within the limits of that material. It is not merely simple translation (although it can be just this in some instances), nor is it a "free-for-all" (as discussed below) where one interpretation is as good as another. Interpreting involves saying something not already said by the given material or situation. It also involves saying something either with certainty or with probability, and differentiating between these.

Since "single-item information does not initiate a thought process" (to use

Sir Frederic Bartlett's phrase), for interpreting or gap filling to occur involves the use of "double-item" information. This means that one provides some data or facts and then calls for meanings, translations, and interpretations.

Interpretations have to be defended on the basis of reason (not majority vote). Voting is not an epistemological method that establishes validity (i.e., logic) or truth (an empirical claim). Instead, it is a *procedural* technique that is properly used to break a deadlock on preferences or on such political issues as resolving contract disputes. Since in political life there can be no *solution* to problems (in the same sense that one solves a mathematics problem), but only *resolution* of them, voting is an appropriate procedural technique to employ *for a political problem*. However, it is serious confusion to employ it as *method* for determining truth, whether formal or empirical.

It is erroneous to believe that inferences can be unrestrained in interpreting pictorial, artistic, or literary materials, whereas in numerical and graphic reports inferences are necessarily limited. Regardless of the type or subject matter of the material, interpretation requires reference to the given, and extensions on the given, *within* the limits of that material. To interpret is to understand reports of all sorts: numerical, pictorial, graphic, artistic, literary. This includes maps, charts, graphs, demonstrations, exhibits, pictures, poems, and stories.

There are a variety of ways in which interpreting may be practiced:

1. Data are presented, and the accuracy of preset interpretations is evaluated.
2. Data are presented to students, and they make some interpretations. These are then reflected back to them for evaluation as to appropriateness and accuracy.
3. Data are presented to students, and interpretations are made (as in 2). These interpretations are then compared with actual interpretations of others made in an original case. For instance, the findings of a celebrated trial, as well as the evidence, are presented. Or, the experiment of a noted scientist is reproduced but not the findings. Or the incomplete geographic data gathered by a famous explorer concerning a then unknown region are presented. (The ultimate findings and the more complete and final-form knowledge are withheld, as interpretations are compared with original interpretations.)

Errors in interpreting include crude errors or distortions of the evidence; overcautiousness or inability to interpolate or extrapolate; leaping beyond the given evidence to unwarranted conclusions—that is, not recognizing the limitations or insufficiency of the evidence.

For practice in interpreting, three-choice exercises are to be preferred over the customary two choices of true or false. In such exercises, the symbols *S, NS,* and *I* are used in the following ways:

> S = There is evidence that *supports* an assertion.
> NS = The evidence and the assertion are in contradiction, hence the assertion is *not supported*.
> I = The evidence is *insufficient* either to verify or to refute the assertion.

Some exercises are presented using only *S* and *I*.

The five-choice exercise is much more complex. In addition to the three symbols described above two additional symbols are used:

> PS = The assertion is probably supported.
> PNS = The assertion is probably not supported.

There are differences in data requirements for *S* and *NS* and for *PS* and *PNS*. In the latter there is a clear indication of a trend in the data, but not *all* the data are available. Hence there is a gap to be filled (*interpolation*) or an extension to the data to be made (*extrapolation*). It is, however, to be stressed that the lack of all the data is not equivalent to insufficiency of data. Although *PS* and *PNS* do not require all the data for support, they do require *some*, and are not to be confused with possibility—that is, what the mind can imagine or invent. In other words, interpreting is *not* imagining or creating.

Exercises in Interpreting Evidence

LANGUAGE

Have the students read the following excerpt from Mark Twain's *Autobiography*. They should then consider each of the fifteen statements listed after it and mark each statement using the symbols *S* or *I*, as defined in the introductory part of this section "Comprehending and Applying the Operation."

> All the negroes were friends of ours, and with those of our own age we were in effect comrades. I say in effect, using the

phrase as a modification. We were comrades, and yet not comrades; color and condition interposed as a subtle line which both parties were conscious of and which rendered complete fusion impossible. We had a faithful and affectionate good friend, ally, and advisor in "Unc'l Dan'l," a middle-aged slave whose head was the best one in the negro quarter, whose sympathies were wide and warm, and whose heart was honest and simple and knew no guile. He has served me well these many, many years. I have not seen him for more than half a century, and yet spiritually I have had his welcome company a good part of that time and have staged him in books under his own name and as "Jim," carted him all around—to Hannibal, down the Mississippi on a raft and even across the Desert of Sahara in a balloon—and he has endured it with the patience and friendliness and loyalty which were his birthright. It was on the farm that I got my strong liking for his race and my appreciation of certain of its fine qualities. This feeling and this estimate have stood the test of sixty years and more, and have suffered no impairment. The black face is as welcome to me now as it was then.[27]

1. Blacks were not discriminated against in Twain's boyhood.
2. In effect, all blacks were Twain's comrades.
3. Unc'l Dan'l served as the model for Jim.
4. Mark Twain admired and respected Unc'l Dan'l.
5. As a child, Mark Twain did not discriminate according to color.
6. Unc'l Dan'l lived in the black quarter.
7. The characteristics that Mark Twain admired are all found in Unc'l Dan'l.
8. Life on the farm helped shape Mark Twain's attitude toward blacks.
9. The word "condition" in this passage refers to a slavelike status.
10. By "complete fusion," Twain meant complete acceptance and equality.
11. In older age, Twain still felt admiration and liking for blacks.
12. Unc'l Dan'l has been a source of literary study for Mark Twain for many years.
13. Twain qualified his acceptance of blacks.
14. Twain always regarded blacks as separate but equal.
15. Twain does not discriminate against blacks socially.*

---

*The correct answers are as follows: 1. *I*; 2. *I*; 3. *S*; 4. *S*; 5. *I*; 6. *S*; 7. *I*; 8. *S*; 9. *I*; 10. *I*; 11. *S*; 12. *S*; 13. *S*; 14. *I*; 15. *I*.

SOCIAL STUDIES

1. Present the students with the situation that follows: You are a representative from New York, serving in Congress in the summer of 1807. In the local newspaper you read the following news story, which is accompanied by a sketch (see Figure 3.5).

FIGURE 3.5. Artist's Sketch of Incident at Sea.

The British ship of war *Leopard* unlawfully attacked the U.S. frigate *Chesapeake* in Chesapeake Bay for refusing to submit to a search for British deserters. During the engagement, three American seamen were killed and eighteen wounded. Four men were seized by the British as deserters, although only one was a British subject.

Although President Jefferson has decided not to summon Congress, you are anxious to learn all you can about the incident. The only first-hand information you have is the "artist's sketch," which is supposed to have been drawn by someone at the scene of the incident. Assume that the sketch faithfully depicts a frigate carrying an American flag, a ship of war carrying a British flag, and a British officer and an American seaman standing aboard the frigate. On the basis of the information provided by the sketch, consider the following statements. If the sketch alone supports the statement, mark it *S*, or supportable. If you think that the statement cannot be made on the basis of the sketch alone, mark it *I*, insufficient evidence.

1. The British ship of war *Leopard* seizes the U.S. frigate *Chesapeake*.
2. The British officer's arrogance angers the American seaman.
3. An officer and a seaman are aboard the frigate.
4. Three of the men taken by the British as deserters are Americans.
5. The seaman has his arms raised.
6. The *Chesapeake* refused to submit to a search for British deserters.
7. The ship of war is flying a British flag.
8. The British are impressing American seamen.
9. The frigate is listing.
10. The dead and wounded are lying on the deck of the frigate.*

2. A group of students, all history majors in college, was asked to draw some inferences from these data alone:

November 1860—Election of Lincoln as President of the United States

December 1860 to February 1861—Secession of six southern states

March 1861—Inauguration of Lincoln as President of the United States

April 1861—War between the states

---

*The correct answers are as follows: 1. *I*; 2. *I*; 3. *S*; 4. *I*; 5. *S*; 6. *I*; 7. *I*; 8. *I*; 9. *I*; 10. *I*.

The following are their inferences. Ask your students to examine them for validity and relationship to the data. They should mark each statement S (supported by the data) or NS (not supported).

1. The election of Lincoln caused the secession of six southern states.
2. The inauguration of Lincoln caused the Civil War.
3. "War between the states" implies separate, equal bodies fighting one another.
4. Lincoln's election ended the possibility of peaceful resolution of differences.
5. Lincoln did not cower in the face of the southern states.
6. The person of Lincoln was detested by the South.
7. "War between the states" indicates that there were two nations.
8. Secession was a result of a proposed plan, and war was a result of carrying out that plan.
9. Some action by Lincoln may have caused secession.
10. Lincoln was in favor of preserving the Union.
11. Southern states nullified the U.S. Constitution.
12. Lincoln was elected by a minority.
13. In the absence of further data, interpretations that I make are in the nature of probabilities.
14. The South was responsible for the Civil War.
15. If Lincoln had not been elected, there would not have been a Civil War.*

3. In this exercise and the following two exercises, a probability factor is introduced that makes matters more complex. In the exercises, one has to distinguish between no evidence, some evidence (but not sufficient to make things certain), and sufficient evidence to establish certainty.

Present this information to the students: The illustration in Figure 3.6 shows the candidates' names on a voting machine before a national election in the United States. Barry M. Goldwater is a conservative Republican candidate for President. Kenneth B. Keating, a candidate for the Senate, does not support Goldwater. Ask the students to evaluate the following statements based only on the above information and that supplied by the figure. They should mark each statement S (supported by the evidence); PS (probably supported); I (insufficient evidence); PNS (probably not supported); or NS (not supported). A more detailed discussion of the use of these symbols is

---

*The correct answers are as follows: 1. *NS*; 2. *NS*; 3. *S*; 4. *S*; 5. *NS*; 6. *NS*; 7. *NS*; 8. *NS*; 9. *S*; 10. *NS*; 11. *S*; 12. *NS*; 13. *S*; 14. *NS*; 15. *NS*.

FIGURE 3.6. Electoral Choices on a Voting Machine

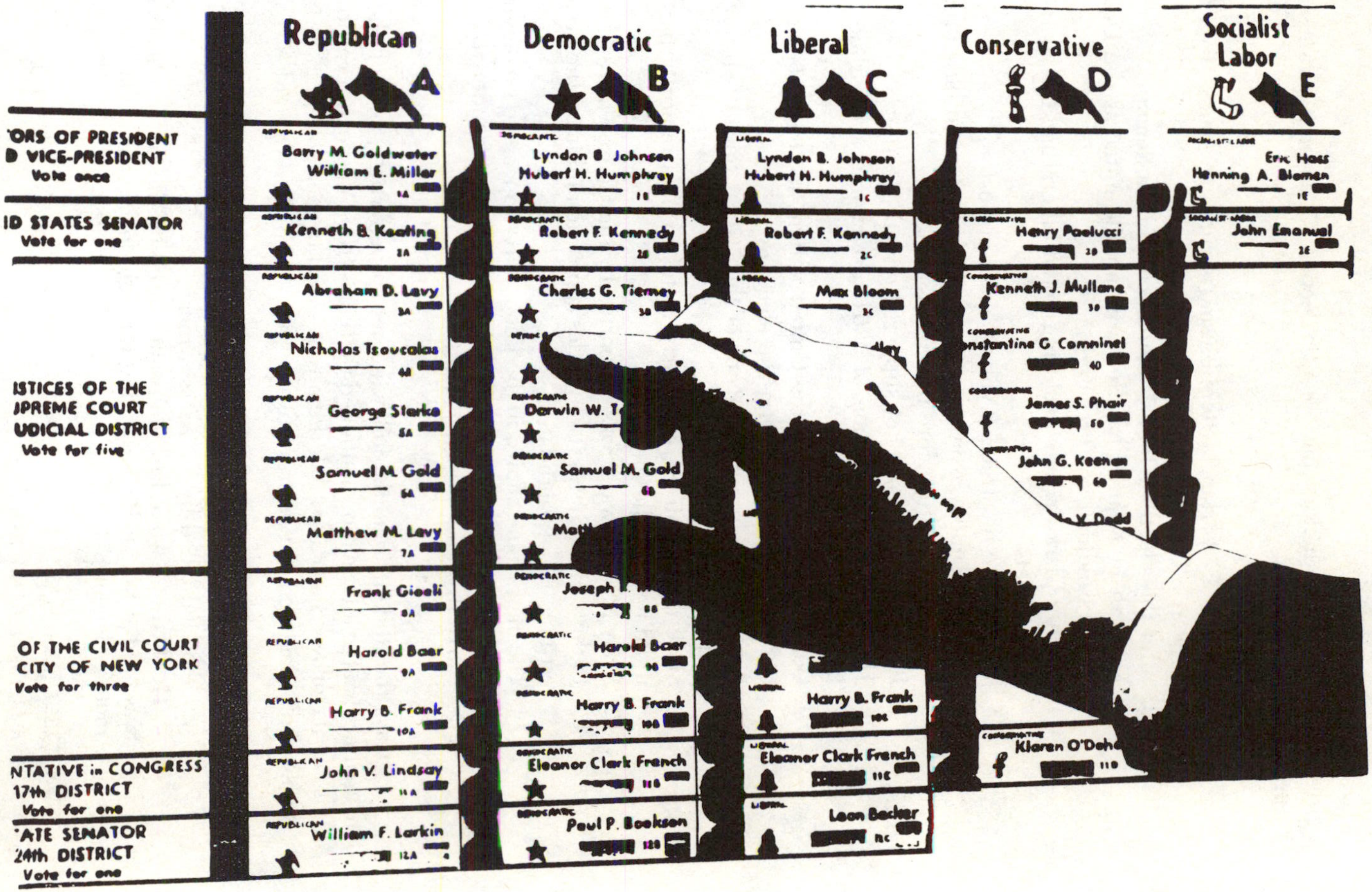

presented in the introductory part of this section, "Comprehending and Applying the Operation."

1. William F. Larkin, a Republican, is running against Paul D. Becker, a Democrat.
2. After this election, John Emanuel could be a Senator.
3. Kenneth B. Keating has the same middle initial as the Democratic candidate for President.
4. Eleanor Clark French is running on the Liberal and Democratic party tickets.
5. This picture illustrates a voting booth in Boston.
6. Senator Kennedy won the election and went on to be a presidential candidate before he was assassinated.
7. Barry Goldwater did not support Kenneth Keating.
8. The presidential election of 1964 turned into a landslide for Johnson.
9. Goldwater's position on the United Nations and on Social Security Bill no. 8647 cost him the election.
10. Lyndon B. Johnson's concept of the "Great Society" brought him victory in the election.
11. Since the Socialist Labor party seems to be a minority party, it did not win the election.
12. Barry M. Goldwater was supported by the Conservative party.
13. In the United States, two parties appear to nominate the greatest number of candidates.
14. The man's hand shown in the photograph appears to be moving toward the lever of one of the first seven names under row A.
15. Harry B. Frank lost this election.*

4. Have the students read the following newspaper article, and tell them to assume that the information contained therein is true. A list of interpretive statements follows the article. Ask them to respond to each statement using the symbols identified in the previous exercise: *S, PS, I, PNS,* and *NS.*

DALLAS, November 22, 1963. President John Fitzgerald Kennedy was shot and killed by an assassin today.

He died of a wound in the brain caused by the rifle bullet that was fired at him as he was riding through downtown Dallas in a motorcade.

---

*The correct answers are as follows: 1. *NS;* 2. *S;* 3. *S;* 4. *S;* 5. *NS;* 6. *I;* 7. *I;* 8. *I;* 9. *I;* 10. *I;* 11. *I;* 12. *I;* 13. *PS;* 14. *PS;* 15. *PNS.*

Vice-President Johnson, who was riding in the third car behind Mr. Kennedy's, was sworn in as the 36th president of the United States 99 minutes after Mr. Kennedy's death.

Shortly after the assassination, Lee H. Oswald, who once defected to the Soviet Union and who has been an active member in the Fair Play for Cuba Committee, was arrested by the Dallas police. Tonight he was accused of the killing.

Oswald, 24 years old, was also accused of slaying a policeman who had approached him in the street. Oswald was subdued after a scuffle with a second policeman in a nearby theater.

Mr. Johnson, who was uninjured in the shooting, took his oath in the Presidential jet plane as it stood on the runway at Love Field. The body of Mr. Kennedy was aboard. Immediately after the oath taking, the plane took off for Washington.

1. President Kennedy was killed in a motorcade through downtown Dallas.
2. The man who assassinated President Kennedy disliked him.
3. John F. Kennedy was the thirty-fourth President of the United States.
4. Lee Oswald was a patriotic American.
5. Lee Oswald assassinated the President as part of a Communist plot.
6. Love Field is in or near Dallas.
7. Mr. Johnson became president ninety-nine minutes after the death of President Kennedy.
8. The Fair Play for Cuba Committee is a Communist organization.
9. Oswald scuffled with three policemen.
10. Lee Oswald was an active member of the Fair Play for Cuba Committee.
11. A revolver bullet killed President Kennedy.
12. Oswald did not like the policies of the Fair Play for Cuba Committee.
13. Mr. Johnson flew to Washington in the Presidential jet plane.*

5. Present Figure 3.7 to the students, and tell them to assume the information therein as a given. Ask them to respond to each of the statements that follow using the symbols identified earlier: *S, PS, I, PNS,* and *NS.*

1. Because of the time-saving element, more people travel by plane today than by railroad.

---

*The correct answers are as follows: 1. *S*; 2. *I*; 3. *NS*; 4. *PNS*; 5. *I*; 6. *PS*; 7. *S*; 8. *I*; 9. *NS*; 10. *S*; 11. *NS*; 12. *PNS*; 13. *PS*.

FIGURE 3.7. Travel Time from Pittsburgh to Philadelphia at Various Periods

(Each clock represents four hours of travel time.)

1812

1834

1854

1920

TODAY

2. A person traveling from Pittsburgh to Philadelphia today can save more than 140 hours of traveling time as compared to a traveler in 1812.
3. Between 1812 and 1854, travel by coach decreased, whereas travel by railroad increased.
4. Different types of locomotives were used between 1834 and 1920.
5. Travel by rail was faster between Pittsburgh and Philadelphia in 1840 than in 1850.
6. Travel time between Pittsburgh and Philadelphia will continue to decrease.
7. The increase of speed in rail travel between Philadelphia and Pittsburgh between the years 1834 and 1920 was due to the use of better-grade steel in the tracks.
8. Both Pittsburgh and Philadelphia have nearby airfields today.
9. The appearance of the two cities (Pittsburgh and Philadelphia) altered between 1812 and today.
10. In every corner of the world today, travel time is decreasing.
11. Travel time by rail beween Pittsburgh and Philadelphia increased by more than two days in 1854.
12. While travel time was decreasing between Pittsburgh and Philadelphia, it was also decreasing in other parts of the United States between 1834 and 1920.
13. Invention of the steam engine was the cause of the great saving of time in traveling.
14. The Philadelphia-Pittsburgh Railroad Company had faster trains in 1920 than in 1900.*

SCIENCE

1. Have the students study Table 3.1 that gives the results of an experiment on the interaction between an acid and a base. Tell them to accept the results as given—that is, to assume that they are accurate. Then on the basis of these data alone, they should mark each statement S (supported by the data), NS (not supported), or I (insufficient data).

1. An acid and base can react to neutralize each other.
2. The acid and base used in this experiment have unequal concentrations or normalities.

---

*The correct answers are as follows: 1. *I*; 2. *S*; 3. *I*; 4. *S*; 5. *PNS*; 6. *PS*; 7. *I*; 8. *PS*; 9. *S*; 10. *I*; 11. *NS*; 12. *PS*; 13. *I*; 14. *I*.

TABLE 3.1.   Results of Experiment on Acid and Base Interaction

Trial No.	Volume Used (ml)		Effect of Resulting Solution on	
	Acid	Base	Red Litmus	Blue Litmus
1	25	18	Turned blue	None
2	20	8	None	None
3	15	5	None	Turned red
4	90	36	None	None
5	7	2	None	Turned red
6	25	50	Turned blue	None

3. If the volume of the acid used is larger than the volume of base used, the resulting solution will be neutral or acid to litmus.
4. The products of the reaction of an acid and a base are a salt and water.
5. The reaction of an acid and a base evolves heat.
6. One milliliter of this base will neutralize 2.5 milliliters of the acid.
7. A given acid and a given base react according to the law of definite proportions.
8. The solution resulting from trial number 2 would have no effect on methyl orange indicator solution.
9. The concentration or normality of this acid is 0.4 times the normality of the base.
10. The solution resulting from trial number 3 contains a greater weight of hydrogen ions (as acid) than the solution resulting from trial number 5.*

 2. Present the passage below to the students. Tell them to assume that the information is authentic and accurate, and ask them to list the inferences that they believe may be drawn from it. That is, what statements may be made with a great degree of certainty?

Resistance met Harvey's discovery of the circulation of the blood, Pasteur's work on microbes, and Semmelweis's discovery that physicians spread the infection of childbed fever from one mother

---

*The correct answers are as follows: 1. *S*; 2. *S*; 3. *I*; 4. *I*; 5. *I*; 6. *NS*; 7. *I*; 8. *I*; 9. *NS*; 10. *S*.

to another. Resistance was also offered against the discoveries of anesthesia, the work of Darwin, and the work of Freud. The sternest resistance sometimes comes from people who are "supposed to know better." For instance:

- Francis Bacon, a champion of the then new (seventeenth-century) experimental science and one of its foremost popularizers, wrote that truth claims have to be examined thoroughly; that they neither should be accepted on mere authority nor rejected on mere improbability or novelty, until such thorough examination. Yet Bacon could not bring himself to accept the theory that the earth revolves around the sun.
- Galileo could not persuade astronomers and physicists of his day to look into his new invention, the telescope. (When some did, they could not see the same things that Galileo saw.) Galileo thought that they had closed minds. Yet Galileo himself could not accept his colleague Kepler's evidence that the planets move in an elliptical orbit around the sun. Moreover, Galileo did not believe a theory current in his day—that people accused of witchcraft generally were more likely to suffer from mental illness than be consorts of the devil.
- Pasteur waged a battle against physicians for the acceptance of the germ theory of disease. Yet at the height of his fame Pasteur addressed a distinguished group of scientists and told them that scientific methods could never be applied to the study of the emotions. (Some of Freud's work was already being discussed at the time.)

From the inferences that the students believe are supported by this evidence, ask them to go beyond it to suggest an explanation (theory) that would account for the evidence as given.

MATHEMATICS

1. Present the four figures below to the students, and ask them to respond to each of the statements that follow. By reference to the figures alone, they should mark each statement S (supportable), NS (not supportable), or I (insufficient evidence).

         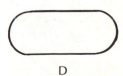

A   B   C   D

1. Four figures are presented.

2. Figure A has more space within it than does Figure B.
3. Figure D has more space within it than Figure B.
4. Figure C has more corners than Figure A.
5. Figure B has fewer corners than Figure A.
6. Figure A has a more useful shape than Figure C.
7. Figure B more nearly resembles Figure A than does Figure C.
8. All the figures are closed.
9. Figure D more nearly resembles Figure A than it resembles Figure C.
10. Figures C and B have the same amount of space within them.*

2. Present the following principle to the students:
   If R is true and R implies G, then G is true.
Ask the students to translate this principle by illustrating it with geometric figures and by using sentences to explain it.

FINDING ASSUMPTIONS

Comprehending and Applying the Operation

Assumptions are starting points in a line of reasoning for which no defense is offered. In order to be reasonable, an argument requires some assumptions or presuppositions—that is, propositions that *must* be believed in order for the truth or falsity of what is later stated to be considered. Some see it as a kind of "enabling legislation" in that it permits thought and argument to go forward.

In order for the main argument or conclusion to be accepted, one *must* accept its underlying assumptions. Without such acceptance, the argument (or conclusion) would not be reasonable, nor could it even be set forth. For instance, to do science it must be tacitly assumed at the very outset that there is an ordered and intelligible universe in which events and phenomena can be replicated. This is not something that goes on in one's mind consciously, but it is, nevertheless, a taken-for-granted presupposition; that is, when looking for causes of some effect, we assume *necessarily* that the event can take place again. It is what may be termed a bedrock assumption; nothing can be built above unless this rests at the very bottom of the structure.

The goal in finding assumptions—whether the content is empirical or logical—is to make explicit what is implicit. For example,

---

*The correct answers are as follows: 1. *S*; 2. *NS*; 3. *I*; 4. *NS*; 5. *NS*; 6. *I*; 7. *S*; 8. *S*; 9. *NS*; 10. *I*.

1. *Empirical content*: "This test is within the capacity of all average ten-year-old children. It has been administered to every ten-year-old in the class, and all but a few of the dullest have passed it." To believe this conclusion, what else must be believed?
2. *Logical content*: "What is the best way to get from New York to California?" Answer: "To fly." This answer intrinsically defines the term *best* as *fastest*. It *assumes* the meaning of *best*. This assumption is absolutely necessary as a logical gap filler to support the argument: That is, one *has to* believe that *best* = fastest, *if* one answers "to fly."

Sometimes, the term *assumption* is used pejoratively: "I don't make assumptions; I only deal with facts." At other times, it refers to a tentatively held conclusion or a conclusion held with reservations. Here, the term refers to the structural supports of a logical argument or the foundational base upon which certain empirical findings rest.

Assumptions fill a gap in an argument. This "filler" involves credibility and simplicity and is integrally connected to the argument. Frequently it subsumes the argument or provides the bedrock upon which it rests. For instance, the argument that no one has to hear a tree fall in the forest for it to have occurred requires a gap filler or presupposition. It rests upon the realist assumption that things can *be*, without being known. Without this as underlying structure, there can be no argument.

There is no formula by which one learns to find assumptions. Assumption finding is essentially a creative activity in discovering what is not stated. Through repeated practice in interpolation, one begins to recognize necessary links between assertions. The basic question that has to be repeated is: What else must be believed if one is to believe this?

In the operation of finding assumptions, there is a natural unification of intellectual and pedagogic method, of coming to know and a means of teaching and learning.

Exercises in Finding Assumptions

1. The content in this exercise would be considered empirical. Present the following passage to the students. Ask them, In order to believe the conclusion that is drawn in it, what else must be accepted, prior to it or along with it?

> Class A was taught a literature course by its teacher, who used techniques of teacher explanation, student recitation, and note taking with a text. Class B, matched in general ability, was taught

the same course by a different technique, quite new to the school, by an enthusiastic visiting teacher. At the end of the semester, Class B's *knowledge of literature* was shown to be significantly superior to Class A's. A statistician explained that in no more than five cases in a hundred would it be likely that such a result could occur by chance alone. *Therefore, the method used in teaching Class B was unquestionably superior to the method used in Class A.*

The assumptions that must be taken for granted if the conclusion is to be accepted are as follows:

The factor of novelty is unimportant.

Teaching technique and teacher personality are separable and distinct.

The tests for general ability in matching classes are valid and reliable.

The tests measuring achievement in literature in both classes are the same. Furthermore, validity and reliability of these have been established.

Have the students read the following passage and consider what else they would want to know before they accepted the conclusions in it. (That is, what are the assumptions supporting the conclusion?)

Report from a central Manhattan medical group: A recent six-year study by a team of scientists from Iowa State College of a group of boys 12–14 years of age showed that those who ate a satisfactory breakfast made better grades, were more alert in class, and were more responsive than those who omitted or skimped on breakfast.

2. The content in this exercise would be considered logical. Ask the students to find the *necessary* assumptions underlying this statement (they are logical gap fillers): "Nothing is wrong if it feels good." Some sample student responses follow:

How something feels is a test of goodness.

Good/bad depends on subjective feeling.

The meaning of "wrong" is assumed to be clear and understood.

The meaning of "good" is assumed to be clear and understood.

Any action can be good.

Something is wrong if it feels bad.

Present this statement to the students: "If X has an experience, X will learn"; that is, having an experience is equivalent to learning taking place. Ask them, Which of the following assumptions *must* be accepted if the foregoing statement is to be accepted?

A. It is illogical to say that one does not learn from experience.
B. If an experience occurs, then learning occurs.
C. There is agreement on the meaning of the term *experience*.
D. The experience is one that can be repeated.
E. There is something called *nonexperience*, and it is a kind of state we can be in.
F. In a state of nonexperience, we're unsure whether or not learning can occur.

3. Present each of the statements below separately to the students, and ask them to list the *necessary* assumptions supporting the statements. The statements may or may not be true. Nevertheless, grant that they are.
A. "Spare the rod and spoil the child."
B. We had dinner at John's house.
C. If the pupil did not learn, the teacher has not taught.
D. If the patient wasn't cured, the doctor did not treat.

4. Have the students read the following passage, and ask them, In order to believe this, what else would you have to believe or know?

A company employs 18,000 workers. Recently, four workers were dismissed from the company after more than ten years of service. All four were over age forty. The four claimed that they were being discriminated against because of their age.

Then present this statement: "If one examines a given occupational category and finds *no* members of Group C in it, it is proof positive that they have deliberately been excluded." Ask the students, If this statement is to be accepted, what else must be accepted?

5. Present the following passage to the students, and tell them to accept the information as a given:

In keeping with an effort to distribute employment opportunities more widely, certain procedures are being followed by some. These include the examining of a given occupational grouping for its composition in terms of ethnic or gender identification, or a similar examination based on a physical characteristic.

Thus, Occupational Classification Z was examined to determine the extent of representation by Group G. Groups D and J were found, but not Group G. It was held, therefore, to be sufficient evidence that Group G had historically been deliberately excluded. (Otherwise, its relative absence now could not be explained.)

One class listed the assumptions below as necessary to conclude that Group G had historically been deliberately excluded. Ask your students to assess each of them to determine whether it is *necessary* as a logical gap filler.

A. "Deliberate" exclusion is defined as an exclusion that is not performance-related.

B. Members of Group G have been willing to gain entry into Occupational Classification Z.

C. Members of Group G have, in fact, tried to gain entry into Occupational Classification Z.

D. Members of Group G are distributed widely enough in given localities as to be available for placement in Occupational Classification Z.

E. Members of Group G have the requisite qualifications called for in the particular Occupational Classification Z.

F. Occupational Classification Z did not want to consider Group G for membership in its ranks.

G. Groups D and J were favored on non–performance-related grounds.

H. Entry into Occupational Classification Z is related to group membership.

I. The future hiring of members of Group G would be on individual grounds and not on group membership grounds.

J. It is not easy to secure firmer evidence on policies of deliberate exclusion other than by noting the presence or absence of groups within a particular occupational classification.*

LANGUAGE

Have the students read the following letter-to-the-editor that dates from the 1960s.

> I am writing about the letter you received on December 31st from Sidney F. He is entirely correct in saying that people of foreign countries have a poor concept of Americans. I happen to know this for a fact.
>
> Last year, I spent a school year in Puerto Rico. While I was there, I met many people in school and out. I can safely say that I found a basic fault in most of them.

---

*Answer: Only *I.* would not be necessary.

This fault was that they generalize too much. If they saw an American sailor drunk, they would say that Americans are drunks. If they read in a newspaper that a restaurant refused to serve a Negro, they say that Americans are prejudiced.

Don't misunderstand me. I'm not saying that all Puerto Ricans are this way; just too many of them. But these people aren't the only ones. I have found this fault in too many people of too many nationalities. In my opinion, Americans also have this fault. If Americans hear of a revolution in any part of the world, the very first thing you hear is that those involved in the revolution are all troublemakers.

The only reason for this fault in many people is just plain simple ignorance. People don't know all of the reasons or facts for things happening. As a result, the people comment on the small part they know. If they would wait, gather all the information, study it and then, and only then, comment on things, the people of the world would all understand everything and each other better and I think this would result in more world unity.

Ask the students to examine the assumptions that follow. Which of them support the conclusions in this letter? What other assumptions can be found? (The content here would be considered logical rather than empirical.)

1. One's experience is a method for determining fact.
2. Everything can be understood.
3. More world unity can be achieved through gathering *all* the information.
4. The basic fault—as this person found it—*is* basic.
5. Ignorance accounts for this basic fault.
6. A basic fault—a tendency to absolutize—is the very first thing that one hears.
7. Faults—as described in this letter—have only one reason for their perseverance.
8. Such faults are correctable.
9. What one knows is a fact.
10. Too much generalizing is not desirable.

SOCIAL STUDIES

Some students were asked this question: If we could remake history, in your judgment would it have been wiser to have held open sessions at the Constitutional Convention of 1787? Many students answered no. Here are some of the reasons they gave:

1. People would have found fault with the Constitution.

2. The Constitution might never have been written.
3. There would have been disturbances.
4. Our present-day government would not be as strong.
5. It would just make things more confusing, and nothing would be accomplished by the interference.
6. The people wouldn't want the new idea.
7. The Constitution would never have been adopted.
8. The federal government wouldn't have had a chance.
9. Nothing would have gotten done.

Ask your students to list the assumptions upon which these statements rest.

SCIENCE

Have the students read the following paragraph and identify the assumptions necessary for the statement to be judged true or probably true.

> Some unfamiliar type of force must hold the protons and neutrons together in the nucleus. They cannot be held by electrostatic attraction because the similarly charged protons would repel each other; and neutrons, being neutral, are not subject to electrostatic attraction. The force cannot be gravitational either because calculations show it would be too weak. The forces between nuclear particles have very short range, somewhat smaller than the diameter of the nucleus.[28]

Some students who tried this exercise responded with the assumptions that follow:

1. An atom can be divided into smaller particles.
2. Some of these particles must be concentrated in a nucleus.
3. Two of the particles that are concentrated in the nucleus are protons and neutrons.
4. Some of these particles carry an electric charge.
5. All protons carry the same charge.
6. All neutrons are uncharged.
7. Like charges repel each other.
8. Uncharged objects cannot be held by the same force that attracts charged objects.
9. Objects will not remain together unless held together by some attractive force.
10. Every object attracts other objects in the universe (law of gravitation).

11. The force of attraction mentioned in the previous assumption is calculable.
12. The diameter of a nucleus is calculable and known.
13. The only familiar types of forces are electrostatic and gravitational.

MATHEMATICS

1. Ask the students, What assumptions underlie the conclusions in the following passages? Or, what else must be believed if one is to accept the conclusions given?

   A. Ed, who was a nonswimmer, saw a sign on a pond that read: "Average depth, three feet." He reasoned that it would be safe for him to wade in the pond, since he was five feet tall.

   B. Tom, who was a good swimmer and diver, saw a sign at the edge of a lake that read: "Average depth, nine feet." He reasoned that it would be safe for him to practice depth diving there.

   C. A man arrived in Chicago ten hours after a crime was committed in New York. The fastest train from New York to Chicago makes the trip in twelve hours. Tom reasoned that this man could not have committed the crime in New York.

   D. If A is ten miles from B, and B is fifteen miles from C, how far is A from C? Jim's solution was: $10 + 15 = 25$.

   E. Here are some weights of boys in a fifth-grade class (in pounds):

Henry	88	James	86
Albert	86	Robert	84
William	82	Richard	82
John	78	Andrew	78
Edward	76	Ronald	74
Stephen	74	Gerald	72

   John concluded that on the average a boy in fifth grade in this school weighs 80 pounds.

2. Have the students try to determine what assumptions underlie each of the responses to the following statements or questions. (Sample answers have been provided for the first two items.)

   1. Write the smallest number you can think of using only the digits 4 and 1.

      Student A: 14
         Assumption: Digits can only be used once. "Number" refers only to the set of whole numbers.
      Student B: ¼. ¼₄

2. How many numbers are there between 21 and 53?
>   Student C: 31
>> Assumption: "Number" refers only to whole numbers.
>   Student D: Infinite
3. Three points determine _____.
>   Student E: a plane
>   Student F: many planes
4. Lines that do not intersect are _____.
>   Student G: parallel
>   Student H: skewed
5. Three planes intersect at _____.
>   Student I: a point
>   Student J: one line
>   Student K: three lines
6. A line intersects a plane at a _____.
>   Student L: point
>   Student M: line
7. A train travels 180 miles in three hours. How far did it travel in one hour?
>   Student N: 60 miles
>   Student O: 90 miles
>   Student P: X miles

INQUIRING: DEVISING PLANS

Comprehending and Applying the Operation

The operation of inquiring involves seeing how knowledge is constructed and participating in the construction or criticism (assessment) of knowledge. Bloom's taxonomic term, *synthesis*, approximates what is intended here, but it does not envelop it. Inquiring actually impinges on a congeries of related operations: explaining; generalizing and generalization testing; hypothesizing and theorizing; criticizing and evaluating; problem solving and theory construction. It is, therefore, necessarily a very broad operation. The prosaic designation "devising plans" is not a happy one, yet it seems to be closest to what goes on as one inquires—that is, as procedures for verification or refutation and schemes for assessment are developed. As may be seen in the exercises and illustrations that follow, there is an emphasis on seeing how conclusions are arrived at, checking the validity of existing parcels of knowledge, as well as a stress on the devising of procedures—that is, the requirement of a method for making judgments and for coming to know.

That one may come to see how knowledge may be discovered and augmented through theory construction is a hoped-for by-product.

The operation of inquiring often involves expressing what it is that one does *not* know, which usually is rather difficult. Indeed, if one is able to do this, one is already on the way to knowing. Part of the difficulty includes determining how data are to be developed or treated. Within the very tasks of inquiring and devising plans may be found a natural unification of intellectual and pedagogic method.

At different times, inquiring also includes

1. Hypothesizing: setting forth a prediction or projection of effects or consequences that will occur as a result of given conditions or circumstances.
2. Explaining: offering a generalization or building a theory that seems to account for a phenomenon or series of events.
3. Criticizing: making a judgment based on some internal criterion or, sometimes, an external one.
4. Analyzing: studying given conclusions, judgments, and generalizations to see how they were arrived at.
5. Judging evidence: determining, in the first instance, what evidence is and establishing degrees of evidence; finding corroborating or refuting evidence.
6. Inventing (of a principle): creating a new system of organizing or analyzing material.
7. Evaluating arguments: recognizing the nature of a strong argument, even though one disagrees with the particular position. Apart from presentation and expressiveness, what is it that makes an argument strong or weak?

Over and above the foregoing is the devising of plans of operation: developing procedures and analytic schemes and the creation or selection of a *method* for finding out, for coming to know, and for checking results. In effect, it is coming to see how knowledge has been created, by participating in the very process of creation.

Very frequently involved in almost all types of inquiring is the making of assessments and judgments. To judge means to set up a standard by which one makes a rating on a scale of appropriateness or inappropriateness or on a scale of superior or inferior. Whether one is rating ideas or eggs, the assigning of a rank order is defensible only when clear standards are set forth. To the ancient Greeks, *kritikos* meant skill in making judgments. Our "criticism," properly understood, means that we differentiate between the capricious and the criterial judgment.

In assessing generalizations or conclusions, one is involved in trying to find appropriate illustrations. This means that one has to look for supporting evidence, as well as counterevidence. Now, a generalization is an explanatory principle that connects and unifies many facts, lending clarity and substance to them. It is the facts, in turn, that support the generalization; however, facts by themselves, detached from a generalization, explain little. Are there ways of checking a generalization—that is, of determining how adequately and sufficiently it explains or accounts for a given set of facts? Another way of saying this is to ask, To what extent does the generalization unify discrete data? Judging the adequacy and sufficiency of generalizations involves developing some scheme of assessment such as meaning and translation, illustration, counterevidence in discrete facts, countergeneralizations that test the explanatory power of the generalization, judgment of sufficiency.

Data are often generated and developed in a variety of ways. They are developed *empirically* through observation, or experimentation, or both. In botany, astronomy, geology, we see the former; in chemistry, the latter; in physics, both. Data may also be developed *historically*, by classifying the kinds of sources and documents, by distinguishing the authentic from the spurious, as well as by determining what is fact and what is interpretation. Finally, data are developed *philosophically*, through critical examination of assumptions and deductions in given material, or through the setting forth of original theoretical material that includes such critical examination.

It is important to note that the data are developed *through* these *means of analysis* (method), sometimes systematically, sometimes less so. However, there is another area of human knowledge where the general characteristic of the field or domain is, in fact, a great body of given literature: for example, in religious writings such as the Bible and Koran, in bodies of law (Roman, Anglo-Saxon), in collections of myths, and in national epics. With these, except for the ongoing corpus of law, which undergoes continual addition and revision, it is not so much that the data are to be *developed* as that they are to be *treated*, most often through documentary analysis or literary criticism or through critical examination of historicity or philosophic assumptions.

Inquiry and inquiring do not seem to be very widespread, perhaps because they are not well understood. It is believed that one of the reasons for this is that we are intimidated and paralyzed by the popular expression "explosion of knowledge"; that is, more knowledge has been acquired (and diffused) since 1900 than in the previous 1900 years. It is obvious that even after a lifetime, one cannot individually know very much if by "know" is meant the accumulation and hoarding of collections of information. Although this is obvious, we apparently are unable to free ourselves from the acquisitive sense of knowing, which, in turn, permits us to be intimidated by the "explosion of knowledge." Yet there is a fruitful area of endeavor for individuals to pursue, rather different from the collecting objectives of such social agencies as libraries, museums, and institutes; namely, the invention of explanation and theory that sort out, order, and check the vast accumulations of information extant. In this area, humanity has not produced "explosions." As Whitehead has argued, all education should begin and end in research or inquiry. "First-hand knowledge is the ultimate basis of intellectual life. . . . The second-handedness of the learned world is the secret of its mediocrity."[29]

Codifications and indexing and cataloging of the discoveries and explorations of others into encyclopedias, handbooks, and digests are essentially a conservational operation, albeit a useful one. Such efforts, however, if pursued on a wide scale as an exclusionary pedagogic objective, have negative consequences on inquiring as the discovery of knowledge.

Codifications, when applied to the practice of pedagogy, present a semblance of order, neatness, and logical organization. Thus, one hears of "steps in the scientific method" that become instructional objectives. Another favorite is problem solving through "learning" and following some formalized and stylized procedures. Then, too, in curriculum construction, the logic by which a subject area came to be organized (post hoc) is often used to determine the sequence for presenting the subject to a beginning student. Certain topics are presented first simply because they appear first in the logic of the codification scheme: for example, the cell, the atom, the musical scale, the parts of speech. That it is hindsight that organizes the material in such a systematic way is overlooked or held to be of little account.

The subject matter of logic itself is often taken as a description of the actual processes and operations that occur in "thinking." This is but an extension of what was said in the previous paragraph about hindsight. The codified and systematic subject of logic, as a repository of explanation and information for checking the *products* of thought, is invaluable as an analytic instrument post hoc. Logic, however, is not a description of thought-in-process. The latter is far from being either systematic or orderly.

Exercises in Inquiring

Have the students devise a scheme for assessing the generalizations that follow. (The teacher should refer to "Comprehending and Applying the Operation" at the beginning of this section. Note that agreement or disagreement is not being called for.)

1. If a nation loses a major war, it undergoes major social changes. If a nation wins a major war (such as World War I), the forces of conservatism are strengthened.
2. The waste product of one species of life is very often the food of another species.

3. Customs and beliefs tend to persist long after the conditions giving rise to them have ceased to operate.

4. Business enterprises whose primary goal is economic gain and profit have been the means of extending a better way of life over wide areas.

5. Situations that threaten war grow out of the activities of business and commerce.

6. The mercury column in a thermometer will first drop upon immersion into hot water.

7. The oratorio *The Creation*, by Haydn, describes a God of nature.

8. The Protestant movement of the sixteenth century was a revolt and not a reformation, much as Christianity, in the first century A.D., was a revolt against (and not a reformation of) Judaism.

9. The suicide rate in a given area is related to the size of the cities in the given area.

10. The study of foreign languages is, at bottom, the study of anthropology.

11. Humans reflect the culture that nurtured them, and they carry it with them to new places and establish it in those new places.

12. What has been called the American Way of Life is less a reflection of the vision of the founders of the Republic than of the work of Henry Ford. "If one is permitted to own and drive an automobile, there is more practical freedom *here* than in the abstract freedoms proclaimed in revered documents."

13. Of all the natural elements (water, fire, air, earth), it is the wind that most often appears in poetry and music as typifying death.

14. "Happiness" may be best expressed in one of the art forms, rather than in other ways.

15. Even within the thinking of a single individual (and, a fortiori, a larger social group), two or more cherished values are often thrown into conflict. The supreme value is the one that is protected at all costs from sacrifice to the others.

LANGUAGE

Have the students check (that is, corroborate or refute) the accuracy of the following conclusions:

Duncan, despite his trusting nature, gives clear evidence that he is aware of Macbeth's intentions.

Hamlet has pieced together evidence that his uncle is the murderer of his father. What system may be used to check his piecing together?

SCIENCE

1. This inquiry involves devising a plan to use in investigating the effect of concentration on the rate of the catalyzed decomposition of hydrogen peroxide. Explain to the students that hydrogen peroxide is an unstable substance that decomposes spontaneously into water and oxygen. The rate of its decomposition may be increased by the use of a suitable catalyst. Have the students select a catalyst and devise a procedure by which the rate of the reaction may be followed and measured. They should then investigate the effect of changing the concentration of the peroxide on the rate at which it decomposes. If there is a definite relationship and it is of low-order kinetics, it may be possible for them to theorize the mechanism by which the decomposition takes place. As they devise a plan, tell them to consider the following questions:

> Where may one find suitable catalysts or information about them?
> What kind of procedure is needed to permit one to follow the reaction rate?
> At what point may a conclusion be drawn about the effect of concentration on the reaction rate?

2. Have the students devise procedures for making the following investigations:

A. You want to find out whether or not living organisms spring from nonliving matter. After you have developed your method, you may find it worthwhile to compare it with Redi's experiments in 1688 or Pasteur's experiments in fermentation.

B. You want to find out whether or not objects tend to continue in motion. After you have developed your method for finding out, you may find it useful to compare it with Galileo's.

3. Ask the students to construct a plan for finding answers to the following questions:

A. What are the most common crimes in a given area?
B. Why don't clouds fall?
C. Why is it more difficult to ride a two-wheeled bike slowly than at moderate speed?
D. Why is it usually difficult to write with ink on substances like blotting paper?
E. Why do some lawn sprinklers rotate as they sprinkle?

4. Ask the students to construct procedures to corroborate or refute the following conclusions:

    A. If purebred plants of different strains (A + B) are crossed and the resultant hybrids are again crossed, then in the next generation the plants produced sort out in definite proportions: Some are pure As, some are pure Bs, and some are hybrid ABs.

    B. Putrefaction is not due to spontaneous generation of germs in a liquid like sugared yeast water.

    C. The speed with which an object falls when not impeded is related functionally to the length of time during which it has been falling.

    D. Dew, frost, cloud formations, wind direction, and other signs within nature account for much of existing weather lore—which happens to be fairly accurate.

5. Have the students construct a basis for checking and evaluating each of the procedures listed in the paragraphs that follow. Help them to identify what it is that they would need to know and understand in order to be able to set forth a basis for evaluating these procedures.

    A. In 1593, Galileo constructed a thermometer. It consisted of a glass bulb an inch or two in diameter with a long tube for a stem. To use the thermometer, the tube was slightly heated, and the end of the tube was immersed in water. When the bulb cooled, the water rose a little. Higher temperatures were indicated by a fall of the water in the tube, while lower temperatures were indicated by a rise of water in the tube.

    B. In 1639, Dr. Jean Rey tried to improve on Galileo's thermometer. He filled a similar bulb and part of the stem with water and pointed it upward. Changes of water level in the stem indicated changes in temperature.

    C. Approximately twenty-five years later, the upper ends of tubes were sealed.

    D. Later, alcohol or mercury was used as the thermometric substance.

MATHEMATICS

1. List for students some operations in arithmetic: adding, subtracting, multiplying, dividing. Ask the students to create some principles about when to use each. They should test each principle that they create for validity and reliability. Next have them connect one operation to the other and show how they are related.

2. Present the two situations below to the students. Ask them to develop a plan for finding answers to the questions that follow each situation.

> Joe works in a carpenter shop. He has a board ⅜-inch thick and 42 inches long that he wants to cut into 2½-inch lengths.
> A. Do you need all the information you are given here?
> B. How do you go about finding out how many pieces Joe will have left over?
> C. How do you go about finding out how many pieces Joe will have?
> D. Can you justify your use of a particular operation?

> Jim painted his backyard fence in three days. On Thursday, he painted ¼ of it. On Friday, he painted ⅕ of it. On Saturday, he finished painting it.
> A. How would you find out when Jim painted the largest part?
> B. How would you find out when Jim painted the least amount of fence area?
> C. How would you find out how much Jim painted on Saturday?
> D. Fifty yards of the fence were painted on Thursday. How would you find out how much was painted on the other days?

3. Have the students devise a system whereby they can verbally locate a point on an orange in terms that are easily understood. Ask them how this system could be checked for accuracy and reliability. Have them compare it with the latitude-longitude system for locating and measuring points on the globe.

SOME FINAL THOUGHTS

There are those who believe that there is magic to thinking, in that it is a mysterious process accorded to the select few. The view presented here is that there is no magic and no mystery. As opportunities are provided for reacting to coding and for comparing, classifying, summarizing, observing and reporting, interpreting evidence, finding assumptions, and inquiring, *thinking* processes are engaged. There *are* other operations, and there certainly are other ways of ordering them. What is being asserted here is that thinking consists of at least these many operations, and that, perhaps, it is better to conceptualize it through these operations and processes. Some have conceptualized thinking as a concern with knowledge of the *forms of thought*, as in the subject matter of logic. Unfortunately, such faith in practicing forms of thought by following a formula—for example, the syllogism—is not very well founded. Nor is it a well-founded notion that the teaching of a particular subject such as logic or geometry will result in the easy and wide transfer of a generalized ability in thinking.

These comments are not intended to suggest that thinking involves a simple process. Recourse to an analogy may be helpful here. Somewhat like thinking, speaking is a process that appears to be effortless. Yet, if one had to describe the neural function, the muscular function, and the coordination that go into speaking, it would be seen as a complicated procedure. Indeed, there are speech and voice teachers who indulge themselves in the abstractions of vocal physiology as a means of showing the learner how to correct faults, but it is rare that the learner can benefit from knowledge concerning theoretical function. Moreover, if one had to pause and reflect on the description of the mechanism before one spoke, the result might be some halting and uncertain sounds. Perhaps the individual would be overawed and might respond as did M Jourdain, the unlettered bourgeois, in Moliere's *Would-Be Gentleman*. Astounded at the sudden discovery of a difference between verse and prose, he declared, "On my conscience, I have spoken prose these forty years without knowing anything of the matter." Thus, although teachers may know, or may want to know, a good deal about the neurophysiology of thinking (or even about forms of thought), they do not teach *these*, for it is not the theoretical bases of thinking that are the prime objective of instruction; teachers are, in the main, concerned with providing opportunities for the exercise of particular mental processes.

At this point, it is well to distinguish between teaching *what* to think, teaching *how* to think, and teaching *for* thinking. Teaching what to think is often viewed as indoctrination, and a typical reaction is one of almost automatic recoil. On the other hand, there appears to be widespread agreement that teaching how to think should be the main concern of teachers. Indeed, student criticism of a teacher's efforts is sometimes expressed as, "I want to learn how to think, and she's teaching us what to think."

Learning how to think may be, and frequently is, viewed in a technical sense. One speaks of *logical* thinking, by which is usually meant an emphasis on the deductive process. Or one may hear the phrase *critical thinking*, which is often applied to an ability to analyze and criticize the underlying assumptions of a given position. Sometimes the phrase *reflective thinking* is employed, and here there may be reference to suspended judgment, the widening of the gap between the stimulus of a problem or issue and the response to it. Occasionally one encounters the phrases *experimental* or *scientific thinking*, which may relate to the setting up of a research design. Then, too, there is the phrase *artistic thinking*. Under this heading, one may find such expressions as *adventurous thinking, creative thinking, imaginative thinking, inventive thinking,* and *intuitive thinking*.

In the grouping "logical," "critical," and "reflective" thinking, there is the implication of a verb, suggesting what it is that has to be *done*. This is helpful. Yet in some other groupings or characterizations—for example, *hard* or *soft* thinking—no verb is implied, and it is unclear what one is to *do*. Maybe artistic, exploratory, and scientific thinking would be more widespread if, as these adjectives are offered as objectives, students knew what teachers were asking them to do. "Ways" of thinking, then, as suggested by the employment of a variety of adjectives before the word, refer simply to a manner of speaking—at best, an attitude—hardly to a change in actual process.

Be this as it may, this part has not been concerned with teaching *thinking* or teaching *how* to think. Nor has there been concern with a particular *kind* of thinking, such as "imaginative" thinking, "adventurous" thinking, or "critical" thinking. The focus has been on ways of providing opportunities *for* thinking. What can be done to increase these opportunities? The theory has been put forth that as we stress a wide variety of thinking operations, greater skill in, and maturity of, thinking will be a consequence.

At this point, some persons, like M Jourdain, may retort, "But we have been doing these things all along!" That may be so, but it is the focus that is critical. Like M Jourdain, the teacher is being asked to be conscious of the parts that contribute to a composite whole. Frequently, exercises are assigned on the unexplicated assumption that certain operations and processes are *necessarily* engaged. In this work, a guide has been provided, a checking point and a kind of checklist: If one wants consciously to provide opportunities for thinking, how may this be done? In addition, what may be new here is the theoretical framework that relates thinking operations to behavior.

Even though it has been said before, it is worth emphasizing again that no profound reconstruction of the curriculum is necessary, nor is it being advocated obliquely here. As is apparent, the sample exercises given for the various operations in this part cut across subject-matter lines. The presentation of exercises in a variety of subject areas has been deliberate but is only intended to indicate that one adapts an existing curriculum and helps to develop it in diverse ways and directions. As teachers extend and develop their subjects (*within* the subject organization of studies) and as they invent materials and exercises after the patterns indicated, it is urged that they do so only in a context that suggests a relationship to what is real. That is to say, exercises need not be a type of puzzle, intellectually remote and sterile. Puzzle solving, although providing for mental acrobatics and rare-muscle flexing, has little value in terms of transfer. To maximize the possibility of transfer, the exercise can be one that is closely related to situations actually encountered. Surely the inventive teacher will search out variety and will avoid situations tending toward artificiality and triviality.

As opportunities for thinking are provided, some beneficial by-products can emerge. Economical learning—that which is retained over a longer period—is promoted. There will tend to be an increase in the teacher's zest and enthusiasm; presentations may have more substance and vitality. Probably a concomitant effect will be an alliance between teacher and learner. Students will be less apt to fight the processes of study, for there is challenge to individuals when they are asked to see how knowledge may be created. "What do *you* think?" is a compliment to the psyche. "Listen to what others have thought" may or may not arouse response, since less directly and perhaps only incidentally does it personalize the acts of study. As Quintilian tells us, "Why then is it a crime to discover something new? . . . Seeing that they, who had none to teach them anything, have handed such store to posterity, shall we refuse to employ the experience which we possess of some things, and possess nought that is not owed to the beneficent activity of others?"[30] We know how admirably well schools have served as places to find out what others have thought. Can schools also be "thinking places" where knowledge may be discovered and augmented?

This part closes as it began—with a plea for reconceptualization of intellectual and pedagogic method, the means of acquiring knowledge and the means of communicating it. The separation between them is an artificial one, often fostered by the administrative partitions of intellectual effort at universities, as well as by partitions of departments or schools. Even if one can analytically separate intellectual and pedagogic method, they are reunited empirically; thinking operations or reflective activities are a way of inquiring (into facts) and a way of acquiring (establishing facts). One would think that this should be sufficient justification for widespread assent, yet frequently among the very passionate and ultra-Romantics, there is a distrust of the intellect powerful enough to influence a change in current trends or educational fashions. Rousseau's dictum, "The man who thinks is a depraved animal," comes to mind, as do the oft-heard neo-Romantic admonitions to trust one's feelings (more than one's intellect). The irreducible, bedrock assumption in this work has been, that of all the methods of confronting problems (e.g., impulse/passion, routine, the coin flip, hearsay advice), reflection—defective as it is—offers a probability for success that is much more reliable than these other means.

PART 4

The Role
of the
Teacher

It is easy to criticize schools and criticisms come from almost every quarter, and at almost regular intervals. Schools are criticized for being too lenient or for being too authoritarian. There are too many "frill" subjects and not enough "basic skills"; or we must enrich the curriculum to prepare children for life in the twenty-first century. Teachers should have more freedom to work as "professionals" in their classrooms; or teachers should be given tests to determine if they are sticking to the prescribed curriculum. Almost every group seems to have an idea about how schools should be changed and about what should be happening in classrooms.

Given the heat of the controversy, given the polarities of opinion, given the politically motivated pressures on schools and teachers, given the fears and anxieties of some parents, what *are* teachers to do? It is no wonder that teachers feel overwhelmed and insecure, and that teacher burnout is a common malaise. It is no wonder that there is concern that the best and brightest will leave the profession and go into fields where they are less likely to be ripped apart by opposing factions.

In all of this confusion we present teachers with yet another set of suggestions for change—and we do so without apology, for there is no controversy about the need to emphasize thinking in our classrooms. There is no disagreement that thinking is vital to what is considered effective education in a democratic society. Very few of us will stand up and say we are against thinking. Thus, we are not advocating a new curriculum that has dubious merit for the educational goals that we all affirm. What we are advocating is a set of strategies that will help teachers to attain those goals. We hope the materials in this chapter will help to make these strategies more explicit.

CREATING A CLIMATE FOR THINKING

...chers themselves and the way teachers run their classrooms are at the ... of teaching for thinking. The classroom atmosphere must reflect pro-found respect for individuals as unique human beings. As teachers respect the students, students are encouraged to respect each other.

Listening to Students

The teacher who respects students is willing to listen to students. Listening is a time-consuming activity, but it is one of the ways that a teacher can get at the students' ideas. Classroom procedures have to be planned in a way that will allow students opportunities to be heard. Along with respect for students, teachers need to have an underlying faith in operations of intelligence as a reservoir within people. If students are looked upon as ignorant fools who are in school solely to sop up the "pearls of wisdom" that come from the texts, it is certainly doubtful that much original thinking will result.

Appreciating Individuality and Openness

Teachers who insist that students conform at all times are showing a lack of respect for them and their intelligence. When students are comparing, for example, it is very likely that no two of them will work in exactly the same way. There may be as many different comparisons as there are students in the classroom. In teaching for thinking programs, there is no one comparison that is "right." The purpose of thinking activities is to involve students in a thinking act—not to find the "right answer." When thinking is involved, there is an openness, not a finality. There are possibilities for the "new" and the "unique" that may not always be anticipated. Each student's contribution is a precious thing, for it represents an effort to think. If each student were to compare in the same way, or if the teacher were to have a list of expected outcomes, then the processes of thinking would be sacrificed for some kind of guessing game with the correct answer as the goal.

Encouraging Open Discussion

Respect for students and their efforts at thinking are enhanced by discussion. Pupils need opportunities to discuss their ideas, their viewpoints, and their analyses with the teacher and with each other. Teacher-student interactions may encourage discussion and give students opportunities to make decisions, to examine alternatives, and to act in accordance with their decisions.

Promoting Active Learning

Traditionally many teachers have used didactic modes of teaching. This involves explaining, telling, and showing how. Teaching in this mode is a process engaged in actively by the teacher. Students listen passively to what is presented in the class. Frequently there are a series of assignments and periodic testing of the students' knowledge of what has been presented. Teaching for thinking requires that students actively engage in the process of thinking. That means more than sitting and listening to the teacher. It means students' being asked to observe and report on their observations; it means looking for similarities and differences in making comparisons; it means classifying and interpreting data, suggesting hypotheses, examining assumptions, and involvement in activities that require the solving of real problems. It means that students not only listen to the teacher's thinking but are themselves actively involved in the creation of ideas. It also means a different interactive style on the part of the teacher.

Accepting Students' Ideas

Where opportunities for thinking are provided, where there is acceptance and discussion of students' ideas, where students are supported and liked, thinking is encouraged. In the teachers' interactions with students, there is an absence of authoritarianism, an encouraging of students to think more deeply, to reflect on their ideas, to consider alternatives. There is a prizing of students and their ideas. In this way the teacher makes it safe for students to think. Learning, and particularly learning that emphasizes thinking, is a fragile thing. It is influenced by emotions, pressures, the health of the student, the dynamics of the class, personal experiences, degrees of self-confidence, teachers' attitudes, and countless other factors. Teachers, aware of the many variables, are called upon to play several roles: to function as catalyst, leader, friend, guide, and authority. It is frequently threatening for students to be asked to question ideas that have been part of their belief systems for many years. The teacher helps the student examine but does so very gently. When a student becomes threatened or upset in relation to thinking, it may be advisable to back off and stop the activity.

It may also be appropriate to reassure the student that "thinking is hard work" and make some indication that the teacher understands the pupil's difficulty. As students become more comfortable with the process of thinking

s they gain more experience with the expectations of thinking, their
lculties are very likely to diminish.

Allowing Time to Think

Students also need time to think, time to assimilate, and even time to
change their patterns of behavior. When thinking is going on, errors occur.
When one thinks, one makes leaps, one makes guesses; one tries ideas to
see if they will work. In a sense, one is experimenting. Thinking does not
usually proceed in an orderly way, step-by-step. When students make errors
in their thinking, teachers can use these as opportunities for learning. When
the processes of thinking are prized, students' chances of learning from their
errors are enhanced. If students get the idea that only correct answers are
prized, they may answer only if they *know* they are "right." Instead of viewing
errors as failures, students may be helped to appreciate how errors may be
used to increase our understanding. It is primarily through the recognition
of error that we are enabled to achieve major insights and proceed with
learning.

Nurturing Confidence

If we are to think, we must dare to think. Daring implies confidence in
ourselves and in our abilities. When we have confidence, we often succeed
in doing tasks far beyond our expectations. When confidence is missing, we
fail in tasks that seem well within our grasp. Confidence grows largely as a
result of experience. It would seem important for teachers to provide opportunities for students to have successful experiences in thinking, so that they
can gain in their confidence as thinkers. As confidence grows, ability often
improves. That is why thinking tasks should be assigned at the students'
level of ability. When students show growth or improvement, teachers'
generally expressed appreciation for their progress will also affirm that their
competence has been recognized.

Giving Facilitative Feedback

Evaluative feedback need not be harsh or punitive. If a student is working
on a particular task and the teacher believes the work could be better, the
teacher might say something like, "This is a good beginning, Sam. I wonder
if there is anything else you can add?" Or, "Sam, you did a fine job on your
assignment last week. I get the idea that perhaps this piece of work you just
gave me does not reflect your real ability. How do you feel about it?"

Sometimes, when teaching for thinking, teachers may be carried away by their own enthusiasm. A teacher may be so intent on getting students to think that interactions and questions may take the form of interrogation and heckling. The students may feel bullied. Sometimes a teacher may put students "on the spot," belittle them, and chastise them for "poor" thinking. Even when the intentions are good and the "right words" are used, a tone of voice may degrade students, threaten them, and put them on the defensive. The words themselves may not be as important as the tone in which they are said. Unless care is exercised, teacher feedback may work against teaching for thinking.

Appreciating Students' Ideas

As thinking is encouraged in the classroom, teachers may be amazed at the high quality of students' work. Occasionally a student from whom not much is expected comes up with a brilliant idea or shows real insight into a situation. At such times teachers may well experience renewed feelings of humility and perhaps say, "I never thought of that" or "I'm glad you brought this up." As students become more discerning, they may catch teachers making errors. At such times it is probably a good idea to acknowledge the pupil's contribution and even to show appreciation of the student's suggestion. Teachers who have good relationships with students, where there is mutual respect, can say, "I made a mistake" without fear of appearing to be reduced in students' eyes. Sometimes a student may ask a question that a teacher is unable to answer, no matter how great the teacher's competency in that area. When teachers can be real people to their students, when teachers can free themselves from the defensiveness of having to appear as *super*teachers, when teachers can reveal that they too are growing and learning, the climate for thinking in the classroom can flourish.

TEACHER–STUDENT INTERACTIONS

In order to help students grow toward becoming more thoughtful human beings, it is necessary that teachers design and carry out a program of learning experiences emphasizing thinking at higher cognitive levels. As we have stated, such a program is best delivered through the selection and use of curricular materials that require higher-level thought, in conjunction with teacher-student interactions that invite and challenge pupil thinking. In order to be effective, a thinking program must also be a part of the daily diet of school experience.

Since the selection of curricular materials has already been extensively discussed throughout this text, it will not be discussed further in this chapter. Neither will daily emphasis on thinking skills in classroom practice receive extensive treatment, since it is obvious that effective delivery of any skill-based program—whether it be reading, or arithmetic, or dancing—cannot be fully achieved in the absence of daily exposure and practice. The discussion in this section, then, will move on to examine teacher-student interactions and the role they play in promoting pupil thinking.

When work on a thinking activity has been completed, the teacher engages the pupils in a process of inquiry about the activity in which pupils are called upon to examine and reflect upon their ideas. Unfortunately, not all questions produce this result. Some questions have been found to be counterproductive to teaching for thinking. Therefore, it is important that teachers not only be aware of the differences about questions but also realize the potential effects of their questions on the development of pupils' ability to think. Pupils are required to think as the teacher uses more responses that promote reflection, that call for analysis of the pupils' ideas, and that ask the students to take cognitive risks in examining extensions of their ideas.[1]

Inhibiting Responses

Some types of teacher responses tend to inhibit pupil thinking. This may occur as a result of one of several types of interactions.

RESPONSES BRINGING CLOSURE

The teacher's response can inadvertently bring closure to the pupil's cognitive processing. The effect of such closure is that the student no longer has to think about the issues. The burden of cognitive processing has been lifted. Closure is likely to occur when

> The teacher agrees with the student.
> The teacher disagrees with the student.
> The teacher doesn't give the student a chance to think.
> The teacher does the thinking by telling or showing the student what to do.
> The teacher cuts the student off.
> The teacher rewards the student's response.

The bringing of closure is seen in the following instances:

> *Pupil:* How shall I do this, Mr. Ivy?

> *Teacher:* Do it this way, Robert. [Teacher tells the student what to do.]

> *Teacher:* What's the difference between these two tapes?
> *Pupil:* One tape has two holes.
> *Teacher:* Right! [Teacher agrees.]

> *Teacher:* What do you call those figures?
> *Pupil:* Statues.
> *Teacher:* Very good, Robert. [Teacher rewards the response.]

RESPONSES UNDERMINING CONFIDENCE

Some types of responses undermine the students' confidence in their ideas. The effect of undermining responses on the students is that they become afraid to offer new ideas, opinions, or thoughts, for fear that they might be criticized. Responses that undermine students' confidence include

> Putting down the student's idea
> Heckling, ridiculing, being sarcastic
> Rejecting hurtfully

The following examples illustrate how this occurs:

> *Teacher:* What would be a good way to proceed?
> *Pupil:* Well, we could start by each of us writing down what we think is important.
> *Teacher:* We don't have all year to do this, Ronald. That would take too much time. [Teacher puts down student's idea.]

> *Pupil:* There are round ice cubes and square ice cubes.
> *Teacher:* If you don't have something intelligent to say, Susan, just keep quiet. [Teacher rejects hurtfully.]

Limiting Responses

Some types of questions tend to limit pupil thinking. These include questions that require students to retrieve specific information that the teacher seeks. While information questions also elicit thinking, it is the kind of thinking that occurs at lower skill levels. Retrieving specific information requires little initiative or originality. Nor does it demand that students exercise the higher-order processing skills.

These types of questions emphasize the students' coming up with a single, correct answer. Therefore students' thinking is limited to that narrow response. Putting limits on pupils' thinking occurs as a result of interactions such as the following:

> *Teacher:* Who can tell me the names of three Pacific states?
> *Pupil:* Idaho, Washington, and Oregon.
> *Teacher:* Not quite right, Philby. Idaho does not border on the Pacific Ocean. [Teacher looks for single, correct answer.]

> *Pupil:* I've thought of a new way to multiply fractions.
> *Teacher:* You can show us your way, Timmy, but, boys and girls, remember the *right way* to do your multiplication. [Teacher emphasizes single, correct procedure.]

> *Teacher:* Now who remembers the name of the first Bill of Rights? Remember, it happened in England a long time ago. [Teacher leads pupils to right answer.]

Teaching for Thinking Responses

Some types of responses call for students to process data or to originate ideas. When students are required to do this, they are more likely to engage in cognitive functioning at higher levels. This type of higher-order thinking requires more originality and initiative. It requires students to take cognitive risks and to "work out" their ideas in an active mental exercise. In the presence of such responses pupils are asked to think for themselves, to think their own ideas and to take ownership of those ideas.

The effect of these higher-order responses on pupils is not always immediately satisfying. First, some pupils may be rusty in the "cognitive functioning department" and may need lots of thinking opportunities before they become skillful at these tasks. Second, some pupils may have already succumbed to the "right answer" style of learning and may initially feel very unsafe in the presence of questions that allow for many potentially correct answers. Third, some students may have already learned to be dependent upon the thinking of others and may falter when asked to function on their own initiative. It is also true that the requirement to think for yourself creates a certain amount of tension and anxiety, more so if you have had limited experiences with the process. "Will I be able to perform well?" is a question that we silently ask ourselves in any learning situation. When the task is more rigorous or when we have had insufficient experience at the task, it is not surprising that we begin by being very, very cautious.

Should a teacher's higher-order responses meet initially with stony stares and silence from the pupils, it may be discouraging and disquieting until we remember that our students, like the rest of us, need time, patience, understanding, and the teacher's diagnostic awareness of existing impediments to their growth before they can become expert in the new tasks of thinking and able to function on their own.

There are several categories of responses that serve to promote higher-order thinking.

REFLECTIVE RESPONSES

Some responses require students to examine their ideas at a surface level, "replay" them in their heads, and assume ownership for them. These "reflective responses" are the *core* of teaching for thinking interactions. There are several types of responses that produce this result:

1. The teacher may give a clarifying response in which the student's idea is "played back" to him or her. For example,

> *Pupil:* The whales are an endangered species. We should really be concerned that they may become extinct.
>
> *Teacher:* You think that we should perhaps take some action to prevent the whales from being eliminated totally.

2. Some responses may issue an open invitation to students in the class to express their own ideas. For example,

> *Teacher:* We've heard some ideas from Marco and Christopher. Would anyone else like to tell what they think?

3. Some responses ask students to elaborate on their ideas. For example,

> *Teacher:* Tell me a little more about that, Sylvia.

RESPONSES CALLING FOR ANALYSIS

Certain responses call for deeper examination and greater cognitive risk, and therefore produce greater tension. Responses that require analysis should be introduced in nonthreatening ways and sensitively interspersed with reflective responses. Students are called upon to analyze their ideas when teachers

1. Ask for examples:

> *Pupil:* Some animals live on land and some live in the water.
>
> *Teacher:* Can you give some examples of those kinds of animals, Polly?

2. Ask for a summary of what has been said:

Teacher: We've heard the discussion of how the Indians have worked to block the timbering industry on Meares Island. Would someone please summarize the kinds of strategies being used by the Indians in their fight?

3. Ask about inconsistencies:

Student: I'm really in favor of making intermediate algebra a required course for everyone in this school, but I'm going to vote against it.

Teacher: There seems to be some inconsistency between your belief statement and your action, Sean. Can you explain it?

4. Ask about alternatives:

Student: Well, we just didn't raise enough money during our campaign to buy the class its own computer. I guess that's that.

Teacher: I wonder. Perhaps it's possible to think about some alternative plans of action.

5. Ask how data might be classified:

Teacher: There are 27 pairs of shoes in this pile. I wonder what kinds of groupings can be set up to classify these shoes?

6. Ask that data be compared:

Teacher: When Simon dropped his parachute, it landed very quickly, after only a few seconds. When Jessica dropped hers, it took much longer for it to reach the ground. What comparisons can be made about these two parachute trials?

7. Ask what data support the idea:

Teacher: Jason, you said earlier that you thought that dogs had feelings. Can you give us any evidence to support your idea?

8. Ask about assumptions:

Student: It took Car A only 30 minutes to get there, so the route Car A took is clearly better.

Teacher: What kinds of assumptions do you have to make to believe that Steven?

CHALLENGING RESPONSES

Certain questions require students to extend their thinking into new and unexplored territory. Here the student is at the greatest cognitive risk, and consequently under greater tension. Challenging questions need to be used thoughtfully and sparingly, since their overuse may be counterproductive. Several types of responses that challenge a student's thinking include

1. Asking the student to generate hypotheses. For example,

Teacher: You have examined the aerial photo of Sun City and made some observations of its geographical configurations. What might be some of the attractions of living in such a town? What are your ideas?

2. Asking the student to interpret data. For example,

> *Teacher:* You were talking about the amount of television viewing among preschool-age children. What do you suppose this means for what these children are learning?

3. Asking the student to make judgments and to specify criteria for those judgments. For example,

> *Pupil:* Frank's story was the best. I think it should go into the class newspaper.
>
> *Teacher:* What was there about his story that made it so good, Melvin?

4. Asking the student to apply principles to new situations. For example,

> *Teacher:* In your work with these foods, you have discovered that milk, left in this jar in the room over a period of four days, will turn sour. What might this mean for other foods in that food group? What are your ideas about it?

5. Asking the student to make predictions. For example,

> *Teacher:* So you have found that heavy things sink. I wonder what this big piece of wood will do when it's placed in the water?

6. Asking the student to formulate a way to test a prediction (hypothesis, theory). For example,

> *Greg:* The heavy part is on the thing, and the heavy part pushes it down, 'cause it weighs more than the other part.
>
> *Teacher:* Greg, you're saying that if you put something heavier on the wood that weighs more than the wood, it will make the wood sink. How could you test your theory?

An outline of the various types of teacher responses discussed in this section is presented in Table 4.1.

LEARNING TO WATCH OURSELVES TEACH

It is difficult for many of us to take a hard look at what we are doing and see ourselves as we really are. The way we actually respond to students may be very different from the way we think we are responding. Yet if we commit ourselves to the educational goals implicit in teaching for thinking, we must move speedily toward a more thoughtful, systematic, and nondefensive examination of our actual classroom interactions.

TABLE 4.1 Teacher Responses and Their Effects on Students' Thinking

Type of Response	Type of Thinking Required
Inhibiting	
Brings closure	Terminates cognitive processing
Promotes fear	
Limiting	
Requires recall of information	Requires student to retrieve
Manipulates student thinking	information; emphasizes
Gets student to give the	remembering, recalling
"right" answer	
Teaching for thinking	
Calls for student to reflect	Requires student to process data;
Asks student to examine ideas	originate ideas; create new
more deeply	frameworks
Challenges students' ideas	

One way of doing this is through listening or watching ourselves work, and by becoming more consciously aware of our interactive patterns.[2] Training oneself to respond more reflectively and less didactically and judgmentally is not an overnight task. It requires perseverance, systematic practice in skill development, and the ability to overcome avoidance behavior that generally accompanies new skills acquisition. It also requires the appreciation that complex and sophisticated skills such as these really do require long-term practice. To help in this task, we have included a coding sheet (Figure 4.1) and an analysis form (Figure 4.2). These self-assessment tools, which have been developed over years of work with teachers, should serve to help in the analysis of interactive style, in pointing out areas of needed growth, and in providing a means for long-term skill development.

In working on your skill development, a tape recorder or video cassette recorder are obvious tools. Tape yourself as you teach, for ten minutes a day. Then, after school, play back your tape and listen to what you are saying, observing each response and noting the type of response it is. Use the coding sheet (Figure 4.1) to tally your responses. Each time you hear yourself responding to a pupil's statement, determine what kind of response it is and place a check (√) in the appropriate category. When you have coded all your responses, you will have a profile of your interactions with your students. Use the analysis form (Figure 4.2) to help you increase your awareness of your interactive style. You might undertake this self-help program over the course of a two-week trial period, doing some taping, listening, coding, and analyzing every day. Should you do this, the likelihood is great

FIGURE 4.1. Coding Sheet for Tallying Teaching for Thinking Responses

A. *Responses That Inhibit Thinking*
   1. Responses that bring closure:
      Agrees/disagrees _____
      Doesn't give student a chance to think _____
      Tells student what teacher thinks _____
      Talks too much; explains it his or her way _____
      Cuts student off _____
      Other closure responses _____
   2. Responses that undermine student's confidence:
      Heckles/is sarcastic/puts idea down _____

B. *Responses That Limit Thinking*
      Looks for single, correct answer/method _____
      Leads student to "right" answer _____
      Tells student what to do _____
      Gives data _____
      Other limiting responses _____

C. *Teaching for Thinking Responses*
   1. Responses that promote reflection:
      Repeats statement so student can consider it _____
      Paraphrases statement/reflects main idea _____
      Asks for student's idea _____
      Asks for more information _____
      Other responses requiring reflection _____
   2. Responses that encourage analysis:
      Asks for an example _____
      Asks about assumptions _____
      Asks how the idea originated _____
      Asks about the value of the idea _____
      Asks about alternatives _____
      Asks that comparisons be made _____
      Asks for data to be classified _____
      Asks for data to support the idea _____
   3. Responses that challenge:
      Asks for hypotheses to be given _____
      Asks that data be interpreted _____
      Asks for criteria to be identified _____
      Asks that principles be applied to new situations _____
      Asks for predictions _____
      Asks how a theory may be tested _____
      Asks for the creation of new schemes _____
      Other challenging responses _____

FIGURE 4.2. Analysis of a Teaching for Thinking Activity

1. Describe the thinking activity that you used.

2. What thinking operation was being emphasized?

3. What major concept or skill was being developed within the framework of the thinking activity?

4. What were some good features of this practice session?

5. What were some weaknesses of the session?

6. What new insights did you acquire about teaching for thinking from doing this practice task?

7. What specific aspect of your teaching for thinking strategies needs more practice for the next session?

that you will begin to notice a marked change in the quality of your interactions with students. And if you were to carry out this self-training program over a six-month period, the likelihood is also great that you will begin to notice some marked changes in pupil behavior. The data suggest that in the presence of these interactive responses, pupils will begin to show an increase in reasoned, thoughtful, self-initiating behavior and a decrease in those behaviors that we associate with dependency and deficits in thinking skills. Only you can decide if such self-training is worth the effort.

When two teachers in a school can join forces and work together on improving their teaching for thinking interactions, the results are likely to be more fruitful in several ways. Each can help the other in analyzing the process. Each can help with suggestions and in finding solutions to difficult situations. Each can serve as a partner in a support system emphasizing personal and professional growth. Two are a team; three, a group. And with five teachers in a school undertaking such self-training, we might begin a small revolution and change the entire system.

Examples of Teacher–Student Interactions

In helping teachers to build teaching for thinking into their classroom programs, we have often used videotape demonstrations to show how some teacher-student interactions work to heighten pupil reflection and how others work to diminish thoughtful responses. As a substitute for videotape, the following transcripts may provide examples of different interactive styles.

TEACHING FOR THINKING APPROACH:
SOCIAL STUDIES, ELEMENTARY LEVEL

This teacher has prepared a series of photographs showing people of different ages, from birth to old age. In this transcript, she is asking the children to make some observations about what is seen in the photographs.

> *Teacher:* Tell me what you see in the pictures.
>
> *Russ:* People.
>
> *Teacher:* Say a little more about that, Russ. [Asks pupil to elaborate.]
>
> *Russ:* They're all different ages.
>
> *Teacher:* What clues in the photograph tell you that the people are different ages? [Asks for supporting data.]
>
> *Stephen:* Well, that man. You can tell.
>
> *Teacher:* Hmmm. How can you tell? [Asks for supporting data.]
>
> *Stephen:* Well, when you get older, your hair goes a little white, and you get a few wrinkles.
>
> *Teacher:* So the man's white hair and his wrinkles suggest that he is older. [Reflects pupil's idea.]
>
> *Stephen:* Yeah.
>
> *Russ:* It looks like the pictures show a guy growing up, at different stages of his life.
>
> *Teacher:* Tell me a little more about that, Russ. [Asks pupil to elaborate.]
>
> *Russ:* From when he was born, to when he was getting a bit older, here, and he's just about our age here. I guess he's got a girlfriend there, and then he's married, and then he's old over there.
>
> *Teacher:* So you think that this set of pictures is telling a story about growing up. [Reflects pupil's idea.]
>
> *Russ:* Yeah.
>
> *Teacher:* What are some things you know about growing up? [Asks that new ideas be offered.]
>
> *Joanne:* You get older.
>
> *Teacher:* I see. [Accepts the idea.] Anything else? [Invites additional ideas.]
>
> *Marlene:* You mature more.
>
> *Teacher:* I see. [Accepts the idea.] What do you mean by mature, can you tell us? [Asks for a definition.]
>
> *Marlene:* Well, the way you act. When you get older, you should act like an older person.

Teacher: How does an older person act, I wonder? [Asks for criteria.]

Marlene: Normal. Not cuckoo like me.

DIDACTIC APPROACH:
SOCIAL STUDIES, ELEMENTARY LEVEL

In this transcript the teacher is using some photographs from the social studies picture series. She is attempting to elicit specific information from the children as to what they should be observing. Her interactions with them emphasize the identification of specific information. She also rewards correct answers and negatively rewards incorrect responses.

Teacher: Tell me what you see in the pictures.

Bob: People.

Teacher: How many people do you see? [Asks for specific information.]

Margaret: There are seven.

Teacher: Are you sure? Count again. [Leads pupil to the right answer.]

Margaret: [Counts.] Eight. I mean eight.

Teacher: That's right. [Rewards the answer.] Now who can tell us which one is the baby? [Asks for specific information.]

All: [In chorus, and they point.] That one.

Teacher: Very good. [Rewards the answer.] And which one is the little boy? [Asks for specific information.]

All: [In chorus, pointing.] That one.

Teacher: Good, [Rewards the answer.] What's the little boy doing? [Asks for specific information.]

Arnoud: He's on the swing. Swinging.

Teacher: Very good, Arnoud. [Rewards the answer.] Do you think he is having a nice time? [Asks for pupil's opinion.]

Arnoud: [Mumbles.] Un huh.

Teacher: Speak up, Arnoud. Let's all hear your answer. [Puts student down.]

Arnoud: Yes.

Teacher: Please put your ideas in a whole sentence, Arnoud. [Puts down student's response.]

Arnoud: He's having a nice time.

Teacher: And what is happening over here? [Asks for specific information.]

Bruce: They are together.

Teacher: Who? [Asks for specific information.]

> *Bruce:* The boy and girl.
> *Teacher:* Does anybody else have a better answer? [Puts down student's idea.]
> *Jackie:* The boy and girl are walking in the park.
> *Teacher:* Thank you, Jackie. That is much better. [Rewards the right answer.]

TEACHING FOR THINKING APPROACH:
SCIENCE, SECONDARY LEVEL

This shortened transcript was made from the interactions that occurred between a teacher and a group of secondary school students who were asked to make some observations of a photograph showing human hair under magnification. In this interactive process, it becomes clear that the students determine the direction of the inquiry through their responses. The teacher asks very few questions that merely require the recall of information. She asks several questions for which there is more than one possible answer, and she does not impose her own views on the students. She talks less than half as much as the students do and is as interested in what they say to each other as in what they say to her.

> *Teacher:* What can you tell me about what you see in the photograph?
> *Jean:* Looks like a magnification of something.
> *Teacher:* What in the photograph suggests to you that it might be a magnification? [Asks for supporting data.]
> *Jean:* I guess the way it's portrayed in the picture . . . the size of it. It reminds me of a forest, . . . but it's not a . . .
> *Megan:* It's not an angle.
> *Jean:* It's not an angle of it.
> *Megan:* It's not realistic.
> *Brock:* It's fuzzy.
> *Jean:* It's fuzzy.
> *Teacher:* Could we have one at a time, because it's very hard for me to interact with you when several people are talking. And I want to get all of your ideas. [Manages behavior.]
> *Jean:* It just reminds me of something I would think would be magnified. Something like hair . . . or . . .
> *Teacher:* Something like hair, which might be magnified. [Reflects student's idea.]
> *Jean:* Yeah.
> *Teacher:* It's the angle of the photograph that—[Reflects Jean's earlier idea, but is cut off by pupil.]

Jean: That I wouldn't think of it as a forest because of the way the shapes are moving, all sorts of angles.

Teacher: Because of the way—[Attempts to reflect, but is cut off by student.]

Jean: Because of the way they are overlapping.

Teacher: The figures overlapping suggest to you that it would not be a forest. [Reflects.]

Jean: Something like hair or a web.

Teacher: Something like hair where everything kind of overlaps. [Reflects.] I see. [Accepts student's idea.] Anyone have any other ideas? [Invites other pupils to respond.]

Bob: It seems like a forest at first, but when you look at the bottom, it doesn't look like a forest floor. It seems like it isn't really ground that you would walk on. It is sort of waves. It's not really ground.

Teacher: You're saying that it can't be the ground. [Reflects.]

Bob: Yeah.

Teacher: I see. [Accepts.] Anyone have any other ideas? [Invites other pupils to present their thoughts.]

Paul: The background. You can't see back, like into a forest. You can't see back into the trees. It might be a dark night, but this bit looks like it is quite light on top. But the magnification can't see very far . . . toward a field or something like that, and that background could be forest or something like that.

Megan: The lack of shadows.

Teacher: So, Megan, you're saying the lack of shadows, and Paul, you are saying the background itself suggests that it is not a photograph of a forest. Those are the clues that you are using. [Reflects.]

Megan: Um hum.

Teacher: Paul, earlier on you suggested that this was a photograph made by an electron microscope, and I was wondering what clues you were using to make that deduction? [Asks for supporting data.]

Paul: Mainly just the coloring. The really bright whites and blacks. Really contrasty. And also because it looks so magnified.

Teacher: It looks highly magnified. [Reflects.] What about it suggests to you that it is highly magnified? [Asks for additional supporting evidence.]

Paul: Well, mainly it is this here. The ground part of it looks like there aren't enough shadows to make it look like it is sticking up, or fronds, or plants, or anything like that. It looks smooth, not with high enough magnification to see the pores or something like that.

Teacher: Not with high enough magnification to see the pores. [Reflects.] So you're working on a theory that this is something specific. You have an idea that you know what this is. Would you like to say more? [Invites student to interpret data.]

Paul: Well, a piece of rat skin with bristles on it.

Teacher: Rat skin with bristles. [Reflects.]

Paul: Yeah.

Teacher: I see. [Accepts.] Anyone want to support or refute Paul's idea? Yes, Wayne, was that your hand up? [Invites other ideas.]

INTERACTIONS CALLING FOR LOWER–LEVEL THINKING: SCIENCE, GRADE 7

In this transcript the teacher is working with the students to have them understand how, in the process of building a city, we alter the natural environment.

Teacher: O.K. What I would like to do with you today is a little activity that demonstrates how a city develops, and I would like to do that by telling you a story about a man named Sam. I want you to imagine that Sam lived about 150 years ago. That was before white people lived around here. And let's say that the story takes place in Washington state. O.K. So Sam lived in a city, and he decided that he wanted to go up into the wilderness area. O.K. So here he is along the stream, and I'm going to draw a picture of Sam in his canoe. And here he is, and he has a paddle. O.K., and he's just coming along here, and he gets into this area, and he thinks, "My this is such a beautiful area I'd like to stay here." Now, thinking that this is about 150 years ago, and this is a place like it would have been around Seattle, what things do you think he would see when he got here?

Brian: Trees.

Teacher: Trees. [Repeats student's answer.] And what else? [Invites additional answers.]

Collin: Burnt-down trees. Like if there had been a fire.

Teacher: Right. [Rewards student's answer.] There could have been some burnt-down trees too, because that's a natural thing that happens. [Tells the student what he thinks.]

Larry: Animals.

Teacher: Animals? What kinds of animals? [Asks student to make his answer more specific.]

Larry: Squirrels, chipmunks, raccoons, I guess.

Teacher: Raccoons. [Repeats student's answer.] What else? [Asks for additional answers.]

Larry: Bears, I suppose.

Teacher: Mm hmm. [Agrees with student.]

Larry: Deer.

Teacher: Right. [Agrees with student and rewards.]

Sean: You could probably see salmon. But you could see the mountains, too.

Teacher: O.K. Salmon, mountains. [Accepts student's answer.] Do you think salmon might live in the streams here? [Looks for answer.]

Sean: Maybe.

Teacher: What other kinds of things would live in the streams? [Does not acknowledge Sean's response; does not help him work out his idea.]

Sean: Trout.

Teacher: Trout. [Repeats answer.] What else? [Looks for additional information.]

Sean: Humpback salmon.

Teacher: Humpback salmon or trout. [Repeats answer.]

Eleanor: Airplanes.

Teacher: Would there be airplanes 150 years ago? [Leads pupil to the correct response.]

Eleanor: No.

Teacher: O.K. [Accepts student's altered answer.]

IMPLICATIONS OF TEACHING FOR THINKING

The applications of some of the ideas in this book may have far-reaching results. It may lead to situations similar to the opening of Pandora's box. When students apply thinking to their lives and studies, in a sense they are set free. German students have an expression for this freedom. *"Die Gedanken sind frei"*: Thoughts are free. Freedom, to some, implies lack of control of behavior. To others it means extreme skepticism, cynicism, or even rudeness. To some it means license. There is a degree of unpredictability about thinking. There is no assurance as to what conclusions our students will reach. There is no way of knowing how students will act in relation to their thinking. It might be helpful, therefore, to conclude this chapter by examining some of teachers' frequently expressed questions, concerns, and fears regarding teaching for thinking.

Lack of Response from Students

"What if you ask a wonderful question and the pupils don't respond?" There is nothing quite so demoralizing for a teacher as a lack of response from students.

"Now boys and girls, how do you think the sound got onto this tape?"

No response. Interminable silence. Finally the teacher leaps in to break the tension and gives the answer. Everybody, including the teacher, visibly relaxes. Whew! Let's not try that again.

There have been rumblings offstage to suggest that teaching for thinking is stressful for students and that to reduce this stress we should teach in more didactic ways. There *is* more comfort in certainty and, arguably, ambiguity does increase dissonance. It is a cunning trap, and we think the teacher ought to be on guard and aware of what lies behind the claims—specifically with reference to students' experiences and their response (or lack of response) and the long-term payoffs in terms of pupil learning.

It is true. Some pupils *do* feel uncomfortable, *at first*, in the presence of tasks calling for original thinking. Some pupils do feel uncomfortable and unable to respond when a higher-order question is raised. This is not a sign that we should abandon the teaching for thinking approach. It is a sign that it is an approach that is unfamiliar to pupils and that they have had insufficient experience with it. It is the lack of experience and the uncertainty of what is expected of them that contribute to the stress. As they grow in their experience and understanding, so they will grow in their assurance and comfort.

It is very much the same for some people with other new experiences. For example, the beginning of a new school year with a new teacher may result in higher levels of stress and anxiety for some students. Their behavior may show this stress in their "holding back," in their increased timidity, in their reluctance to respond. When this occurs, we do not suggest that schools be done away with; we instead help those pupils to become oriented to the new situation. We provide them with experiences that enable them to feel more comfortable. The more familiar they become with the new situation, the more stress is decreased, and the more responsive they become.

It is more helpful to approach students' stress and lack of response diagnostically, for to diagnose is to increase our understanding of the "whys" and to point in the direction of corrective measures. When pupils fail to respond, it is likely for one or more of the following reasons.

1. Students may be entirely unaccustomed to working on activities where many different answers are both appropriate and expected. Their programming in doing exercises that require single, correct answers may have been very extensive. If this is the case, introduction to an activity that is more open-ended may cause a great deal of confusion and anxiety as pupils try to "psych out" what it is the teacher wants.

2. Some students may be "hung up" on teacher approval. They have successfully learned to give the teacher exactly what the teacher wants. If they have no clues to the "right answers," how will they get the approval they badly need?

3. Students may not have enough information to be able to do certain activities with real insight. For example, if we ask primary-grade pupils to hypothesize about how sound is transferred onto magnetic tape, they are likely to have inadequate conceptual understanding of the scientific principles involved to be able to come up with appropriate and meaningful responses. To ask pupils questions that are out of the realm of their experience certainly heightens stress. Level of suitability of the thinking activity is an important consideration.

4. Students may shrink from questions like, "What's your idea, Margaret?" because they believe, from past experience, that what the teacher is really asking is "What's the right answer to this, Margaret?" If they are uncertain of what the teacher wants, they may be unwilling to take the risk of getting the answer wrong. They have not yet learned that each pupil's idea will be valued and that it is the ideas that are being sought—not *the* "right" answer.

5. Students may have difficulty, initially, with questions like "What examples support that statement?" or "How do you interpret those data?" because these questions represent a greater challenge to students' thinking and require both experience in the process as well as confidence in one's ability to take cognitive risks. (See the section "Teacher-Student Interactions," earlier in this chapter.)

6. Students may already have succumbed to insufficient experience with thinking, just as they would have succumbed to inadequate diet. They may be acutely dependent, very underconfident, unable to comprehend, and fearful. If these behaviors are seen, it is quite likely that pupils will feel rather uncomfortable when called upon to generate their own ideas and take cognitive risks. They are already in deficit, and to ask them to function on their own will probably result in lack of response, confusion, and demoralization.

It is the most astonishing nonsense to suggest that a "cure" for the ills just described will come with a further reduction of opportunities for students to think for themselves. It is tantamount to saying that we will try to cure malnutrition with a diet of bread and water, because starving people will have too much difficulty in digesting protein. To alleviate stress symptoms seen in pupils who are initially uncomfortable in the presence of teaching for thinking activities and higher-order questions, we must do much the same as we would in other teaching contexts, specifically:

1. Make sure students understand the nature of the activities. Help them to understand what each task involves and what is expected of them. Generally students do not learn this after a single telling. They will need to hear it reaffirmed many times.

2. Introduce new material slowly. Take the students through the new material in slow steps. Provide careful, sequential orientation to the material.

3. Provide material in which students can experience success almost immediately.

4. Be reassuring when you notice students feeling stressed. Tell them that you understand that thinking is hard work and that you have confidence in their ability to undertake this work.

5. Don't abandon the course of action after only a few tries. Understand that much experience on task is needed to produce the results sought.

6. Don't expect miracles. It may take months of daily practice in a teaching for thinking program to develop some students' skills as thinkers and to see a reduction of those patterns of behavior associated with diminished thinking capability.

7. Select activities for which pupils have at least some background information. Students cannot process data unless they have some data to begin with.

8. Use challenging questions judiciously and sparingly. Emphasize (especially at first) those questions and responses that promote reflection and those that encourage analysis of ideas.

The old saying "The proof of the pudding is in the eating" may be a good rule-of-thumb test of what we do in the classroom. For whatever program we try, we need but look at the behavior of our pupils to know how our efforts have borne fruit. If we see the fruits of our teaching in increased dependency, conformity, and a low tolerance for ambiguity, then to what purpose have we taught? If we see the results in students who become able to function on their own, who face new problems with self-assurance and confidence in their ability, who see new experiences as challenging rather than threatening, then surely our teaching has made a substantial difference to the quality of their lives.

Evaluating Student Performance

"How do you evaluate students' work?" One of the questions teachers frequently ask is, "How do you mark thinking activities?" Following that, teachers also ask, "How do you give feedback to students that will contribute to their growth as thinkers?" Parents and administrators also want to know, "How can we tell if students are improving in their thinking abilities?" Knowing the answers to these questions can be valuable information for a teacher embarking on a teaching for thinking program.

MARKING

The response to the question of marking is at once the easiest and the most difficult. It's easiest, because the answer is, "You don't." It's the most difficult because it represents a distinct departure from traditional teaching practices.

"What? Not *mark* a student's work? Unheard of!" Before you toss this book into the fireplace, allow us to argue the case.

Although a case can be made for marking papers in instances where the criterion of correct-versus-incorrect is the main issue and where it is relatively clear that correct responses get credits and incorrect responses get demerits, the correct-versus-incorrect criterion is more ambiguous in certain other performance areas. A student's art, for example, may be more difficult to assess in terms of right and wrong. A student's poetry is another instance where the criterion of correct versus incorrect is inappropriate.

In the latter two instances, we are not judging whether something is correct or incorrect. We are instead judging quality of thought, creativity of thought, artistry in execution, skill in execution, originality, and similar qualities. In assessing these performance skills, we are on much shakier ground. Although it is clear that in student answers to a spelling test most words are either spelled right or wrong, it is far less clear that a student's poem is good or bad. Two expert reviewers judging the same book will see it differently and will place different values on that same book. Gene Siskel, the television film critic, may say of a film, "See it, by all means," whereas Roger Ebert, his long-time associate in film review, may disagree, saying, "It's terrible!" When we are attempting to judge by the criterion of quality, we find that the perception of quality resides chiefly in the eyes of the beholder.

But so what! What does it matter if teachers perceive quality differently? Isn't it part of the teacher's professional responsibility to make that judgment? Yes . . . but! With such a potential margin of error, suppose the teacher is . . . *wrong*, when he or she downgrades young Picasso for his odd-looking drawings, young e e cummings for his noncapitalizations, or young James

Joyce for his run-on sentences. Will such grading practices subvert the very imaginative and creative processes that make these artists' works new, original, and inspiring? The data tell us that this is a very clear and present danger.

When we examine a student's responses on a thinking activity, we are not judging matters that are unambiguously correct or incorrect. We are seeing the products of the student's thinking processes—the creation of ideas. In that sense, student responses are creative responses and are therefore judged by the quality criterion, "Is this good?"

Since the answer must be so subjective, we are already on dangerous ground. A grade here is not only capable of being called into question but also may thwart the very creative generation of ideas that the teacher seeks to promote. For once a teacher sets himself or herself up as the expert on quality control in thinking, all ideas must agree with that teacher's standard of *good* if they are to receive high marks. It is the path toward promoting high levels of conformity—and students who get high grades are likely to be those who agree with the teacher's ideas.

GIVING FEEDBACK

"But is there no feedback that a teacher can give?" Are there ways in which teachers' evaluative feedback can serve the more productive goals of promoting increased thought?"

Assuredly, yes: There are valuable and appropriate ways in which teachers' feedback can serve these ends. When teachers read students' papers, they will want to invite pupils to reflect more upon their ideas. Students may be encouraged to make analyses and deeper examinations. Pupils may also be invited to avail themselves of the teacher's help when specific difficulties are noted. All of these types of comments are offered in a nonpunitive, considerate manner. Here are some examples of this kind of diagnostic and extending feedback:

> "Dimitri, I see you are having some difficulty with the operation of hypothesizing. I'd like to help you with this. Please come and see me."
>
> "Whew! You've really worked hard on this classification. I can see that! You may want to rest a bit before you think about some other ways to classify this information."
>
> "You have come up with one valuable hypothesis, Phylo. There may be other hypotheses that you'll want to consider—perhaps about the weather, or about the distance, or about the location. Think about it a little more, and see what comes to mind."

vill also appreciate knowing that the teacher values their creative
ments such as "I really liked the way you worked through your
thought your idea for a story title was brilliant!" may be very
encouraging for pupils. One can see immediately, however, that there is
considerable difference between offering the judgment "This is good" and
saying, "I really liked it!" *Vive la différence!*

DETERMINING STUDENT GROWTH

"But how do I know they're improving?" Teachers know that students
are improving in reading by observing their performance on reading tasks.
It is not very different with thinking skills. There are two primary indicators
of quality. One is pupils' performance on thinking tasks. Improvement here
is reflected in the quality of the response and in the ways in which students
are able to process data. In such assessment, the teacher exercises his or
her judgment about the quality of student performance and develops criteria
to use as in other curriculum areas where quality of response is to be determined. The second indicator of improvement is pupil behavior. Is the behavior less impulsive? Are certain students more willing to try things out on
their own? Do more students seem to have a greater understanding of events
around them? Do they begin to see alternatives? Do they seem to value
inquiry? Are they growing more skeptical, more questioning? Do they suspend judgment? If such signs appear in their behavior, then it would be
reasonable to assume that they are profiting from their work. More formal
assessments of students' behavior may be made by using the behavioral
measures included in Appendix A.

Waiting for Results

"How long does it take to see results?" All of us need to feel that we are
successful in what we do. Teachers are no exception; they need and want
tangible evidence of their success in teaching. It pleases us immensely when
a student who has been struggling with a particular mathematical function
learns to perform it with ease; when the shy, retiring tenth-grader with
whom we have been working begins to move out of his shell to make contact
with his peers. What about tangible evidence of increased skill in thinking?
The suggestions in the preceding paragraph may help to point to evidence
of success. In some students, results will begin to appear in a few short
weeks. In others, results may not appear in as many months. As different
students learn other skills at varying rates, so will they vary in the time it
takes for them to learn comparing, observing, classifying, and other thinking
skills. We hope that teachers will be able to be patient enough to allow the
time needed to cultivate thinking.

Perils of Freedom

"Teaching for thinking is too open. It's scary!" Thinking invo~~~~ ~~~ ination. It involves looking for assumptions, attributions, extreme statements, bases of belief, and evidence. As students scrutinize, they may very well begin to criticize each other, their teachers, their textbooks, their principal, and even their parents. They may uncover prejudices, values, and taboos. They may develop contempt for certain textbooks. Is this bad? One answer is that it depends upon the way they do it. One needs to distinguish between freedom to think and license in behavior. Does freedom mean we can do anything we want? Oliver Wendell Holmes said that freedom of speech does not give a person the right to yell "Fire!" in a crowded theater.

When students are engaged in teaching for thinking programs, they may become much more questioning of assumptions and much less believers-on-faith. Is this what we want? Can we have it all? In that excellent old film *Inherit the Wind*, the defense attorney pleads to the jury that his client be allowed the "right to think." When we think, we gain important ground in knowledge and in furthering the advances of humankind, but we also pay some prices. We may learn to fly—but as we do, the birds lose their wonder. These are hard decisions to make, and teachers are faced with having to make them. We may have thinking students, but we will certainly lose much of our ability to bend them to our authoritarian rules. We have to decide.

If we decide in favor of thinking, there will be benefits, of course. We establish a universe of discourse that helps us to work together and understand each other. This does not necessarily mean that people will agree just because they are thinking. But where there is disagreement, differences can be pinpointed by examining assumptions, beliefs, evidence, and values. There can be disagreement without personal attacks, calling names, using insults, being rude, or becoming emotional. Sometimes profound respect can grow for the other person, even though we do not agree with him or her completely. If teachers expect them to, students can function within a universe of discourse where there is mutual respect between students and teacher. The openness of thinking can be liberating, instead of threatening.

Teacher Expectations and Student Behavior

"Will students' behavior change in other teachers' classes?" Sometimes students who have learned something new become "hotshots" or "show-offs." They may seek to confound their friends and bait adults. In a departmentalized school setting they may try to put one of their teachers on the spot. A reality of education is that different teachers emphasize different things. The more teachers students come in contact with, the more it may become

necessary for them to shift gears from class to class. One teacher may emphasize thinking, another concepts. One teacher may emphasize product, another process. Sometimes these teachers do not have first-hand contact with each other. Students may have trouble with these differences. However, as students get the idea that thoughts are free but behavior is not always free, and as they grow toward the maturity that comes with competence in thinking, they are likely to become better able to cope with the realities of teacher' differing expectations.

Academic Skills

"Does thinking interfere with learning academic skills?" What happens to the rest of the curriculum when thinking is emphasized? As we have stated, the available research suggests that there is no loss in academic achievement as teachers emphasize thinking in connection with the regular curriculum. Actually some studies indicate not only no losses in academic achievement but, in some cases, dramatic gains. The individual children being studied *and* the classes of which they were members showed gains in achievement test scores.[3]

In another group of investigations, researchers have pointed to data suggesting that higher-order questions actually interfere with learning—that they cause an increase in anxiety and a decrease in achievement. Barak Rosenshine, a leading advocate of "direct instruction," has used these data to further support his position that direct instruction is the key to gains in pupil learning.[4] At first glance, such data would seem to contradict all the claims we have made about teaching for thinking. Yet, when the surface is probed and one examines the question more deeply, some important discoveries are made.

First, higher-order (challenging) questions must be used skillfully. As we have indicated earlier in this chapter, to use too many challenging questions in one lesson will not allow sufficient opportunity for pupils to reflect and to examine in depth. Challenging questions must be interspersed with responses that require reflection and questions that call for examination of the students' ideas. An overuse of challenging questions can certainly be counterproductive to pupil growth in thinking skills and concept development.

Second, challenging questions can provoke anxiety in students who have been accustomed to performing in the recall-of-information arena. If pupils have learned to be very successful at coming up with just the very answer that the teacher wants, they are likely to become highly agitated when asked a question for which there is no information they can draw on and for which they have to generate ideas of their own.[5] This initial feeling of stress is diminished over time as pupils become more experienced with this mode and as they gain confidence in their ability to think.

We can look at the data from an inexperienced person's use of a hammer and conclude, quite accurately, that using hammers results in swollen thumbs, bent nails, and great frustration. The same is true of examining the results of teaching for thinking. Such data should be examined diagnostically and critically so that we can grow to understand how teaching for thinking interactions, used skillfully, contribute to increased competence and how, used inappropriately, they can be mystifyingly unproductive in facilitating pupil learning.

Teacher Relationships

"What will happen to my relationships with my fellow teachers?" As teachers teach with an emphasis on thinking, what will happen to their relations with other teachers in the school? The answer probably depends upon the quality of the relationships before the program in thinking began. A teacher who had good professional relationships before probably will continue to have them. Of course, if teachers become boastful or arrogant and claim to have solved the problems of the world, they may not endear themselves to their fellow teachers. On the other hand, if teachers see themselves as learners, searching for knowledge, and if they do not become emotional when differences of opinion occur, they may well find that their relationships with fellow teachers even improve.

Relationship with the Administration

"What can I expect from the administration?" Administrators are primarily concerned with the smooth running of the school. When teachers are teaching effectively, when students are eager about attending classes, when parents believe the school is doing an important job, when problems are at a minimum, administrators are usually satisfied.

Almost everybody is *for* thinking, and administrators are no exception. Today, more than ever before, they are in favor of a curriculum in which thinking is emphasized. Therefore, as teachers incorporate thinking activities into their programs and as students become more challenged by their educational experiences, it is likely that teachers' efforts will be welcomed. As students gain skill in using thinking operations to some purpose, the results will speak for themselves. An ineffective teacher is often the source of much concern to an administrator. An effective teacher is often a source of security and satisfaction.

Relationship with Parents

"*How will parents respond to the program?*" A primary concern of most parents in relation to school is whether or not their children are learning. Anxiety over learning is expressed in many ways. "Will my daughter succeed?" "Will he pass?" "Will she get into college?" "Will he be a success in life?" In one way or another, these questions are related to learning. When parents have the idea that their children are not learning, problems may well develop. When parents have the idea that their children are learning, they tend to support schools and their children's teachers. There is much evidence that teaching for thinking enhances learning. As students gain skill with thinking, they grow in their enthusiasm for school, their studies, and their teachers. The parents' anxiety about their children's progress tends to diminish as they see the results.

Doing Well Versus Meaning Well

"*But does this mean me? I already do that all the time!*" As teachers read about thinking, a frequent reaction is, "This makes sense to me. I do it all the time." Sometimes a teacher is asked, "What did you do today to emphasize thinking in your classroom?" The response is, "I do it all the time in so many ways I just can't think of any examples." Some teachers believe that because they mean well, they do well. But do they always do as well as they mean to? How can they be sure? The technique of tape recording teacher-student interactions is one way of finding out whether we are practicing what we preach. The two self-assessment instruments provided in Figures 4.1 and 4.2 can also help teachers to examine diagnostically what it is they are actually doing when they say they are teaching for thinking. Some teaching guidelines have also been suggested. Questions for teachers to consider have been raised. It is hoped that these suggestions will lead to some fruitful introspection and soul-searching, bringing what teachers *say* and what teachers *do* into closer congruence.

Here Today, Gone Tomorrow

"*Is this just another new educational fad?*" It often seems as if society is searching for easy answers or panaceas. Each year publishers come out with *the answer* to "all" our teaching problems. Of course, publishers want to sell their books, and they may be inclined to overstate the case. Too frequently the answers become fads that are discarded when *new* answers become available. Teaching for thinking is not offered as a panacea nor as the solution to "all" educational problems. There are some occasions when thinking may not be appropriate. It is not suggested that teaching for thinking be the sole objective of the school. The authors see teaching for thinking as an approach to the curriculum, needing effective and judicious application at the kindergarten through twelfth-grade level and beyond.

Uncovering New Learning Problems

"I keep discovering students' learning problems. Is this good?" The saying "ignorance is bliss" may apply to teaching for thinking. If a teacher's only contact with students is as a lecturer to a large class, the chances are that neither recognition nor identification of learning problems will occur. The teacher probably will not notice the students as individuals. It is when teachers associate closely with students that they become aware of their problems. It is when teachers give students opportunities to reveal their behavior that behavioral symptoms may be identified. Teaching for thinking programs may therefore result in the surfacing of learning difficulties that have hitherto gone unnoticed. When such problems emerge, it may be an indication of a teacher's greater awareness of the functioning of each student. It is only when the problems emerge that we have any chance of dealing with them effectively.

Encountering New Teaching Problems

"Will teaching for thinking create more problems for me?" No classroom program is completely trouble free. No matter what teaching method is used or what curriculum is taught, problems are likely to develop. Teaching for thinking is no exception. If teachers are autocratic and rigid in their teaching, problems will develop. If teachers are democratic in their teaching, other problems will develop. If teachers are permissive, still other problems will develop. No matter how classes are taught, teachers will face problems. If teachers are very successful, they may be the object of envy. If teachers are inept, they may be the object of contempt. Furthermore, teachers may be subjected to a certain amount of criticism no matter what they do in their classrooms. In extreme cases, on a single day a teacher may be criticized for being too strict, too lenient, too easy, too hard, giving too much homework, boring the class, telling too many jokes, and so on. Sometimes the school and teachers become scapegoats for the frustrations of the public. Life itself involves problems, challenges, striving, difficulties. As long as problems and criticisms are part of life, let us accept them. They do not diminish the satisfaction that comes from teaching for thinking.

CONCLUSION

Teachers have dozens of excuses for not initiating teaching for thinking programs. Thinking takes time. There isn't enough time in the day. There's too much curriculum to cover. Thinking is too disrupting. It teaches students to be too critical. It gives too much power to the students and undermines the teacher's authority. Students need to learn the right answers. After all, that's what they are going to be tested on. You can't ask pupils to think unless they spend their school years accumulating the information they need to think with.

In the past twenty years, we have probably heard them all. And we have also seen the products of such avoidance behavior: students who tell us that they have been handicapped by their school experiences. In spite of test scores that admit them to college and university, many students say that they feel quite inadequate when asked to do their own thinking. In the rationalizations of teachers, we have paid a terrible price: the diminishing of our most precious human resource.

Where teachers have struggled to develop their competence as teachers of thinkers, there are different stories to tell. There are gains in pupils' ability to function competently and successfully as independent, thoughtful learners. Students' ability to work together in small groups is dramatically improved. Teachers and students feel liberated in the process, and the classroom is an alive and exhilarating place.

It is the teacher who is the key to emphasizing thinking in the classroom. Explicitly and implicitly, the role of the teacher is the theme of this chapter. It is easy to stifle thinking. It is much harder to encourage it. It is easy to think *for* the students. It is much harder to give students opportunities to think for themselves. Yet, if emphasis on thinking is one of our educational goals, we as teachers must find ways of providing the means for delivery. To teach for thinking is to open the doors of the mind and to cultivate the most potent human tool that we have. To empower students as thinkers: There can be no greater teacher's gift.

PART 5

In Support of Thinking

THEORY AND HYPOTHESES

If colleges, universities, or special schools set themselves up as responsible agencies for the preparation of teachers, it must follow that there are principles or theories that are to be taught. Ideally these principles or theories give direction to what teachers will do in the classroom as they meet those situations that are in some way related to their theoretical preparation. We need to assume also that the preparation of teachers is directed toward the kinds of problems that are present in typical teaching situations. Those problems of concern to teachers almost always involve behavior of one kind or another on the part of students.

In some circumstances students behave in ways that make it difficult for them to learn. Sometimes their behavior makes it difficult for other students to learn. Teachers who take seriously their responsibility to promote learning tend to be frustrated when learning is inhibited. They want guidance in these situations; they want to know how to help students who are in difficulty. If there is sound theory in the field, teachers accept this as a guide. If one theory does not succeed, a teacher may want to try another theory, and still another. There have been relatively few *theories* in the field of education that have been helpful to teachers in the solution of behavior problems related to learning. The available evidence is fairly clear that we do not accomplish very much in our efforts to modify the values of children or of young adults. The same might be said of thinking-related behaviors. If one examines the textbooks that are used in teacher-preparation courses, one finds that theory, as defined in this volume, is conspicuous by its absence. In this same connection it should be said that in the area of education, theory tends to be thought of as something that is nebulous, up in the clouds, away from reality, something almost irrelevant to the practical concerns of the day. It is almost never conceived as a clear statement of relationships between two or more variables. It is almost never seen as something that suggests hypotheses that can be tried by the classroom teacher.

In this volume, however, we have said that certain behaviors of students are related to their lack of experience with thinking. We have stated that the behaviors such students typically exhibit in thinking situations—impulsiveness, extreme dependency, missing the meaning, failing to concentrate, overassertiveness and dogmatism, and rigidity—are indications that the students have failed to develop the habits that are appropriate to successful conduct in thinking situations.

We have also presented a wide variety of operations that give students opportunity for thinking. These include comparing, summarizing, classifying, interpreting, criticizing, and others. Many illustrations of such thinking operations that have applications to elementary and secondary school settings have been presented. The most significant hypothesis derived from our theory suggests that as students engage in these thinking operations regularly and consistently for at least one semester, the behaviors indicative of immaturity tend to decline. Given students with behavior like that described, and given a teacher who wants to test the theory, thinking operations may be easily carried out with the methods suggested in this text. Under these circumstances teachers do not have to take these materials on faith. They are in a position to *test* what has been offered. Here is a hypothesis that can be tested by teachers who use it, and as they test it with different students in different situations, they will be testing the soundness of the theory as it operates in their own classrooms with the students they teach.

In deciding to test the hypothesis with respect to particular students, teachers are warned to make a two-pronged investigation before starting. First, one should make sure that no health problems are affecting the student's performance. It is wise to consult with parents and review school medical records. In some cases the results of annual physical checkups may be available. We need to take more seriously the idea that ill health affects behavior, and particularly those behaviors related to learning. Second, a teacher should make some assessment of the student's emotional stability. If students have deep worries, these will probably get in the way of their learning. The surface manifestations that are significant indicators of emotional problems include persistent and unusual aggressiveness, persistent and unusual withdrawal from group activities, unusual meekness or submissiveness to other students, symptoms of psychosomatic illness that are confirmed by a physician, and patterns of behavior that regress to earlier age levels. Where physical or emotional illness is involved, these need attention before any great program for an emphasis on thinking is launched.[1]

If we could assume that the questions of physical and emotional illness have been answered, the next step would be to identify some students who, according to the theory, are very much in need of intensive work. The Teacher Rating Instrument developed by Wassermann is designed to assist teachers in assessing their students' behavior in thinking situations (see Appendix A).[2] This instrument consists of a number of paragraphs describing typical student behaviors in thinking situations. In using the instrument, the teacher reads each profile and mentally identifies the students in the class who exhibit the behavior described. When the Teacher Rating Instrument is used in beginning-of- and end-of-year assessments, teachers have a record of students' growth in thinking capability.

While filling out these behavioral profiles, teachers may have some doubts about relying on memory in making such important judgments. To check the validity of their recall, teachers might focus on the students whose behavior seems to be related to the descriptions in the profiles and observe their behavior each morning and afternoon for a period of about one week. If corroborating evidence is found, teachers may be more confident about proceeding.

School records may also contain anecdotal material or behavioral judgments that may add to the identifying data. Teachers who worked with the students the preceding year may have recorded some judgments about their thinking-related behavior. The teacher may also consult with other teachers who taught the students in previous years. If there are other teachers now working with the student, comments may also be solicited from them. The principal of the school may have additional information. One can be more certain when the same kinds of data come from different sources.

There are other ways to obtain evidence about behavior related to thinking. The Profile of Student Performance, included in Wassermann and Raths' *Thinking and Learning Programs*, which are sets of classroom materials emphasizing pupils' thinking skills development, identifies "positive" and "negative" characteristics of students' behaviors on thinking tasks.[3] In addition, there are pencil-and-paper measures like the Watson-Glaser Critical Thinking Appraisal, the Torrance Tests of Creative Thinking, *Judgment: Deductive Logic and Assumption Recognition*, and the Ross Test of Higher Cognitive Process, all of which provide data about specific aspects of students' thinking capabilities.[4] But we would prefer to rely upon observations of behavior. Excellent teaching helps students to mature, and as they mature, they behave differently. We think it is much more important to know that a student's excessively dependent behavior upon the teacher is diminishing than it is to know what score he or she has made on a pencil-and-paper instrument that purports to measure one or more aspects of thinking. Fortunately, an either-or choice need not be made. In the section following, dealing with research, we present evidence suggesting that teaching for thinking does produce increases in test scores that relate to thinking, along with observable changes in students' patterns of behavior related to thinking deficits.

In this respect another factor deserves emphasis. Many statements of educational objectives indicate changes that teachers want to make in the behavior of students. The implication is that the teacher changes the student. We believe that the decision for change should be left in the hands of the student. In teaching for thinking, a teacher does not urge or exhort students to change their ways or to mend their manners. The theory requires that students be given many, many opportunities to think, under the guidance of an informed, competent, compassionate teacher. It is our hypothesis that under these conditions students form new habits of behavior. As they gain skill in comparing, as they practice summarizing, as they learn to classify, as they criticize, as they learn to interpret materials, as they themselves learn to hypothesize, they are forming habits of behavior that are ordinarily called *thoughtful*. They begin to develop ways of responding that are at variance with those characterized as immature. The change in behavior may be cultivated by the teacher, but it is the students who choose the expressions they will use.

In this chapter, the theory has been reexamined, and hypotheses to test the theory have been suggested. Suggestions have been made for ways of identifying students whose behavior shows deficits in thinking. The next step is to appraise the students' progress by the collection of evidence after a semester of learning with an emphasis on thinking.

The Teacher Rating Instrument (see Appendix A) could be used again at the end of a semester's trial. Evidence from the classroom teacher's observations may be obtained, in addition to relevant evidence from other teachers who have had opportunities to work with the students in question. Thinking tests could be administered again. All the evidence thus collected could then be pooled and a judgment made about progress, lack of progress, or uncertainty as to whether progress was made. The research conducted thus far with this theory indicates the behavior of more than 80 percent of the students will change significantly after one semester of such work.

RESEARCH FINDINGS

One of the earliest studies bearing upon the theory was conducted by Rothstein.[5] He undertook an investigation to test the hypothesis that as teachers use thinking activities, such as those presented in this book, students' test scores on thinking would change significantly and that thinking patterns in essay-type assignments would show improvements among the experimental group. In his study Rothstein used a number of assignments that involved comparing and interpreting, and he utilized coding techniques. He devised exercises in problem solving and decision making for the area of social studies in the secondary school. His experience supported the idea that this approach is a way to stimulate thinking and that actual increases in thinking test scores take place. In addition, Rothstein reported an increased interest on the part of students in classroom work and in social studies generally. One or two students, accustomed to more conventional types of assignments, were persistent objectors to questions that involved thought. These exceptional cases wanted work that could be "learned" in a homework assignment. They wanted to read and reread such assignments, and they wanted to be asked information-type questions the following day about what they had read.

Shortly after the completion of Rothstein's work, a more controlled study was initiated by three elementary school teachers who were working together in the same school. One of them taught grade 3, another taught grade 4, and the third taught grade 5. Using their own classes, Machnits, Jonas, and Martin undertook three separate but parallel studies of the relationship of certain behaviors of children to thinking.[6] Each of them included cases that related to areas other than thinking, but each also had individual children who were taught as if an emphasis upon thinking were clearly needed. The results of these three studies supported the general notion that when there was an emphasis on thinking, the behavior of the children in the experiment changed during the work of one semester. These three investigators also undertook to determine whether there was any loss in the usual subject matter achievement if thinking were emphasized. The various standardized tests that measure performance in reading, study skills, and other subjects indicated that the children who took part in the experiment, as well as the other children in the classes in which thinking was stressed, made more than the average gains achieved by several previous classes at the same level of instruction.

Following these studies, Cartwright developed a comprehensive resource unit for use at the college level that included a heavy emphasis upon thinking operations.[7] His collections of criteria and illustrative examples represented a further contribution to possible trials of the theory under more controlled conditions.

In 1962 Wassermann completed "A Study of the Changes in Thinking-Related Behaviors in a Selected Group of Sixth Grade Children in the Presence of Selected Materials and Techniques."[8] She tested the hypothesis that when materials and techniques designed to stimulate thinking are applied, a change will result in thinking-related patterns of behavior. At the beginning of her investigation, the characteristic thinking behaviors of each of the children was identified by their former teachers, by their peer group, by themselves, and by the investigator. An objective test relating to thinking was also used as a basis for estimating certain thinking abilities.

Nine children identified as having extreme patterns of certain thinking-related behaviors at the close of their previous school year were placed in Wassermann's sixth-grade class the following September. In her program, the children were provided with daily opportunities to participate in activities involving comparing, classifying, criticizing, summarizing, and the other operations described in Parts 2 and 3 of this text.

At the close of the semester the behaviors of these children were once more assessed by their teachers, by their peers, by the children themselves, and by the thinking test, which was administered again. The results were conclusive. In terms of before-and-after scores on the thinking test, there was an improvement that was significant at the 2-percent level. The behavior patterns changed in very significant ways. Each of the nine children showed a positive change in the behavior by which he or she had initially been identified and in his or her total behavior. These results were significant beyond the 1-percent level, and the evidence clearly supports the theory put forth in this volume. The same kind of positive change was revealed in the peer ratings, and this, too, was significant beyond the 1-percent level. The scores of the experimental group of students on the Stanford Achievement Test, Form KM, administered in April of the school year, showed no loss in academic performance; for some of the children, the achievement gains were significant.

In addition to the before-and-after scores and ratings, Wassermann's research includes case studies of the nine children in the experimental group. The detailed, almost day-by-day record of the way in which each child participated in the thinking program contains many suggestions for the classroom teacher.

Wassermann's investigation was a before-and-after study of nine children. No outside controls were employed. It was assumed that if anything of great significance happened in the course of engaging in a program emphasizing thinking, the results would be immediately visible in rather significant changes in the behavior of the children. At this point in the testing of the theory, there seemed to be a need for a more closely controlled study, and this was undertaken by Ruth R. Berken in 1963.[9] Berken was a member of the Bureau of Curriculum Research of the New York City school system. She applied for and was granted permission to conduct the study in several elementary schools on Manhattan's West Side. With some slight revision, Berken used the same techniques for identifying children as had been used by Wassermann. Nine fifth- and sixth-grade teachers participated in this study. These teachers were members of a seminar course Berken taught on the use of assignments emphasizing thinking. When these teachers began the process of selecting children, they identified twenty-seven matched trios—one child for the experimental group, and one for each of *two* control groups. One set of the control-group children was selected from the same classes as the children in the experimental group. Another set of control-group children was selected from classes outside of the experimental group. In addition to the matching of thinking-related behavior, the sets were also matched in terms of grade level, sex, academic achievement, I.Q. level (within five points), and economic status of the family. The children in each matched trio manifested one of the thinking-related behavior patterns.

The children selected for the experimental group were encouraged to carry on extensive work in thinking activities. With the control groups, no single effort or intensive work in thinking experiences was undertaken.

The results thus have bearing upon "control" children in the same classroom and "control" children outside of the experimental classroom. Berken reported that there was a significant difference between both control groups and the experimental group. On the rating scale used, there was a gain of three or more points by twenty-four out of the twenty-seven pupils in the experimental group; a similar gain was achieved by only three out of the twenty-seven control-in-class pupils. These results were significant at the 1-percent level and give additional support to the theory.

In terms of the before-and-after self-ratings of the same students, there was again a very significant difference, of the same order as has been described. In the self-ratings, twenty out of the twenty-seven students in the experimental group thought they had improved, whereas none in the control groups thought they themselves had. The peer ratings demonstrated again a significant difference between the control and experimental groups, and this evidence is also consistent with the theory. Berken's study gives added support to the idea that where children with certain behaviors are helped to focus on assignments that involve thinking, their behavior changes. The students themselves report awareness of change, their peers assess them more positively, and the teachers see positive changes in their behavior.

Still another kind of research has bearing on this theory. Stern undertook a study entitled "The Perseverance or Lack of It of Specified Behavior among Children in Selected Elementary Schools in Nassau County, New York."[10] Among the behaviors studied were those that in this book are described as "thinking related." In one of the schools there was a perseveration of 84 percent in the many behaviors related to deficits in thinking. If two or more of the behavior patterns were chosen for comparison, two of the schools in Stern's study showed a perseveration rate of 80 percent. He notes that even if one takes the 71-percent level (the average) of perseveration, this is relatively high if we think of the elementary school as a place that has significant influence on the growth and development of children. In other words, where little or no emphasis is given to thinking in the curriculum, there is much less likelihood that significant change in the thinking-related behavior of children will take place.

What has been proved by all these studies? A theory is not something that can be proved in the absolute sense. In almost all the studies the investigators have operated on the hypothesis that there *is* a relationship between consistent and persistent exposure to thinking exercises and resultant behavior. On the basis of these studies we can be reasonably sure that if teachers work with students in ways that put an emphasis upon thinking, changes will take place in the behavior of students. We cannot be specific in attributing the cause of the change. What can be said is that as teachers work in these ways with students, certain kinds of behavior will diminish in frequency and certain other kinds of behavior will develop.

What about the element of chance in all of this? If the results of only one study were available, we might be tempted to say that these improved behaviors represented unique responses to enthusiastic teachers, or else that the so-called Hawthorne effect was operating—that almost any "new" procedures would produce a change. The testing, however, has been tried out with a number of teachers. It has been tried out in a variety of situations where students did not know that they were taking part in an experiment. The final ratings were made by teachers and students without their knowing which children were in the experimental group. Stern's study supports the other findings for control groups, since between 70 and 80 percent of the children described as having certain behavioral characteristics tended to be similarly described a year later. In the several studies not only did the students who took part in the experiments improve significantly, nearly *all* the students in the classes involved in the experiments improved. It is reasonable to infer that teaching that emphasizes thinking will, in other situations, with other students, produce positive and welcome changes, and it is predicted that this emphasis on thinking will receive wide attention in the years ahead.

THE VALUE OF THINKING

This entire volume has been concerned with a theory that relates behavior to thinking. Great emphasis has been put upon the importance of thinking in our daily lives, and we have taken the position that schools ought to be places where students have extensive opportunities to develop their thinking capabilities. To this end, hundreds of examples of ways to emphasize thinking at the elementary and secondary levels have been given.

How does thinking help us? There are a number of ways to go about making a decision. Sometimes we do it by hunch or intuition. Sometimes we do it by consulting an authority. At times we do it by examining what has been done in the past. Some seek divine guidance when they are facing a problem of great consequence. A few seek advice from astrologers and fortune-tellers. Some people look for help in established policies, or rules and regulations.

Of all the methods that are known for solving problems in terms of human needs, human values, and human concerns, *thinking* represents the one best method available. This is not to say that the processes emphasized here will inevitably lead to a correct or even to the most appropriate conclusion. Thinking is not an absolute guarantee for an adequate solution to a problem. Where hundreds of problems are to be solved and a higher average of success is sought, then thinking is the single best approach. Where there is freedom to think, there is also freedom to correct past errors. Where there is freedom to think, there is the possibility that new and better hypotheses will be proposed for testing. Where there is freedom to think, ideas not yet heard of may have opportunity to be voiced, to be discussed, to be modified, and to be tried. Our faith is in a process that is to be used by people in solving the problems that face us and in identifying problems to which we have been insensitive heretofore.

Much is said about the monopolistic characteristics of our culture, and the bureaucracy and increased emphasis on technology. The more pessimistic outlook suggests that these elements control us, that these *determine* our thinking—that we can do nothing but drift with the times. Throughout history, humans have reconstructed their environment. They are still capable of doing it. Where we can clearly see what it is that we want for our culture and where deliberate processes of thought are employed, our culture can be modified in ways that more nearly represent our heart's desire.

There has been a tendency in the past to associate almost all learning difficulties with emotional disturbance. If students lean heavily on authority figures for guidance, it is assumed that there were problems in their relationships with their parents when they were infants. If students "cannot concentrate," it is suggested that psychological therapy is needed. There is an analogy here with the medical profession. Not so very long ago, physicians tended to believe that all, or almost all, illness was caused by germs. We now acknowledge the presence of many causes. Some will say that this book deals with profound emotional problems, and does so superficially, because of its orientation toward thinking processes. We must be clear about this matter. We agree that emotional security is very important and that some behavioral disorders may be traced to emotional insecurity. We do *not* believe that *all*, or *almost all*, behavioral problems have their roots in emotional imbalance.

CONCLUSION

Americans are very proud of their public schools. True, they criticize the schools severely at times, but beneath the criticism they also identify closely with them. In no other country of the world are fathers and mothers as closely involved with what goes on in the schools as they are in the United States.

The administrators of our schools are required to have professional training. Teachers also are required to secure an understanding of students at the several age levels, as well as an understanding of the subjects they teach. A majority of the public is convinced that our schools have made a great contribution to the welfare of the nation and to its resources in terms of identifying and solving the many problems that now confront the nation.

Yet, although there is commitment on the part of teachers to excellence in education and to furthering the growth of children, there seems to be a lack of commitment on the part of society to mobilizing the resources that would help these teachers to achieve their purposes. For example, if an emphasis upon thinking is an objective, one would expect that graduate schools, colleges, and trained supervisors would be helping the teachers day by day, in very specific and concrete ways, to build a curriculum that would reflect this emphasis upon thinking. In fact, however, the emphasis is not upon the operational procedures that would help to carry out this purpose but rather on the formulation of statements of purpose. Perhaps this book will be helpful in its emphasis on actual procedures that can realize our goals.

In a larger sense, the book attempts a significant contribution to what may be called a "way of life." As a country we are committed to a deep respect for the individual. We are also committed to a doctrine that is best expressed as "faith in intelligence." We have indicated in our Constitution that we believe in sharing our problems and our ideas in the widest possible manner, thus ensuring the participation of all of our people in decisions that affect their lives.

Thinking often adds to tensions already experienced. Society is threatened in many ways by freedom of thought. The very structure that is cherished becomes a subject of reflection and possible change. Consequently, it takes more than "freedom to think" to handle the tensions that are created by such a society as ours. It takes competence in thinking. It requires excellence as an ideal for those who emphasize thinking. As we continue to pledge ourselves and each other to the ideals of democracy, we must also pledge that we will use every resource to provide that excellence in the education of our youth. Just as we want them to be free to identify the problems of concern to them, so do we want them to have those experiences that can contribute greatly to the competence of people in problematic situations.

To translate these majestic purposes into classroom practices that can further these goals; to present educational theories relating to the achievement of these purposes; and to do it in ways that suggest hypotheses that can be tested in any or every school of the country is the hoped-for contribution of this text.

As we see it, the good life is associated with zestful living, and zestful living is, over and over again, associated with a life that both creates problems and creates opportunities for working with the problems. Man may be a reed, but as has been said, "he is a thinking reed"; and where he can think, and where ideas can be put to test in the marketplace, life is richer and life is better. Where our schools have these aims, and where teachers have the competence to put these aims into operation, school life too will be richer and better for teachers and students.

APPENDIX A

Teacher Rating Instrument

Notes to the teacher: After reading each profile, complete A by writing in the names of students whose behavior is clearly described in the profile (i.e., you are certain). Under B, write the names of those students whose behavior may *possibly* reflect that described in the profile (i.e., you are not certain; there is some element of doubt).

1. *Profile of the very impulsive student.* These students typically act without thinking. When a problem or activity is introduced, these students leap into action first. They don't seem to have a plan, nor do they consider alternatives. The mode of operation is *doing*—and sitting down to "think things out" does not seem to be their pattern of behavior. Impulsive students do not engage in reflection.

Associated with impulsiveness is the idea of rapid and random movements, of acts directed by little more than whim or caprice. Action itself seems to be much more important than thinking about possible modes of action. To be up and doing is so prominent in the behavior of these students that the purpose or goal of the doing is neglected.

    A. This pattern of behavior sounds very much like

    B. This pattern of behavior sometimes describes

2. *Profile of the very dependent student.* These students typically want help with practically everything they undertake. They find it hard to begin work without asking for help in getting started. Once they have begun, help is again requested. Often such students say, "I'm stuck!" or "What shall I do now?" or "I don't know what I'm supposed to do."

These students' insistent calling on the teacher for help is a strong characteristic of their inability to carry out tasks independently. When the teacher's help is not available, these students may just sit there and do nothing until help is forthcoming.

A. This pattern of behavior sounds very much like

B. This pattern of behavior sometimes describes

3. *Profile of the loud, dogmatic, and overly assertive student.* These students seem to have "all the answers," and they are unyielding in their conviction that they are *right*. Such students reject discrepant data; their minds are made up. These students stick to their positions regardless of the facts. There is a quality of inflexibility about the way they think. We generally consider them as intemperate, unreasonable, and insensitive to the feelings of others. They don't listen to alternatives. In fact, they seem reluctant to acknowledge that there are alternatives.

These students are apt to impugn the motives of those who oppose their views. Their language is frequently studded with extreme words, such as *always, everybody, nobody, never*. They may generalize loosely about races or nations or religious groupings. We sometimes think of them as authoritative; that they try to dominate other people; that they are rash in their judgments, close-minded, intemperate, or unreasonable in presenting their ideas.

A. This pattern of behavior sounds very much like

B. This pattern of behavior sometimes sounds like

4. *Profile of the rigid, in-a-rut student.* These students typically want to stick to doing things in the same old ways. They don't like new or different ways of doing things. The fact that a problem or task is new and calls for new procedures doesn't make a difference. These students try to force old methods onto new problems. When that procedure doesn't work, these students complain that the problem is at fault.

These students are most comfortable when carrying out routines. They can learn lessons and formulas, but they have great difficulty in applying the principles of what has been learned to new situations.

A. This pattern of behavior sounds very much like

B. This pattern of behavior sometimes sounds like

5. *Profile of the student who misses the meaning.*   These students don't seem to understand. They miss the point—of a lesson, an assignment, a story, a joke. Such a student might say, "I don't get it." We think of these students as people who "don't listen" and who don't pay attention. Actually, the problem is that they are not able to interpret data intelligently or "sort out" cognitively what is happening. It is as if their ability to process data has been seriously impaired.

A. This pattern of behavior sounds very much like

B. This pattern of behavior sometimes describes

6. *Profile of the student who can't concentrate.*   The dominant charac-teristic of these students is their tendency to use means that are inconsistent with or inappropriate to the ends being sought. It's not that these students don't have any ideas. They do have ideas about what they want to do, but the paths that they take to arrive at their goals may be silly or illogical, impractical, or even irrational. There seems to be an absence of cognitive awareness in choosing these paths. Their choices do not reveal a great deal of thinking about the connections between means and ends but rather suggest an indiscriminate and random selection of means. Perhaps that accounts for the fact that the goals these students set are seldom realized.

A. This pattern of behavior sounds very much like

B. This pattern of behavior sometimes describes

7. *Profile of the underconfident student.*   These students lack confidence in expressing their thoughts. During class or group discussion, such students rarely volunteer information, not because they have nothing to say but because of fear of exposing what they are thinking to public scrutiny. At the end of class, these students might say privately to the teacher that they did

have an idea but were concerned about how it might have been received by the group. Underconfident students are not necessarily shy; they rather lack confidence in their ability to think and are fearful about exposing their thoughts to possible criticism.

    A. This pattern of behavior sounds very much like

    B. This pattern of behavior sometimes describes

    8. *Profile of the student who actively resists thinking.*   These students typically scorn thinking as a preferred mode of operation. They believe that action is more important and that thinking is for the "intellectuals." Classmates who are seen as intellectually advanced are held in contempt. When asked to do some thinking, these students reject the process. "It's the teacher's job to tell us what to do" may be the response these students give. Such students see their function as acting rather than reflecting. They make strong value judgments about "people who think," and those judgments are clearly negative.

    A. This pattern of behavior sounds very much like

    B. This pattern of behavior sometimes describes

APPENDIX B

Annotated Bibliography

As you scan this list of readings and note the publication dates of some works, it may be tempting to dismiss them as old and therefore no longer relevant to current concerns about thinking. On the contrary, most of the related readings included below are now considered "classics," and the ideas presented in them are as rich and substantial today as ever before. It is also instructive to note that although the reading list has been updated for this second edition, no new seminal work in thinking has been published in twenty years.

RELATED READINGS

Scholarly Books

Bartlett, Sir Frederic. *Thinking*. New York: Basic Books, 1958.
> A thorough and detailed analysis of thinking by an eminent psychologist dealing at length with experiments in the mental processes of interpolation and extrapolation. The author delineates everyday thinking and adventurous thinking, the thinking of the artist, and the thinking of the experimental scientist.

Black, Max. *Critical Thinking*. New York: Prentice-Hall, 1946.
> This college text with a heavy emphasis on logical analysis provides many fine illustrative materials on fallacies.

Bloom, Benjamin S. *Taxonomy of Educational Objectives: Part I, Cognitive Domain*. New York: Longmans Green, 1956.
> An attempt at classifying the goals of teaching: knowledge, comprehension, analysis, synthesis, application, and evaluation; essentially, the work is derived from an analysis of the materials used in the Progressive Education Association Eight-Year Study.

Bruner, Jerome S. *The Process of Education*. Cambridge, Mass.: Harvard University Press, 1961.
> The author sets forth the thesis that it is the structure of a subject that should be taught. It is his contention that the history of how the discipline came to be should occupy a central role in the process of education.

Bruner, Jerome S., Jacqueline Goodnow, and George A. Austin. *A Study of Thinking*. New York: John Wiley and Sons, 1961.

>An inquiry into the processes of categorizing and conceptualizing. Human capacity to categorize is seen as a necessity. We group things into classes and respond to them as classes. Concept attainment, a result of categorizing, enables us to learn more readily.

Bury, J. B. *A History of Freedom of Thought*. London: Oxford University Press, 1922.

>The author traces the history of man's emancipation from passion and prejudice. He indicates that there is no linear progress but merely illuminating flashes of freedom of thought. (The books of Robinson and Russell listed below deal with similar themes.)

Conant, James B. *On Understanding Science*. New Haven: Yale University Press, 1947.

>Through the presentation of case histories from the diaries of famous scientists, the author offers a historical approach to the understanding of science hoping to acquaint the nonscientist with the methods of science. "Understanding science" is, according to the author, acquiring a special point of view, knowing what science can or cannot do.

Dewey, John. *How We Think*. Boston: D. C. Heath, 1910.

>This book is now a classic. It was a pioneering and systematic examination of thinking—the method by which things acquire significance—and its relationship to teaching and learning.

Dimnet, Ernest. *The Art of Thinking*. New York: Fawcett World Library, 1955.

>This is a highly literary presentation of thinking as art. The author's wit and engaging style make for pleasurable and enlightening reading.

Hullfish, H. Gordon, and Philip G. Smith. *Reflective Thinking: The Method of Education*. New York: Dodd, Mead, 1961.

>Reflective thinking is presented as the method of teaching and learning. Leaning heavily on epistemology, the book offers a theory of learning and suggestions for the promotion of reflection.

Hunt, J. McVickers. *Intelligence and Experience*. New York: Ronald Press, 1961.

>The author examines the assumptions of fixed intelligence and predetermined development. He describes changes in our thinking about the development of intelligence and logical thinking and how the experiences of living contribute to this development.

Judd, C. H. *Education as Cultivation of the Higher Mental Processes*. New York: Macmillan, 1936.

>This is an outstanding classic on the subject of thinking. It provides one of the earliest psychological discussions of mental processes, their definition and distinctions. In addition, it illustrates ways of putting emphasis on higher mental processes.

Keyser, C. J. *Thinking about Thinking*. New York: E. P. Dutton, 1926.

>A highly analytical discussion of empirical and autonomous thinking, which is described as "human" thinking. Other kinds of thinking, whether by humans or not, are characterized as subhuman. The book is the scientific counterpart of Dimnet's presentation of thinking as art.

Raths, Louis E., Merrill Harmin, and Sidney B. Simon. *Values and Teaching*. Columbus, Ohio: Charles E. Merrill, 1966.
> This book creates new concepts of the relationship between thinking and valuing, and it suggests classroom procedures for making value development operational in classrooms.

Robinson, James H. *The Mind in the Making*. New York: Harper & Row, 1950.
> The author sees the collective rational efforts of man to solve his problems as a historical development of mind. He regards creation of more mind as a distinctive function of the school.

Rokeach, Milton, *The Open and Closed Mind*. New York: Basic Books, 1960.
> Probing into the nature of prejudice and dogmatic thinking, the book sheds light on the processes by which we construct and organize our belief systems.

Russell, Bertrand. *Understanding History*. New York: Wisdom Library, 1957.
> Written with an acid pen, the book contains a valuable essay on free thought. It makes a good companion to the books by Bury and Robinson.

Russell, David H. *Children's Thinking*. Boston: Ginn, 1956.
> This is a compilation of earlier research findings in thinking from various fields. The author attempts to create a structure in which theories of child development, educational psychology, and the psychology of thinking are combined into a unified theory.

Schön, Donald A. *The Reflective Practitioner*. New York: Basic Books, 1983.
> The author examines five professions—engineering, architecture, management, psychotherapy, and town planning—to show how professionals go about solving problems.

Thomson, Robert. *The Psychology of Thinking*. Baltimore: Penguin Books, 1959.
> This is a lucidly written psychological inquiry. It presents thinking as a collection of skills (one of which is reflection) that is the coordinated result of simpler functions. How the higher-level functions are developed is not yet clear. The book makes a good companion to the volumes by Bartlett and Judd cited earlier in this section.

Whitehead, Alfred N. *The Aims of Education*. London: Williams & Norgate, Ltd., 1950.
> This is actually a collection of lectures written in elegant style by the eminent philosopher. The author is concerned with educational goals and the means of attaining them.

Popular Books

Carroll, Lewis. *Alice's Adventures in Wonderland* and *Through the Looking Glass*. New York: Macmillan, 1930.
> These literary gems, enjoyable in their own right, are sometimes overlooked as a resource in thinking materials.

Chase, Stuart. *Guides to Straight Thinking*. New York: Harper & Row, 1956.
> In a very easy-to-read style, the author builds the book around an analysis of fallacies drawn from formal logic.

De Bono, Edward. *Lateral Thinking: A Textbook of Creativity*. Harmondsworth, England: Penguin Books, 1970.

The author presents ways of helping children learn to think imaginatively. The materials have easy application to elementary school classrooms.

Feuerstein, Reuven. *Instructional Enrichment*. Baltimore: University Park Press, 1979. The author introduces a nonverbal way of working with students to help them acquire higher-order thinking skills. The material is especially suitable for students with limited language skills.

Gould, Stephen Jay. *The Mismeasure of Man*. New York: W. W. Norton, 1981. This book is about the abstract conception of intelligence as a single entity; its location within the brain; its quantification as one number for each individual; and the use of numbers to rank people in a single series of worthiness. Highly readable, the book examines the misuse of measures of intelligence and is recommended reading for those who would place credence in such measures.

Hayakawa, S. I. *Language in Thought and Action*. New York: Harcourt, Brace, 1947. Hayakawa places heavy emphasis on semantics and problems of communication. With an engaging, highly readable style, the author analyzes language as the expression of thought.

Huff, Darrell. *How to Lie with Statistics*. New York: W. W. Norton, 1954. This small volume in soft cover is well illustrated and humorous. The author draws attention to common errors in going beyond data, especially those data presented in the form of charts and graphs.

Keyes, Kenneth S. *How to Develop Your Thinking Ability*. New York: McGraw-Hill, 1950. This is an easy-to-read and profusely illustrated book. The author draws heavily from semantics to offer a popular guide to thinking. He attempts to teach moderation in the use of language.

Stebbing, Susan L. *Thinking to Some Purpose*. Baltimore: Penguin Books, 1950. This is a more serious treatment of a guide to thinking in the Chase and Thouless vein. The author, a logician, talks about moderation, propaganda, illustration and analogy, and stereotypes.

Thouless, R. H. *How to Think Straight*. New York: Simon & Schuster, 1947. Like the preceding, this book is a popular guide to informal logic. It is an early work in its field, a revision of an older study. It gives the reader a chance to practice avoiding fallacies.

Wassermann, Selma. *Put Some Thinking in Your Classroom*. San Diego: Coronado, 1978. Working from the theoretical base established by Louis Raths, the author presents a framework for carrying out thinking operations in the elementary school classroom. This is a practical resource for teachers who wish to learn more about how to implement teaching for thinking in classroom practice.

Books in Specific Content Areas

Biggs, Edith, and James R. McLean. *Freedom to Learn: An Active Approach to Mathematics*. Reading, Mass.: Addison-Wesley, 1969. A process-oriented approach to the teaching of mathematics, emphasizing inquiry and "hands-on," active learning in promoting the understanding of mathematical concepts in the elementary grades.

Fraenkel, Jack R. *Helping Students Think and Value in the Social Studies*. Englewood Cliffs, N.J.: Prentice-Hall, 1973.

> Weaves the components of learning goals, subject matter, curriculum activities, and teaching strategies into a coherent whole, with emphasis upon promoting pupil thinking and valuing. Suitable for elementary and secondary programs.

Lowenfeld, Viktor. *Creative and Mental Growth*. New York: Macmillan, 1960.

> A classic in the teaching of art, the book emphasizes understanding of the mental and emotional development of children in relation to their creative processes. Suitable for elementary and secondary teachers.

Moffett, James. *A Student Centered Language Arts Curriculum, Grades K–12*. Boston: Houghton Mifflin, 1968.

> Presents the idea that oral and written language, and indeed, all expressive experiences, are central in the educative process. Emphasizes the learner's own production of language as central to teaching and learning in the language arts.

Rowe, Mary Budd. *Teaching Science as Continuous Inquiry*. New York: McGraw-Hill, 1973.

> Provides elementary teachers with a knowledge base to implement an inquiry-based science program with a conceptual system for thinking about physical and biological phenomena.

RELATED RESEARCH

Berken, Ruth R. "A Study of the Relationships of Certain Behaviors of Children to the Teaching of Thinking in Grades Five and Six in Selected Schools in West Side Manhattan." Doctoral dissertation, New York University, 1963.

> The teaching for thinking theory was tested in a controlled study involving nine teachers. The results of this investigation support the theory.

Bloom, Benjamin S., and S. J. Broder. *Problem-Solving Processes of College Students*. Chicago: University of Chicago Press, 1950.

> This is an investigation into thought-in-process. The study involves an analysis of transcripts of college students who used thinking "out loud" in response to selected problems.

Brownell, William A. "Problem-Solving." In *The Psychology of Learning*. Forty-First Yearbook of the National Society for the Study of Education, Part II. Chicago, 1942.

> This classic work presents the characteristics of problems. The author distinguishes between problems seen as applications of principles to new situations and problems seen as puzzles and exercises.

Cartwright, Roger. "An Account of the Development and Application of a Resource Unit Stressing Thinking for a Course: ETA 2: Values, Teaching and Planning." Doctoral dissertation, New York University, 1961.

> In this study, a resource unit for college teachers was developed that put an emphasis on thinking operations. Both the making of the unit and the creation of appropriate assignments are described in detail.

Chess, Edith. "The Manner in Which Two Samples of Ninth-Grade General Science Students Analyze a Number of Selected Problems." Doctoral dissertation, New York University, 1955.

> The investigation is somewhat similar to the study by Bloom and Broder. It attempts to analyze thought-in-process as recorded on tapes by children as they worked out loud to solve specific problems presented to them. Some implications of the study are worth noting: Similarity of mental product does not mean similarity of mental process; instead of failing to learn, students sometimes learn something different from that which is intended; teacher delineation of problems is not necessarily meaningful, since different problem statements persist in the thought processes of the student.

Fawcett, H. P. *The Nature of Proof. Thirteenth Yearbook of the National Council of the Teachers of Mathematics*. New York: Teachers College Press, 1938.

> This was a pioneering investigation that focused on the use of nonmathematical materials in the teaching of mathematics. The author was concerned with those aspects of demonstrative geometry that served to illustrate the *nature* of proof rather than its *content*, the traditional emphasis in geometry courses. Fawcett demonstrated that even for the so-called "thinking subjects" there is little gain in thinking ability unless there is focus upon thinking itself. His work antedates those by latter-day champions of having students discover rules rather than memorize them.

Glaser, E. M. *An Experiment in the Development of Critical Thinking*. Contributions to Education, No. 843. New York: Teachers College Press, 1941.

> The well-known Watson-Glaser Critical Thinking Appraisal, used in this study for the first time, is the most distinctive contribution of the work. The experiment, somewhat staged, is less convincing than the materials used. The latter are heavily weighted in the areas of propaganda analysis and syllogistic reasoning.

Jonas, Arthur. "A Study of the Relationship of Certain Behaviors of Children to Emotional Needs, Values and Thinking." Doctoral dissertation, New York University, 1960.

> This study, closely related to those of Machnits and Martin (see below), was carried out in a suburban New York school. Fifteen children were studied in relation to their behavior associated with thinking. As the teachers of the three experimental groups emphasized thinking over a four-month period, the behavior of the children in the experimental groups changed significantly in comparison to the children in the control groups. Neither the experimental children nor the experimental classes as a whole performed less well on tests of academic achievement. Jonas' study was carried out with a grade 4 class. Machnits and Martin conducted their studies with grades 3 and 5, respectively.

Lewis, H. "An Experiment in the Development of Critical Thinking through the Teaching of Plane Geometry." Doctoral dissertation, New York University, 1950. Also available in *Mathematics Teacher* 43 (1950).

> Teachers of geometry cannot teach the subject in a traditional way and expect growth in thinking ability in nonmathematical areas. The author gets students to discover and even to create geometric principles. This study, as also demonstrated in the Fawcett, Glaser, and Rothstein investigations, reveals that

experimental groups, although showing marked growth in achievement in thinking abilities, also do better on traditional tests than do control groups. The belief of teachers that it is necessary to emphasize the learning of facts if their students are to pass examinations is not supported by the evidence.

Machnits, Ernest. "A Study of the Relationship of Certain Behaviors of Children to Emotional Needs, Values and Thinking." Doctoral dissertation, New York University, 1960.

See Jonas, above.

Marcham, F. G. "Teaching Critical Thinking and the Use of Evidence." *Quarterly Journal of Speech* 31 (1945).

With the field of literature as a base, the author describes how he provided students with practice in comparing and interpreting sources and using evidence.

Martin, Donald. "A Study of the Relationship of Certain Behaviors of Children to Emotional Needs, Values and Thinking." Doctoral dissertation, New York University, 1960.

See Jonas, above.

Obourn, E. "Assumptions in Ninth Grade Science." Doctoral dissertation, New York University, 1950.

This was an experiment similar to those of Fawcett, Glaser, Lewis, and Rothstein. It emphasized science as discovery and as method rather than as content. The major thinking operation stressed was assumption finding.

Rothstein, Arnold. "An Experiment in Developing Critical Thinking Through the Teaching of American History in the Secondary School." Doctoral dissertation, New York University, 1960.

This work confirms the conclusions of earlier investigations that there is no loss in students' mastery of subject matter when emphasis is put on thinking, whereas there is a distinct gain in thinking achievement. A great part of the work is devoted to illustrations of curricular materials emphasizing thinking and guidelines for ways in which materials may be constructed and used are set forth.

Secret, Dennis, Hans Strechel, and David Swetnam. "An Experimental Study in Chemistry 11." Three master's theses, Simon Fraser University, 1973.

These studies, carried on in individual schools, but as parallel investigations, measured the growth in students' logical reasoning during one semester of Chemistry 11. Six chemistry teachers and about 150 students participated. Three teachers emphasized thinking within the Chemistry 11 curriculum. The other three teachers acted as controls. Students' gains were measured on tests of logical reasoning in pre- and post-settings. Experimental groups showed significantly higher scores on both tests of logical reasoning and the provincial chemistry examinations than control groups.

Stern, Ira LeRoy. "The Perseverance or Lack of It of Specified Behaviors Among Children in Selected Elementary Schools in Nassau County." Doctoral dissertation, New York University, 1962.

Stern investigated the types of problem behaviors that we have described in this text. Where nothing specific is done for students exhibiting such behaviors, they tend to persist in the following year.

Taba, Hilda, Samuel Levine, and Freeman Elzey. *Thinking in Elementary School Children*. Final Report of Cooperative Research Project No. 1574, U.S. Office of Education, April 1964.

> In an effort to arrive at learnable and teachable aspects of thinking, this study identified three cognitive tasks: (1) concept formation; (2) interpreting data; and (3) applying known concepts, generalizations, and data when hypothesizing or constructing a theory.

Wassermann, Selma. "A Study of the Changes in Thinking-Related Behaviors in a Selected Group of Sixth Grade Children in the Presence of Selected Materials and Techniques." Doctoral dissertation, New York University, 1962.

> In this investigation, certain behavioral patterns that relate to deficits in thinking were identified in a group of nine sixth-grade pupils. It was found that after daily exposure to thinking tasks, these nine children showed significant changes in their behaviors.

Wassermann, Selma, and George Ivany. "Project Science-Thinking." Unpublished research report, Simon Fraser University and the Vancouver School Board, 1984.

> Twenty primary-grade teachers participated in a one-year study examining the relationship between learning outcomes in science and thinking, and classroom applications emphasizing a teaching for thinking approach. Where teachers used teaching for thinking practices effectively, learning gains were significant. This study pointed to the need for more effective in-service training programs for teachers in using these instructional strategies.

APPENDIX C

Curriculum Materials

The Thinking and Learning Programs listed below are sets of classroom materials based upon the Raths' thinking operations. Each program is designed for a specific grade level and contains more than one hundred thinking activities representing all subject areas. Posters and charts provide instructional examples for introducing thinking operations to students. In addition, materials are also included that help teachers use higher-order questions to promote group discussions.

Wassermann, Selma. *The Primary Thinking Box*. San Diego: Coronado, 1978.

Wassermann, Selma, and Louis E. Raths. *Thinking and Learning*. Level 3. San Diego: Coronado, 1984.

Wassermann, Selma, and Louis E. Raths. *Thinking and Learning*. Level 4. San Diego: Coronado, 1984.

Wassermann, Selma, and Louis E. Raths. *Thinking and Learning*. Level 5. San Diego: Coronado, 1985.

Wassermann, Selma, and Louis E. Raths. *Thinking and Learning*. Level 6. San Diego: Coronado, 1985.

NOTES

INTRODUCTION TO THE SECOND EDITION

1. John Dewey, *How We Think* (Boston: D.C. Heath, 1910).

2. See Education Commission of the States, *National Assessment of Educational Progress. Reading, Thinking and Writing: Results from the 1979–80 National Assessment of Reading and Literature* (Denver: Education Commission of the States, 1981).

3. John Goodlad, *A Place Called School* (New York: McGraw-Hill, 1983). Goodlad's study of 1,016 classrooms across the United States revealed extensive emphasis in elementary and secondary curriculum materials on low-level cognitive (factual) responses and a consistency ("sameness of form") of such emphasis throughout the school sample.

4. Selma Wassermann, "Promoting Thinking in Your Classroom II: Inconsistencies Between Means and Ends," *Childhood Education* 60, no. 4 (March/April 1984): 229–33.

5. John Goodlad, "A Study of Schooling: Some Findings and Hypotheses," *Phi Delta Kappan*, March 1983, pp. 465–70. Goodlad's study found that "the form and substance of the curriculum appeared to call for and make appropriate only some ways of knowing and learning, not others. Students listened; they responded when called on to do so; they read short sections of textbooks; they wrote short responses to questions or chose from among alternatives in quizzes. But they rarely planned or wrote anything of some length or created their own products. And they scarcely ever speculated on meanings, discussed alternative interpretations, or engaged in projects calling for collaborative effort. Most of the time they listened or worked alone. Topics of the curriculum were something to be acquired, not something to be explored, reckoned with and converted into personal meaning and development."

6. Ibid. Goodlad cites that "about 70% of the instructional time involved verbal interactions or 'talk'—with teachers, on the average, 'out-talking' their entire classes of students by a ratio of about three to one." About 7 minutes, out of a total of 150 minutes, of talk involved teachers' responses to individual students.

7. Stewart Brand, *Whole Earth Software Catalog* (New York: Quantum Press/Doubleday, 1984).

8. Seymour Papert, *Mindstorms* (New York: Basic Books, 1980). Papert predicts that the computer presence will alter significantly what is happening in schools.

9. Benjamin Bloom, *Taxonomy of Educational Objectives: Cognitive Domain* (New York: Longmans Green, 1956).

10. David Aspy and Flora Roebuck, *Kids Don't Learn from People They Don't Like* (Amherst, Mass.: Human Resource Development Press, 1977). A number of studies were conducted to assess the relationship of interpersonal skills with a variety of pupil outcomes. Teachers offering high levels of interpersonal functioning achieved significant positive gains in areas of pupils' emotional, intellectual, and interpersonal growth.

11. Goodlad, *A Place Called School.*

12. Papert, *Mindstorms.*

13. Ibid., p. 9.

14. Bernard Asbell, "Writers' Workshop at Age Five," *New York Times Magazine*, February 26, 1984.

PART 1.   A THEORETICAL FRAMEWORK

1. Louis E. Raths, Merrill Harmin, and Sidney B. Simon, *Values and Teaching* (Columbus, Ohio: Charles E. Merrill, 1966).

2. Louis E. Raths and Anna P. Burrell, *Meeting the Needs of Children* (Columbus, Ohio: Charles E. Merrill, 1972).

3. R. W. Tyler, "Permanency of Learning," *Journal of Higher Education* 4 (April 1933): 203–4; J. E. Wert, "Twin Examination Assumptions," *Journal of Higher Education* 7 (March 1937): 136–40.

PART 2.   APPLICATIONS IN THE ELEMENTARY SCHOOL

1. The reader is also referred to Selma Wassermann and Louis E. Raths, *Thinking and Learning Programs* (San Diego: Coronado, 1984). These sets of thinking activities for classroom use are grouped according to subject areas.

2. Nancy Bawden, "Don't Tell Anyone   But," unpublished poem, reprinted with permission of the author.

3. Melanie Zola, *Peanut Butter Is Forever* (Scarborough, Ontario: Nelson, 1984), p. 36; reprinted with permission of the publisher.

4. Mary Budd Rowe, *Teaching Science as Continuous Inquiry* (New York: McGraw-Hill, 1973), p. 2.

5. Melvin Berger, *Science and Music* (New York: Whittlesey House, 1971), p. 2; reprinted with permission of the author.

PART 3.   APPLICATIONS IN THE SECONDARY SCHOOL

1. Charles H. Judd, *Education as Cultivation of the Higher Mental Processes* (New York: Macmillan, 1936).

2. Benjamin S. Bloom, *Taxonomy of Educational Objectives: Part I, Cognitive Domain.* (New York: Longmans Green, 1956).

3. Arthur Schopenhauer, *Counsels and Maxims*, trans. T. B. Saunders (New York: Macmillan, 1905), p. 149.

4. Reprinted by permission from the *London Times* of October 19, 1959.

5. ©1959 by the New York Times Company. Reprinted by permission.

6. ©1960 by the New York Times Company. Reprinted by permission.

7. Reprinted by permission from Wide World Photos, Inc.

8. Alfredo Moreno Espinosa, *Compendio de Historia de España* (Barcelona: Editorial Atlante), pp. 339, 341, 343, as cited in Arthur Walworth, *School Histories at War* (Cambridge, Mass.: Harvard University Press, 1938), pp. 58–59. Copyright 1938, by the President and Fellows of Harvard College. Reprinted by permission of the publishers.

9. W. B. Guitteau, *History of the United States* (Boston: Houghton Mifflin, 1937), p. 17.

10. F. P. Wirth, *The Development of America* (New York: American Book Company, 1936), p. 34.

11. D. S. Muzzey, *History of the American People* (Boston: Ginn, 1936), p. 41.

12. Espinosa, *Compendio de Historia de España*, p. 350, as cited in Walworth, *School Histories at War*, p. 61.

13. Pedro A. Bleye, *Compendio de Historia de España* (Madrid: Espasa-Calpe, S. A., 1933), pp. 115, 123–24, as cited in Walworth, *School Histories at War*, p. 62.

14. T. J. Wertenbaker and D. E. Smith, *The United States of America* (New York: Charles Scribner's Sons, 1931), pp. 18–19.

15. Espinosa, *Compendio de Historia de España*, pp. 350–51, as cited in Walworth, *School Histories at War*, pp. 62–63.

16. J. G. Saxe, "The Blind Men and the Elephant," from *The Poetical Works of John Godfrey Saxe* (Boston: Houghton Mifflin, 1882), pp. 111–12.

17. *Congressional Record*, November 22, 1943, vol. 89, p. 9919.

18. Mark Twain, *A Connecticut Yankee in King Arthur's Court* (New York: Modern Library, 1917), pp. 323–26.

19. William Harvey, *De Motu Cordis*, as cited in Robert B. Downs, *Books That Changed The World* (New York: New American Library, 1956), p. 144.

20. *New York Tribune*, April 19, 1906.

21. William Allen White, Kansas publisher, 1902.

22. Presbyterian Church of the Confederate States of America.

23. *Chicago Daily Journal*, April 17, 1861.

24. The Synod of North Carolina, November 1, 1861.

25. Adolf Hitler, from a speech made on December 1, 1942.

26. Adolf Hitler, from a speech made on December 31, 1941.

27. Mark Twain, *Autobiography*, ed. Charles Neider (New York: Harper & Row, 1959), pp. 5–6.

28. Charles E. Dull, H. Clark Metcalfe, and John E. Williams, *Modern Physics* (New York: Holt, Rinehart & Winston, 1960), p. 144.

29. Alfred North Whitehead, *The Aims of Education* (New York: New American Library, 1949), p. 61.

30. Quintilian, *Institutes of Oratory*, Book 10.

PART 4.   THE ROLE OF THE TEACHER

1. Theodore Parsons, "Guided Self-Analysis," mimeographed (University of California, Berkeley, 1968).

2. Selma Wassermann, *Put Some Thinking in Your Classroom* (San Diego: Coronado, 1978).

3. Selma Wassermann, "A Study of the Changes in Thinking-Related Behaviors in a Selected Group of Sixth Grade Children in the Presence of Selected Materials and Techniques," doctoral dissertation, New York University, 1962.

4. Barak Rosenshine, "Context, Time, and Direct Instruction," in *Research on Teaching*, ed. Penelope L. Peterson and Herbert J. Walberg (Berkeley: McCutchan, 1979).

5. Selma Wassermann, "The Gifted Can't Weigh That Giraffe," *New York Times*, Education Supplement, November 15, 1981.

PART 5.   IN SUPPORT OF THINKING

1. See Louis E. Raths and Anna P. Burrell, *Meeting the Needs of Children* (Columbus, Ohio: Charles E. Merrill, 1972).

2. The Peer Rating Instrument was developed by Selma Wassermann in "A Study of the Changes in Thinking-Related Behaviors in a Selected Group of Sixth Grade Children in the Presence of Selected Materials and Techniques," doctoral dissertation, New York University, 1962.

3. Selma Wassermann and Lous E. Raths, *Thinking and Learning Programs* (San Diego: Coronado, 1984).

4. *Watson-Glaser Critical Thinking Appraisal* (Yonkers, N.Y.: World Book, 1952); E. Paul Torrance, *Torrance Tests of Creative Thinking, Research Edition* (Lexington, Mass.: Personnel Press, 1966); Instructional Objectives Exchange, *Judgment: Deductive Logic and Assumption Recognition, Grades 7–12* (Los Angeles: Instructional Objectives Exchange, 1971); Catherine Ross and John Ross, *Ross Test of Higher Cognitive Process* (Pacific Grove, Calif.: Midwest, 1982).

5. Arnold Rothstein, "An Experiment in Developing Critical Thinking Through the Teaching of American History in the Secondary School," doctoral dissertation, New York University, 1960.

6. Ernest Machnits, "A Study of the Relationship of Certain Behaviors of Children to Emotional Needs, Values and Thinking," doctoral dissertation, New York University, 1960; Arthur Jonas, "A Study of the Relationship of Certain Behaviors of Children to Emotional Needs, Values and Thinking," doctoral dissertation, New York University, 1960; Donald Martin, "A Study of the Relationship of Certain Behaviors of Children to Emotional Needs, Values and Thinking," doctoral dissertation, New York University, 1960.

7. Roger Cartwright, "An Account of the Development and Application of a Resource Unit Stressing Thinking for a Course: ETA 2: Values, Teaching and Planning," doctoral dissertation, New York University, 1961.

8. Wassermann, "Study."

9. Ruth R. Berken, "A Study of the Relationships of Certain Behaviors of Children to the Teaching of Thinking in Grades Five and Six in Selected Schools in West Side Manhattan," doctoral dissertation, New York University, 1963.

10. Ira LeRoy Stern, "The Perseverance or Lack of It of Specified Behaviors Among Children in Selected Elementary Schools in Nassau County, New York," doctoral dissertation, New York University, 1962.

Index

225